Development Thro

Why, despite an emphasis on 'getting institutions right', do development initiatives so infrequently deliver as planned? Why do many institutions designed for natural resource management (e.g. water user associations, irrigation committees, forest management councils) not work as planners intended? This book disputes the model of development by design and argues that institutions are formed through the uneven patching together of old practices and accepted norms with new arrangements. The managing of natural resources and delivery of development through such processes of 'bricolage' is likened to 'institutional DIY' rather than engineering or design.

The author explores the processes involved in institutional bricolage; the constant renegotiation of norms, the reinvention of tradition, the importance of legitimate authority and the role of people themselves in shaping such arrangements. Bricolage is seen as an inevitable, but not always benign process; the extent to which it reproduces social inequalities or creates space for challenging them is also considered. The book draws on a number of contemporary strands of development thinking about collective action, participation, governance, natural resource management, political ecology and wellbeing. It synthesizes these to develop new understandings of why and how people act to manage resources and how access is secured or denied. A variety of case studies ranging from the management of water (Zimbabwe), conflict and cooperation over land, grazing and water (Tanzania) and the emergence of community management of forests (Sweden) illustrate the context-specific and generalized nature of bricolage and the resultant challenges for development policy and practice.

Frances Cleaver is Professor of Environment and Development at Kings College, London. She wrote the bulk of this book while a Reader in International Development Studies at the University of Bradford.

Development Through Bricolage

Rethinking Institutions for Natural Resource Management

Frances Cleaver

Routledge
Taylor & Francis Group

LONDON AND NEW YORK

First published 2012 by Routledge
2 Park Square, Milton Park, Abingdon, Oxon OX14 4RN

Simultaneously published in the USA and Canada by Routledge
711 Third Avenue, New York, NY 10017

Routledge is an imprint of the Taylor & Francis Group, an informa
business

British Library Cataloguing in Publication Data
A catalogue record for this book is available from the British Library

Library of Congress Cataloging in Publication Data
Cleaver, Frances.
Development through bricolage : rethinking institutions for natural
resource management / by Frances Cleaver.
p. cm.
Includes bibliographical references and index.
1. Natural resources--Management. 2. Natural resources--Co-
management. 3. Environmental agencies--Evaluation. I. Title.
HC85.C54 2012
333.7--dc23

2012001631

ISBN: 978-1-84407-868-4 (hbk)
ISBN: 978-1-84407-869-1 (pbk)
ISBN: 978-1-84977-721-6 (ebk)

Typeset in Bembo
by Fakenham Prepress Solutions, Fakenham, Norfolk NR21 8NN

Printed and bound in Great Britain by
TJ International Ltd, Padstow, Cornwall

I dedicate this book to the memory of my dear friend Mrs Thatshisiwe Nyoni (née Ncube) of Eguqeni and Mpopoma.

Contents

Acknowledgements

Many people have influenced this book in different ways and I am grateful to them all. I particularly thank the brave and hardy people of Nkayi district in Zimbabwe for their hospitality and friendship over the years, sometimes offered in circumstances of extreme hardship. I am also indebted to all those I have lived and worked with in the Usangu Plains in Tanzania, who have been so generous with companionship, information and insights.

I owe a big debt to colleagues too numerous to name who have provided intellectual support at various stages of writing, given me the opportunity to present work-in-progress at seminars and freely shared their own perspectives. Co-researchers on various projects have lived through the highs and lows of fieldwork with good humour as well as shaping and contesting my ideas. Special thanks go to those who read and commented on various chapters of the book, in particular Simon Duncan, Behrooz Morvaridi, Emil Sandström, Sam Wong, Tom de Herdt and Jessica de Koning. The reviewers, Margreet Zwarteveen and Bryan Bruns offered very welcome and incisive suggestions for improving the book – inevitably I did not do justice to them all. Tom Franks has been a stalwart colleague over the years of research in Tanzania, and many aspects of this work are influenced by our collaboration. I am also grateful to Kurt Hall, who provided invaluable intellectual and practical support when I was in the final throes of finishing the book. Hearty thanks also to my family and friends for their love and for staying the course.

Preface

The ideas outlined out in this book have been long in gestation; a process which unfolded through my early career in health service management and my subsequent academic jobs in development studies. Here I introduce some of the key themes of institutional bricolage by drawing on scenarios from rural development in Zimbabwe and in Sweden.

Scene One: A Lion Spirit Ceremony in Chiweshe, Zimbabwe

In February 1987 I was working as an administrator in a mission hospital in rural Zimbabwe. The mission was facing a number of challenges – the financial accounts never seemed to add up and there was some suspicion about where the money was going. The children at the mission school had recently rioted over bad food and oppressive discipline and the hospital vehicles had been involved in a number of serious accidents. The rains that year were both scanty and intermittent and people feared for their crops; many employees were anxious and demoralized.

The missionaries attributed these misfortunes to the workings of evil an power intending to disrupt their good work. Other local people attributed these various problems to the displeasure of ancestral Mhondoro spirits, who had protected the mission through years of civil war but were now displeased at the levels of disharmony between people living there. Accordingly, a big meeting of the spirit mediums for the area was arranged, at which the spirits would be consulted about what people needed to do to resolve these difficulties.[1]

Although it was said that white people were usually prohibited from such ceremonies, my friend the district medical officer and I (both white) were invited to attend. This was made possible by the brokering efforts of the medical officer's driver, who also briefed us on appropriate dress (the colour red was forbidden in the presence of the spirits) and on a suitable offering (maize and black or white cloth). He warned us about the prohibition against bringing 'modern things' such as watches or shoes into the presence of the spirits.

That night we parked at the foot of the hill where the ceremony (which lasted for some days) was being held and walked barefoot to the site in the dark. We arrived at a place full of people, brightly lit by a lamp powered by a car battery. We drank beer from a bowl passed around and listened to the words of the Mhondoro spirit already possessing one of the mediums. The spirit made a number of pronouncements (translated by an assistant) relating to the lack of rain. He welcomed us and said that black and white people must live together peacefully in Zimbabwe like black and white cattle in the same field. He railed against the disrespect of youth – particularly of young girls who aborted their unborn foetuses and buried them in the fields – and he talked about the need to make amends for bad deeds done by the people, and for blood spilled on the land during the liberation war, before the rains would come and the grass could grow. Singing and dancing and more beer drinking followed and at some point in the night we left the ceremony and descended the mountain to find our shoes and Land Rover.

Viewed with the benefit of substantial hindsight, this engaging experience offers a lead into understanding the ways in which people–environment relations are framed in reference to wider moral and social meanings. Such worldviews and associated practices are shaped by tradition, but not determined by it – our presence as white people at the ceremony was made possible by bending the rules, facilitated by the authoritative status of my doctor friend. Our presence was incorporated into the pronouncements of the spirit and used to reinforce messages about conflict resolution and reconciliation. Such ideas were central to 'traditional' Shona worldviews but were also prominent in the post-independence nation-building rhetoric of the Zimbabwean state in the 1980s. The ceremony followed a well-worn pattern through the practices of making offerings, sharing of beer, talking in tongues of the spirit through the medium and dancing. 'Customary' principles of living peaceably together and the reinforcement of patriarchal relations of respect were asserted. But the 'rules' were liberally interpreted, for example in the tolerance of our presence and pragmatic use of the 'modern' light powered by a car battery. Later in the book I will argue that such insights are important for the ways in which we understand people's behaviour towards each other and in relation to natural resources. Similarly, I will elaborate on the idea that authoritative meaning leaks, or can be borrowed between traditional and modern, public and private, global and local domains. This book is not limited to interesting manifestations of adapted 'traditional' culture in African societies – in later chapters I will illustrate the ways in which similar processes manifest, for example, in processes of natural resource management in northern Europe.

Scene Two: Mary the Pump Fitter – Development in Practice

In October 1988, as a student at the University of Zimbabwe, I undertook a study of community maintenance of handpumps in one district for a postgraduate dissertation. For three weeks I lived and worked with a government technician employed to support the implementation of the rural water supply programme and to train communities in pump maintenance. Mary, the peripatetic pump fitter, had a bicycle, a toolkit and a small government allowance. She had been appointed to the job after several years of working in a voluntary capacity at her local health clinic. I cycled with her long distances along dusty roads to fit or mend village pumps, lived on two meals of maize and vegetables a day and was often hot, tired and hungry. As the only two women sleeping at road builders' rest camps, we frequently spent our evenings fending off the unwanted attentions of men.

Mary's technical work was conducted amidst lengthy discussions with waterpoint committee members and other villagers. The newly created committees included a large number of widows and other women heading their households in the absence of men who had been killed in the war or migrated for work. Influential women dominated key positions on the committees. In one case, the chairwoman of the village water committee also chaired the savings club, while the secretary (who headed the wealthiest household in the village) was also vice-chair of the women's league (connected to the ruling party). As well as discussing water issues at length, people often talked to me about how they were going to better their situations and those of their children so as to 'develop the community', to 'build Zimbabwe'.

Mary, at the time one of only two women pump fitters in the country, was a widow with six children to support. Conscientious in her technical duties, she also planned her work to include trading possibilities and to ease travel to her home area at the weekends. The way that Mary and the village waterpoint committees worked well illustrates that the social identities of people undertaking local resource management are as important as their formal institutional or technical roles. Mary had the advantage of a paid job, which gave her a small salary, some social status and the ability to shape water management. The way she conducted this work was influenced by her physical embodiment (affected by the distances cycled, the physical effort of pump fitting, the heat, being the only woman in a camp full of men) and by overlapping aspects of her social identity, notably as a mother of six dependent children.

This example also illustrates the ways in which newly designed institutions (the waterpoint committees) offer opportunities or spaces for people to participate in resource governance but may also reinforce existing social inequalities. In this case, women household heads and widows, marginalized in 'traditional' patriarchal arrangements, were positioning themselves on 'modern' development-oriented committees, partly in anticipation of future opportunities. Nevertheless, committee leadership was dominated by women of elite social and political identities who held similar positions across a variety of institutions. Later in the book, I will discuss further the tension between opportunity and constraint for individuals in institutions. I will argue that in order to understand individual agency and collective action we need to see people as socially located (with overlapping identities and motivations) and physically embodied. Institutions can facilitate or limit individual actions, and people with different social identities experience varying 'room for manoeuvre' within them.

Reflecting on How Institutions Work

I took the experiences of the lion spirit ceremony and of working with Mary the pump fitter with me into my subsequent job in the Ministry of Health, providing planning support to the national rural water and sanitation programme. This was still an era of grand development planning with Zimbabwe's National Master Plan for Rural Water Supply and Sanitation running to eighteen volumes. Systems were being created, models adopted, institutions designed. This water master plan set out a formalized three-tier system for maintenance of water supplies with specified roles for the community as the first tier. After experiencing for myself the social arrangements around resource use, and the ways the maintenance system actually operated at local level, I was highly aware of the disjuncture between designed development interventions and contextualized practices. In a nationwide evaluation study of handpump maintenance, conducted in 1990, I struggled to reconcile the national model with the field evidence I found. This pointed to a picture of government departments struggling with rigid procedures and lack of capacity, often unable to effectively interface with plural, informal and intermittent practices of handpump maintenance at the community level. In a summary of the report I rather lamely concluded that 'The three tier maintenance system is improvised, adapted and lives alongside parallel maintenance systems' (Cleaver, 1990: 115).

The Zimbabwe experiences prompted me to think further about the difference between theoretical models of 'designed' institutions and how institutions work in practice. The variety of local arrangements and improvisations of water management and their relation to other aspects of people's lives seemed to illustrate the complexity of institutional functioning. The role of leaders and of local elites (both traditional and modern) in shaping the way things are done pointed to the ways in which institutions function through the deployment of authoritative resources. The cases also pointed to the need to better understand the ways that interfaces between communities and government work. Finally, I noted both the potential and the limits of community action. In the maintenance study I had come across examples of communities raising labour, money, transport, even improvising their own spare parts, but despite this, often unable to overcome the constraints of remoteness, poverty or unresponsive bureaucracy. For many years after this I assumed that the processes and understandings I had observed (the ways that beliefs in spirits informed everyday practices, how social relationships shaped formal roles and institutional engagement, the interaction between the informal economy and the formal state) were specifically African, or at least particular to developing countries. However, through subsequent decades of work at the interface between academia, policy-making and development practice, I began instead to see some of these processes as generic to institutional functioning.

As the promise of community-driven development became mainstreamed into development policy, a body of scholarship evolved demonstrating that communities can effectively manage natural resources through properly crafted institutions. At the same time literature and evidence grew of the variable experience of community-based natural resource management and the enormous challenges to ensuring its long-term effectiveness. It seemed to me that designed institutions clearly mattered, and had great potential, but that interventions aimed at facilitating their greater effectiveness were fraught with problems because of the inherently social nature of institutional functioning. In thinking further about the nature of institutions and their evolution, I also drew on literature and experiences from northern Europe.

Through the work of scholars at Swedish universities (such as Arora-Jonsson 2005, Sandström 2008) I became aware of a number of studies of community-based natural resource management in Sweden. Here I found fascinating cases of the emergence of local-level institutions, in one of the most developed countries in the world, renowned for a strong welfare-oriented, democratic state committed to the pursuit of social equity. In these studies was evidence of people drawing on the past (or re-inventions of past practices) as a guide to current action, of evolution and re-creation of social and cultural identities, and the assertion of spiritual connections between people and the environment. Here institutions relating to community-based natural resource management were both formal and informal; collective action and common under-standings were forged through everyday relationships and practices as well as through rules and authoritative roles.

Scene Three: 'This Mountain is Our Living Room' – Everyday Struggles to Create Shared Understandings

So, for example, Sandström's study of Ammarnäs village in northern Sweden details the ways in which local people with Sami (reindeer herder) and with Swedish 'settler' identities endeavoured to form common cause to establish local institutional arrangements for the management of the 500,000 hectares of state-owned Vindelmountain Nature Reserve (Sandström, 2008). Despite a history of serious conflict over property rights in the village, the self-styled Ammarnäs Council developed by forging a sense of unity between these groups of people, derived from common place connections and commitments to a local form of sustainable development. This involved asserting fundamental underlying principles of cooperation (very similar to those pronounced by the Zimbabwean spirit medium in Scene One). Sandström quotes a local landowner and member of the council calling on a previous era of cooperation by saying, 'The mountains had brothers and sister living like neighbours until the state created a partition' (Sandström, 2008: 165).

This reinvented idea of unity was strongly asserted to claim the legitimacy of local arrangements for environmental stewardship. As one reindeer herder said,

> It is important that we develop a local management, which is based on the knowledge that has been inherited for generations ... We the Sami together with the settlers know how to manage, since we were here before any of the authorities were here! (Sandström, 2008: 164)

Notable in Sandström's account of the development of Ammarnäs Council is the importance of the meaning of natural resources to people's everyday lives and practices. This is not confined to the economic importance of those resources (which had decreased over time) but rather to ideas about identity and place in the world. One informant pointed out the important place of bears in Sami cosmology, an element not reflected in contemporary state policies of environmental protection. Another Sami emphasized the everyday nature of resource management arrangements:

> the Vindelmountain area is our living room ... It is from here that we earn our living and within this room that we shape the rules for how we live our lives ... no one else should shape the rules in our living room! (Sandström, 2008: 162)

Prominent in this and other cases is evidence that developing shared understandings is critical to the institutionalization of collective action and natural resource management. In these cases arrangements for resource management were shaped both deliberately in formal spaces, and less consciously in routinized daily interactions. Although they constantly asserted the importance of local connections, influential actors also drew on wider political or cultural networks and on national and international discourses of community, democracy and environmental management to give weight and meaning to their actions.

Further Reflections: From Community Management to Bricolage

Although some of the examples cited above are now historic, the importance of community-based management remains undiminished in development policy, which is dominated by assumptions about the positive possibilities of collective action. However, the Zimbabwean and Swedish cases suggest that this is a problematic area which requires some rigorous analysis. So, what kind of concepts or theories can we use to help frame our enquiry into the processes and effects of community-based natural resource management? The dynamic and socially embedded essence of these processes seem to me to be only partially captured in dominant theorizing about institutions and common property resource management, for reasons elaborated later in this book. Nor do the prominent concerns and assumptions of development policy, characterized by an instrumental focus on designing interventions to foster economic growth and counter poverty, provide a good enough basis for such exploration. It is my purpose in this book to outline some of the key challenges to understanding institutions and community-based natural resource management. I aim to address these challenges and to explain institutional functioning by elaborating the concept of institutional bricolage. I hope that this contributes to better understandings of institutional dynamics and so to furthering real and progressive change in the way we attempt to manage human–environment interactions.

Bibliography

Arora-Jonsson, S. (2005) 'Unsettling the Order: Gendered Subjects and Grassroots Activism in Two Forest Communities', Doctoral thesis No. 2005: 70, Swedish University of Agricultural Sciences.

Cleaver, Frances (1990) 'Community Maintenance of Handpumps'. Report to the National Action Committee, Water and Sanitation Studies Fund, Department of Rural and Urban Planning, University of Zimbabwe.

Jestice, P. G. (2004) *Holy People of the World: A Cross-Cultural Encyclopaedia*. Oxford, ABC Clio.

Lan, David (1985) *Guns and Rain: Guerrillas and Spirit Mediums in Zimbabwe*. Berkeley, University of California Press.

Ranger, T. (1985) *Peasant Consciousness and Guerrilla War in Zimbabwe*. London, Scarecrow.

Sandström, Emil (2008) 'Reinventing the Commons: Exploring the Emergence of the Local Natural Resource Management Arrangements', Doctoral thesis No. 2008: 48, Swedish University of Agricultural Sciences.

Spierenburg, M. J. (2004) *Strangers, Spirits and Land Reforms: Conflicts about Land in Dande, Northern Zimbabwe*. Leiden, Brill.

Note

1 In Shona beliefs Mhondoro or lion spirits are thought to be able to possess the bodies of human mediums, otherwise residing in the bodies of young lions. The spirits are those of important deceased ancestors, chiefs or political leaders who have returned to protect their people. The Mhondoro spirits play an important role in rainmaking, ensuring the fertility of the land, the abundance of wild fruits and animals, and the conduct of war. They can advise on collective problems of the community, especially in respect of conflicts, and also undertake divination and healing. Mhondoros acting through their mediums advise chiefs and other living leaders and can intervene on behalf of the community with the High God Mwari. The territories over which they preside may vary from a few villages to a wider area encompassing different chiefdoms. Mhondoro spirits and their mediums have played a significant role in the nineteenth- and twentieth-century political struggles in Zimbabwe. For elaboration of the role and importance of Mhondoro spirits, see Jestice (2004), Spierenburg (2004), Lan (1985) and Ranger (1985) as cited in the bibliography for this chapter.

1 Getting Institutions Right: Interrogating Theory and Policy

Introduction: Why Focus on Institutions?

This book explores the ways in which institutions mediate relationships between people, natural resources and society. It aims to animate theory by showing just *how* the interaction between social structure and individual agency works through institutions. My primary focus is not on designing institutions for better resource management (already the subject of an impressive literature), but rather on understanding *how* institutions work in practice and consequently *why* the outcomes benefit some people and exclude others. This book raises the questions we need to ask if institutions tasked with natural resource management are *also* to promote equity of access and distribution, to further social justice.

Local institutions as the building blocks of 'good' governance?

'Getting institutions right' has become central to development policy in a number of ways. A curious amalgamation of policy ideas paradoxically link market reforms and the individualization of property rights to decentralization and community-based development (Peters, 2004; Osei-Kufuor, 2010). In such approaches, institutions are the channels through which individual and collective action is shaped, social capital built and the weaknesses of state or market provision redressed (Merrey *et al.*, 2007; Osei-Kufuor, 2010). Robust local institutions are seen as fundamental to good governance and democracy, providing the spaces through which people express their needs and call representatives or service providers to account (Putnam, 1994; Cornwall, 2004; Houtzager and Lavalle, 2009). The current international policy consensus in the area assumes that institutions with clear roles, rules and lines of accountability will help to shape desirable governance arrangements of transparency, accountability and probity (Asian Development Bank, 1999; McGranahan and Satterthwaite, 2006; Grindle, 2007). My argument in this book, however, is that these desirable outcomes are not at all assured and that we need to understand why this is if we aim to attain them through development interventions.

This focus on designing the correct institutional arrangements to further good governance and development strongly influences policy approaches concerned with natural resource management at the local level. Here, well-designed institutions are seen as critical to regulating land rights, preventing degradation and depletion of resources (forests, fisheries, rangelands, wildlife, water), managing common property and creating sustainable livelihoods (Woodhouse, 2002). Mainstream approaches suggest that resource management can be strengthened through policy reform, capacity building, and particularly through redesigning *community-level* institutions so as to provide incentives to cooperate (Varughese and Ostrom, 2001; Heikkila *et al.*, 2011).

Ideas about the inefficiencies of the state, the efficacy of local knowledge and action and the need to regulate individual behaviour are combined in a number of interlinked assumptions (see also Blaikie, 2006). Firstly, it is often asserted that communities can most effectively manage natural resources as they are best placed to monitor resource use and so deal with 'open access' problems of overuse. It is argued that they have an advantage in efficient resource use and allocation, being able to draw on their local knowledge of resources, environmental conditions and technology (Cinner, 2011; Ostrom, 2008). Secondly, community management is thought to be pro-poor. The claims are that local institutions can specify a place for marginalized people in decision-making, community norms often include the right for a living for all, and labour-intensive resource management activities may generate economic benefits. Thirdly, community management is seen as contributing to a virtuous cycle of 'good governance', so mitigating state failure. According to this view, it is through participation that people express their needs, call service providers to account and challenge corrupt practices. Fourthly, it is assumed that local traditions of cooperation provide the building blocks of good resource management, but often lack robustness due to informality and lack of clarity in rights incentives and authority structures. Policy approaches to rectify this 'institutional deficit' include formalization and codification of property rights and governance arrangements (for example, in relation to land tenure, see World Bank, 2001: 35–7, quoted in Sturgeon and Sikor, 2004). However, as will be illustrated in this book, this set of linked assumptions does not necessarily hold in practice and the related policy emphases may be misguided. Approaches to implementing local-level resource management tend to overlook the complex and changing interactions amongst community members, the state and service providers; to underestimate the dynamic nature of institutional governance in socio-economic systems (Huppert, 2008; Cleveringa *et al.*, 2009).

Local resource management and its limits

The policy approach outlined above advocates the proper design of local participatory institutions for good natural resource governance. However, there is also a significant literature critiquing participatory approaches in development and community-based management of natural resources in particular. In this it is argued that the costs and benefits of such public participation are not evenly spread, and furthermore that some people find it more difficult to shape the communal rules than others. This literature is therefore more cautious about assuming that local governance will lead to 'good' governance and is concerned with the *limits* of decentralization, with unpacking over-romantic 'myths' of community and with the equity effects of local institutional arrangements (Agrawal and Gibson, 1999, 2001; Campbell *et al.*, 2001; Cooke and Kothari, 2001; Mtisi and Nicol, 2003; Cleaver *et al.*, 2005; Osei-Kufuor, 2010; Wong, 2010). Such questioning is compatible with critical social justice perspectives, which see the mainstream policy concerns with equality of opportunity in livelihood generation as too restricted (Morvaridi, 2008). Instead, advocates of critical social justice analyze the ways that power exercised through societal relationships produces unequal outcomes, and how this can be addressed through the broader redistribution of resources rather than just tinkering with the redesign of local institutions.

By way of introducing some of this more critical thinking on the institutions and community management, consider this sketch of the evolution of one village's water supply scheme (for a more detailed elaboration see Cleaver and Toner, 2006[1]).

The Evolution of a Local Water User Association

Since around 2000 a water users association has managed the supply of piped water in Uchira village in Kilimanjaro, Tanzania, working from an office constructed with financing from a German development agency and through the labour and contributions of the villagers themselves. By 2005 the association had evolved from being a resource-poor sub-committee of the Uchira Village Council into a semi-professional organization able to manage a significant water supply system and to collect sufficient funds to cover day-to-day operations. It was constituted as a community-owned institution made up of paying members, separate from state institutions, governed by a board and managed by a professional team of staff, and was judged a success by the donors. However a number of tensions in its evolution and operation raise questions about community-based management of services and resources.

Who participates?

During the development of the water user association the balance shifted away from voluntary efforts towards professional management. By 2005, paid staff (some recruited from outside the village) included a general manager, an accountant, two technicians, two office watchmen, one intake watchman and an office secretary. At the same time public decision-making became dominated by a minority of residents. Villagers could become full members of the association, with the right to vote in elections and attend board meetings, by contributing labour or finance to the construction of the scheme and thereafter paying a yearly membership fee. However, only a small percentage of water users became full members (145 members of a village population of over 5,000), and these tended to be the wealthier villagers. Positions on the board of the association were dominated by a small elite of 'big potatoes' who were already heavily involved in other village organizations. Other villagers were reluctant to pay for membership when there was little chance of significantly affecting the decision-making dominated by these big men.

The Uchira experience echoes other literature which finds that actual participation at community level is often limited and the equal exercise of voice cannot be assumed. For example, women with small children or older dependents, young women married into an area, people from chronically poor households, or men and women from minority groups often experience participation as costly. Even if able to spend the time and effort to attend formal public meetings, they may be unable to speak effectively or to be heard in fora dominated by powerful members of the community. In such circumstances they may then bypass formal institutions in favour of accessing resources through kin and patronage networks or by stealing and cheating. Equitable participation in community-level institutions cannot be assumed merely because the arrangements are local and nominally open to all.

Attempts to address unequal participation by deliberately facilitating the inclusion of less-powerful people have had mixed results and cannot be assumed to automatically ensure a fairer distribution of resources (Dikito-Wachtmeister, 2000; House, 2003; Tukai, 2005; Zwarteveen and Bennett, 2005; Cleaver and Hamada, 2010).

Efficiency and social justice in tension

Decision-making at community level is not necessarily fair or just in its effects. In the Uchira case the board and management team considered their role to be the *efficient* management of the water system, with no remit for ensuring universal or needs-based access. There was therefore no provision made for graduated fees or for exemptions from contributions (although labour contributions could be transmuted into cash payments by those who could afford it). In practice the designed system of charging for water evolved in unanticipated ways, illustrating tensions between efficiency and equity considerations in community management.

The Uchira water system was formally established to include household connections and public taps. At the public taps elected water attendants were to charge people five Tanzanian shillings per bucket and to claim twenty per cent of their monthly takings back from the association. However, in practice, private attendants at some waterpoints (often in roadside or commercial areas) charged ten shillings per bucket. Some households with their own connections sold water on to neighbours (so potentially undermining the viability of paid attendants at public taps). In the remoter areas of the village households collected water fees (generally held at five shillings) by rota, or paid an attendant a monthly fee, and users unable to pay were sometimes able to obtain credit. Users complained about the fees (higher than when the Uchira Village Council ran the water supply) and grumbled about paying when they had already contributed labour and money to rehabilitate the scheme. However, the water users association managers considered higher fees and the unplanned sale of water from household connections acceptable in terms of ensuring financial viability and greater coverage by the scheme.

The example of the uneven development of the fee system illustrates how decision-making in formal institutions, whilst highly legible to officialdom, only partially reflects the ways in which decisions are shaped. An emphasis on formal rules and sanctions and on the public negotiation of differences overlooks the importance of the social relations on which people depend for their daily life. These may include unequal relations of patronage, reciprocity with neighbours and kin, the commercialization of certain aspects of resource access and the need to avoid open confrontation of difference in the interests of everyday harmony. These social relationships and daily practices, where inequalities and cooperation entwine, also shape community decision-making and resource management. The endurance and robustness of institutions partly depends on their social fit, yet this is also how inequalities (in the form of relationships of privilege and disadvantage) are produced and enforced.

In the Uchira case further tensions were evident in the fluctuating balance between different aspects of community governance, and 'external' intervention. The water association evolved away from its previous incarnation as a sub-committee of the Uchira Village Council partly because the donor insisted on an independent constitution as a condition of continued support. With the donor's financial and technical assistance, the water user association developed far more capacity than the village council and had better offices and facilities. However, it still depended on the council to ensure labour contributions for maintenance, while the boundaries between water management and village government were blurred by the role of influential individuals with positions in both. In this way the evolution of the association reinforced both elite dominance at local level *and* dependency relationships between the community and donor.

Myths of community: the dangers of localism

'Small is beautiful' has become a slogan which encompasses many dominant ideas about natural resource management. Collective action is thought to be more likely at the local level, where relatively homogeneous users share norms, knowledge and an interest in the resource. However, many community-based natural resource management schemes fail in that they tend to reinforce local power structures, to impose non-local views about sustainability and overlook the complexities of how actual communities work (Fleuret, 1985; Blaikie, 2006).

Uchira well illustrates one of the prevailing myths of community management – that local communities are infinitely resourceful. Situated in a relatively wealthy village, well connected to markets and administrative centres, the water user association was able to cover the daily operations of the water supply system. However, it was unable to secure sufficient funds and capacity to ensure long-term maintenance and necessary rehabilitation of the scheme without the support of the donor. In this book we will come across examples of many other communities which, though highly dependent on natural resources, lack the resources to manage them effectively. These limitations include a crippling mix of disadvantages including spatial remoteness from markets and services, environmental marginality and poor communications, transport and infrastructure. Such communities may be characterized by a large proportion of households with high dependency levels and low levels of human capital and assets. Social capital, generated and maintained through association, is unlikely to adequately substitute for the lack of more material assets (Cleaver, 2005).

Participatory approaches can be further hampered by prejudices held at local level, norms of 'a living for all' co-existing with intolerant ideas about the unworthy poor, witches, inferior gender, caste, ethnic groups or religions, as we will see in the following chapters (Joshi *et al.*, 2003; Beall, 2005). The prevalence of patterns of inequality both within and between communities raises the issue of scale. To what extent can *community*-level decision-making and the building of *local* institutions positively effect lasting change in command over resources? The case of Uchira is limited to a village water supply, but as we will see in numerous other cases cited in this book, we face situations where the boundaries (of the village, the managing institution and the natural resource) are not conterminous.

The 'small is beautiful' approach deals with scale by linking of the community-level action to other levels of governance through systems of representation. There is some doubt, though, whether local people, competent in creating institutions and organizing collective action, are also well placed to influence higher levels of decision-making in their favour (Ribot, 2001a; Agrawal and Chhatre, 2007; Mercer, *et al.*, 2008; Nelson and Agrawal, 2008; Meagher, 2010). Indeed, some of these authors analyze the ways in which local co-management arrangements can be manipulated to strip communities of decision-making and resource allocation powers. Influence does not necessarily neatly travel through hierarchically nested layers of representation and this presents another challenge to the efficacy of community management and the scaling up of its effects.

So, we can identify a mainstream policy discourse optimistic about the possibilities of designing local institutions that shape good community-based governance of natural resources. However, there is also evidence of the limits of this model and question marks over its ability to deliver lasting benefits for poor people. Do such reservations then mean that optimism about the possibilities of institutional design is misplaced? To address this question let us probe a little deeper into some of the concepts and assumptions which underlie policy thinking about the *institutions* for community-based natural resource management.

Thinking About Institutions

Institutions are arrangements between people which are reproduced and regularized across time and space and which are subject to constant processes of evolution and change. In other words, an institution 'refers to social arrangements that shape and regulate human behaviour and have some degree of permanency and purpose transcending individual human lives and intentions' (Merrey *et al.*, 2007: 196). Definitions of institutions in the literature vary according to the emphasis put on formal organizational structures or on the 'rules of the game' – the codes of conduct that define practices, assign roles and guide interactions. Uphoff usefully distinguishes between *organizations* that are structures 'of recognised and accepted roles' and *institutions* as 'complexes of norms and behaviours that persist over time by serving collectively valued purposes' (1986: 8–9). Of course, a norm-based institution may also take organizational form (as in marriage or the family) whilst the operation of organizations is governed as much by the prevailing culture (such as ideas about the proper place of women) as by the official roles and procedures.

Institutional schools of thought

For the purposes of this book I divide ideas about institutions and community-based natural resource management into two broad 'schools' of thought: Mainstream Institutionalism and Critical Institutionalism. Mainstream Institutional thinking (MI) includes common property scholarship and is linked to the ideas of New Institutional Economics (North, 1990; Ostrom, 1990). From this perspective, the role of institutions is to provide information and assurance about the behaviour of others, to offer incentives to behave in the collective good, and to monitor and sanction opportunistic behaviour. All these factors aid individual decision-making and choice. In this model institutions are amenable to design; indeed, they can be crafted by the resource users themselves. Common features of robust and long-enduring arrangements are identified as 'Design Principles' which concern desirable attributes of the resource managing community and of governance mechanisms. This approach is privileged in policy, partly because it offers a bridge between neo-liberal economic ideas and the desirability of decentralized local management and 'ownership'.

By contrast, many of the scholars who could be characterized as Critical Institutionalists (CI) question the rational choice and functional assumptions of MI. Instead they tend to emphasize the complexity of institutions entwined in everyday social life, their historical formation and the interplay between the traditional and the modern, formal and informal arrangements (Mosse, 1997; Cleaver, 2001; Lund 2006). In this view, rules, boundaries and processes are 'fuzzy'; people's complex social identities and unequal power relationships shape resource management arrangements and outcomes. Some thinkers adopting this approach emphasize the ways in which local level decision-making is entwined with national and global processes. CI perspectives, though growing in the academic literature, often lack policy purchase, partly because they fail to offer clear direction for policy-makers.

The distinction between the two schools of thought is not always clear cut and other scholars categories contrasting approaches to writing about natural resource management dilemmas in different ways, as Table 1.1 outlines.

Inevitably, such categorization involves a certain amount of caricature – a simplification of the complexities and nuances of people's work. These ways of thinking are not wholly antagonistic and often overlap, though they are underpinned by very different assumptions about the nature of human action and society. Indeed I see the promise of CI as offering ways of steering MI and policy thinking to more fully address issues of power and inequality and to understand *why* designed institutions turn out in unexpected ways. I write this book primarily from a CI perspective with the aim of defining and strengthening this school of thought. I leave it to others to consider the extent to which it is useful

Table 1.1 Institutions and natural resource management: schools of thought

Authors	*Categorizations used in the Commons Literature*
Cleaver (2012)	Mainstream Institutional Approach/Critical Institutional Approach
Mosse (1997)	Economic-Institutional Explanations/Sociological-Historical Explanations
Goldman (1998)	Tragedy Scholars/Anti-Tragedy Scholars
Johnson (2004)	Collective Action Scholars/Entitlement Scholars
Agrawal (2005)	Common Property Scholars/Political Ecology Scholars
Sandström (2008)	Common Pool Approach/Adaptive Resilience Approach/Socio-Historical Approach
Mehta *et al.* (2001)	Mainstream Approach/Emerging or Post-Institutionalist Approach
Roth (2009)	Mainstream Institutional Economics Approach/Alternative Social Anthropological Approach
Bruns (2009)	Building/Crafting/Bricolage/Discourse/Adaptation

to synthesize this approach with MI. So, let us proceed to consider in more detail the salient features of each approach and the explanatory challenges they face.

Mainstream institutionalism

The idea that institutions for common property resource management can be deliberately crafted is epitomized by the work of Nobel laureate Elinor Ostrom (1990, 2005). This work has been hugely significant in countering previous assumptions that resources will inevitably be depleted or degraded (a 'tragedy of the commons') in the absence of individual ownership or state regulation. Numerous case studies demonstrate that such resources are in fact 'owned' as common property by communities who can sustainably manage them. Communities do this through institutions, publicly designing and administering rules of access and distribution. The cases show a great variety of locally formulated arrangements to regulate resource use and ensure that a tragedy of the commons does not occur (Hardin, 1968, 1998; Wade, 1988a for greater elaboration on the tragedy of the commons; see National Research Council, 1986 for common property theorists and recent development of this thinking in Andersson and Ostrom, 2008; Ostrom, 2008; McGinnis, 2010, 2011).

Design principles

Key to Mainstream Institutionalism is the specification of 'design principles'; conditions that are central to the functioning of robust and enduring institutions for common property resource management (Blaikie, 2006; Wong, 2009; Ostrom, 2009; Cox *et al.*, 2010). The case study literature empirically supporting the design principles approach tends to emphasize the formalization of institutional arrangements, the delineation of clear boundaries of resource use and jurisdiction, the specification of inclusive decision-making arrangements, the codification of rules and regulations and the strict exercise of sanctions against free-riders. Overall there is a strong emphasis on transparency, on the principle of user representation and on devising efficient mechanisms for conflict resolution and resource allocation. It is deemed possible both to craft new institutions and to 'make good' the deficiencies of indigenous arrangements through careful design (Wade, 1988b; Ostrom, 1990, 1992, 2005; Ostrom 1980); Bromley and Cernea, 1989). More recently there has been some recognition that design principles cannot be seen as a panacea or a blueprint for institution building. Instead they are presented as potential indicators, as sets of issues to be considered or questions asked when trying to craft more robust and sustainable institutions (Rudd, 2004; Ostrom, 2007, 2008; Ostrom *et al.*, 2007; Cinner, *et al.*, 2011; Heikkila, Schlager and Davis, 2011).

Nature of institutions

Within this school of thought, institutions are essentially arrangements of rules or regulations used repeatedly to shape individual actions: 'Institutions are human-constructed constraints or opportunities within which individual choices take place and which shape the consequences of their choices' (McGinnis, 2011). These configurations of rules (institutions) are designed, negotiated, altered and administered (crafted) at local level to achieve particular goals (sustainable resource management). The focus is primarily on formal and public institutions, but norms have a role as they are seen as concepts of appropriate actions or outcomes in particular situations. The focus of common property scholars is largely on interactions between individuals and community-level institutions as the 'action arena'. Biophysical variables, community attributes and rules are conceived of as 'exogenous variables', effectively external to the local institution. Mainstream institutionalists do recognize that resource management issues that cross scales require specific attention and coordination and have developed the concepts of 'nesting' and 'polycentricity' to accommodate this (Ostrom, 1990, 2010a, 2010b). In response to questions about how local arrangements can be 'scaled up' and linked to other levels of management without losing the advantages of local 'fit', it is suggested that

> the principle that institutions are nested in a polycentric system provides an answer. At each level – from small to medium and large scale – entities govern the complex and dynamic ecosystems based on the most relevant information and with respect to the specific socio-cultural and ecological context (Inforesources Focus, 2010: 6–7; see also Andersson and Ostrom, 2008; Ostrom, 2009, 2010; Wyborn and Bixler, 2011)

An example from Kenya illustrates nested arrangements for water management consisting of 'Water User Associations at the local level, Catchment Advisory Committees for the regional level, and the Water Resources Management Authority at the national level' (Inforesources Focus, 2010: 6–7).

Nature of individual actions

Mainstream Institutionalism is strongly influenced by rational choice assumptions about human behaviour, in which individuals act purposefully in their own interests (assumed to be 'resource appropriation'). As Ostrom puts it, 'institutional rules are often self-consciously crafted by individuals to change the structure of repetitive situations that they themselves face in an attempt to improve the outcomes that they achieve' (Ostrom, 2005: 19). However, in this approach, people's rationality is seen as 'bounded', their strategizing being limited by their ability to obtain and process the necessary information, particularly about the trustworthiness of others. This gives a role for properly designed institutions in which the operation of rules provide individuals with an *assurance* that others will use the natural resource in agreed ways, or be sanctioned. Individuals will then cooperate if they are assured that others are also following the rules. In this way institutions help to reduce the transaction costs of repeated calculative interactions between individuals.

The overall strength of this school of thought is that it has theoretically and empirically demonstrated that the management of common property through collective action is possible; that there are certain conditions which can facilitate this; and that people govern resources through a variety of institutional forms. However, common property scholarship has also been criticized for its narrow focus on *local* institutions and its generally apolitical explanations of social–environmental interactions (Robbins, 2004; Chhotray, 2007). Recent revisions from within the Mainstream Institutionalist paradigm have begun to take into account the complexities of context (Acheson, 2006; Berkes, 2007), the discordant politics (Poteete, 2009) and the unpredictable interaction between social and ecological processes (McGinnis, 2010), all of which affect institutional design. However, despite these efforts and related attempts to refine the theoretical 'public choice' principles that underpin Mainstream Institutional analysis (Vatn, 2009; Aligica and Boettke, 2011), the core assumptions of this school of thought remain intact. Work by scholars from outside this school focuses more critically on the ways in which the wider context shapes institutional arrangements and on developing more socially informed understandings of human behaviour in institutions. Let me now attempt to characterize some of these alternative ideas.

Critical institutionalism

Various critiques have been formative in outlining alternative ideas about how local institutions work to shape resource use. These analyses derive from different disciplinary perspectives (social theory, political ecology, ethnography, legal pluralism, history), do not necessarily engage with each other and are difficult to categorize (see Table x). Some of this work does not focus primarily on *institutions* (see, e.g., Agrawal, 2005; Mosse, 2008) but nonetheless has influenced alternative ways of thinking about the collective management of natural resources. Conversely, valuable insights can be derived from institutional thinking that is not concerned with natural resource management, as for example in organizational theory (Mumby and Putnam, 1992; Scott, 2006). Here, I label all these approaches as broadly belonging to a school of 'Critical Institutionalism'. I use this term rather than the 'Post-Institutionalism' favoured by Mehta *et al.* (2001) to reflect a debt to critical realist thinking which recognizes diversity in social phenomena, the potentially creative effects of individual agency *and* highlights the enduring influence of social structures in shaping individual behaviour and in the patterning of outcomes (Archer, 2000; Sayer, 2000). The label is also appropriate because insights in this school of thought are variously drawn from critical social justice, political ecology and post-structural perspectives.

As the contributions that make up this school of thought are disparate, some work is needed to pull out common themes. It is testimony to the strength and coherence of common property scholarship that I begin by defining alternative thinking primarily in relation to this school of thought.

Nature of institutions

Critical Institutionalist approaches differ from Mainstream Institutionalism because their starting point is often a broad focus on the interactions between the natural and social worlds rather than a narrower concern with predicting and improving the outcomes of particular institutional processes. This results in a number of other differences of emphasis.

In Mainstream Institutional theory the nature of institutions tends to be formal and functional; they are crafted to address a specific dilemma of resource management; effectiveness is equated with clarity of purpose, transparency, public accountability and regularity of operation.

Critical Institutionalists, however, suggest that institutions managing natural resources are only rarely explicitly designed for such purposes and that their multi-functionalism renders them ambiguous, dynamic and only partially amenable to deliberate crafting. Here institutions are seen as both formal and informal; they are often multi-purpose, intermittent and semi-opaque in operation. Access to natural resources may be mediated by a range of institutions. These include designed arrangements of varying degrees of publicness and formality (committees, associations, user groups, burial societies), institutionalized interactions as embodied in kinship and social networks, relations of reciprocity and patronage and in sets of norms and practices deeply embedded in the habits and routines of everyday life.

Critical Institutionalists question the highly focused gaze of Mainstream Institutionalism and the abstraction involved in formulating design principles. By contrast, Critical Institutionalists emphasize the non-comparability of various 'messy' contexts, the inter-relating of global and local factors and the impact of social and economic changes over time (Mehta *et al.*, 2001; Steins, 2001). They variously draw on in-depth ethnographic studies, on the wider sweep of political economy and the *longue durée* of history to situate the formation, operation and outcomes of institutions (Ribot, 2001b; Johnson, 2004; Peters, 2004; Agrawal, 2005; Mosse, 2006, 2008; Fontein, 2008).

Institutional emergence and evolution

For some critics the evolutionary concepts underpinning Mainstream Institutionalism are over-simplified and too static (Rocheleau, 2001). We have seen how Mainstream Institutional thinking equates institutional robustness with clearly delineated formal structures and with the role 'crafting' plays in regularizing repeated interactions, so making good the deficiencies of 'traditional' or informal arrangements (Ostrom, 2000).

Critical Institutionalists suggest rather that it is possible for institutions to operate intermittently, through informal relationships as well as formal structures *and* to be enduring and approximately effective (Berry, 1994; Chase Smith, *et al.*, 2001; Benjaminsen and Lund, 2002; Berry, 2005). Institutional arrangements are partly formed in the practices, norms and relationships of everyday life, may ebb and flow, and may be *both* intermittent and robust (an example would the phased introduction of queuing and rationing of water in times of drought, as illustrated in Chapter 3). The cumulative layering of arrangements renders dichotomous categorizations of institutions (as formal or informal, modern or traditional, state or community, public or private) redundant (Bierschenk and de Sardan, 2003). Institutional blending occurs when, for example, 'informal' or customary institutions emulate state bureaucracies (adopting 'official' stamps and constitutions) and when 'formal' institutional arrangements become blurred when operationalized through social relationships and practices, such as patronage (Benjaminsen and Lund, 2002; Lund, 2009; Lesorogol, 2010). Studies from Latin America, Africa and Asia illustrate

the dynamic evolution of institutions (involving both conflict and reconciliation) that occurs when modernizing states try to impose standard
polices, laws, organizational structures in localities where there may be
very different ideas about equitable distribution and decision-making
and pre-existing norms and arrangements for managing resources (Sikor
et al., 2009; Lesorogol, 2010; Van Koppen *et al.*, 2007).

Nature of human behaviour

Critical institutionalists reject the 'thin' model of boundedly rational
human action adopted by Mainstream Institutionalism, in which behaviour
is either strategic or learnt and a common interest in resource appropriation is seen as the foundation for collective action. Instead, they see
the influences shaping human behaviour as more diverse and complex and
adopt a 'thicker' model of human agency. For them, strategic livelihood
choices (about the use of resources) are critically influenced by social
concerns (such as the need to live in peace with neighbours), by psychological preferences (for example for cooperation over confrontation) and
by culturally and historically shaped ideas about the 'right way of doing
things'. Individuals, invested with complex identities and affinities, may
operate within a number of overlapping but diffuse networks or communities in multiple locations. In this model people can purposefully plan
their actions in relation to the collective, but this is likely to be informed
by 'emotional', 'moral' or 'social' rationalities as well as economic ones
(Scott, 1985; Boelens, 2008). Actions and preferences are also shaped
by non-conscious factors – by taken-for-granted everyday practices and
embedded ideologies. For Critical Institutionalists, the workings of power
and the patterning of inequality means that some people are more able to
shape collective rule making and to benefit from the outcomes than others.

Rather than being designed, or even crafted, institutions are patched
together, consciously and non-consciously, from the social, cultural and
political resources available to people based on the logic of dynamic
adaptation (Chase Smith *et al.*, 2001: 42). As such, institutions are not
'things' but the results of what people do; they must be continually reproduced or re-enacted by people to exist (Rocheleau, 2001). In combining
a highly contextualized focus with an awareness of the wider structural
forces shaping institutions, it becomes clear that no one factor (or group
of factors) is sufficient to explain their success. Rather, institutional
processes are dynamic, play out through very different forms in varying
contexts and, to this extent, elude design (Cleaver and Franks, 2005).

The key elements of the two schools of thought are characterized in
Table 1.2.

Challenges in Understanding Institutions

In characterizing the different schools of thought it is easy to see Mainstream Institutionalism as clear, normative and instrumental and Critical Instrumentalism as providing insights into complexity, negotiability and fuzziness. But both approaches leave us with a number of unresolved challenges in understanding institutions, to which we now turn.

Making complexity legible

If institutions are things people do rather than objects, then they are very difficult to capture in analytical snapshots. A focus on constitutions, the composition of committees, records of rules and sanctions tends to illuminate the more static manifestations of institutional functioning. It is far more difficult to capture the invisible workings of power, the informal bargaining and bending of rules in practice, the worldviews which shape participation and the uneven ways that institutional

Table 1.2 Key features of Institutional Thinking

Features	School of thought Mainstream Institutionalism	School of thought Critical Institutionalism
Nature of institutions	Formal/public institutions in nested layers with horizontal and vertical linkages	Blurring of boundaries and of scales, blending of institutional logics and forms (eg formal/informal).
Formation of institutions	Institutions formed through crafting; design principles characterise robust institutions.	Institutions pieced together through practice, improvisation, adaptation of previous arrangements.
Nature of decision-making	Decision-making and negotiations mainly conducted in public fora	Decision-making and negotiations embedded in everyday life, shaped by history and politics.
Models of agency	'Bounded rationality' models of agency as strategic and purposeful – individuals as resource appropriators.	Agency as relational, exercised consciously and non-consciously – individuals with complex social identities and emotions.
Factors shaping human behaviour in institutions	Information, incentives, rules, sanctions and repeated interactions.	Social structures and power dynamics, relationships, norms, individual creativity.
Outcomes	Institutions can be crafted to produce efficient resource management outcomes.	Institutions evolve to 'socially fit': functioning may result in access to *or* exclusion from resources.

arrangements work for different people. In this sense Mainstream Institutionalists, by specifically adopting a focus on understanding factors *internal* to the workings of public institutions, reduce the scope of this challenge. Ostrom and colleagues do endeavour to capture the dynamic aspects of institutions through tracking 'rules-in-use' – the ways that collective rules are actually applied and adapted in practice. These, however, prove much harder to capture or encode than more formally expressed rules. When Critical Institutionalists both deepen the focus to include social relationships and practices (some of which are implicit and non-conscious) and expand it to encompass wider societal trends, there is a danger of losing explanatory power to depth and breadth of description. Capturing 'institutions-in-motion' is indeed a tricky endeavour implying multi-dimensional long-term studies, and these are only rarely favoured by funding agencies (Berry, 1994).

The practical appeal of Mainstream Institutionalism is enormous. The design principles for robust and long-enduring institutions are frequently reiterated and elaborated in the literature and directly translated into policy and project documents, as guidance for action (Cleaver and Franks, 2008). Ostrom herself has cautioned against using the principles as a *blueprint* for institutional design, both reflecting on their utility and sensibly re-formulating them as 'design questions' (Ostrom, 2005, 2008 and 2010a). However, clarity is seen as desirable in policy; it helps to choose between options, reduce uncertainty and maintain a focus on specific interventions and outcomes. Adopting a design principles approach seemingly offers a practical solution to the conundrum of ensuring efficient and sustainable use of natural resources without excessive intervention by the state (Mizrahi, 2003; Meinzen-Dick, 2007; Asian Development Bank, 2009; Ostrom, 2010a). It has also been argued that the reliance of common property thinking on rational choice, game theory and evolutionary psychology fits well in an intellectual climate which values positivism, methodological individualism and formal modelling (Johnson, 2004).

However, critics suggest that this clarity is only achieved through over-simplification, by assuming that institutional design begins with a clean slate and occurs within clear (local) boundaries. Indeed, some suggest that the very abstractions and simplifications necessary to policy formulation also render such policy un-implementable at the level of messy social reality (Lewis, 2009).

By contrast, the complexity analyses offered by Critical Institutionalism have far less appeal to those concerned with development interventions. The emphasis on 'messiness' in the shaping of institutions offers a way of exploring complexity but without the 'locking down' of this into practical guidelines, it is an approach which often remains illegible to policy-makers (Blaikie, 2006; Mosse, 2006). Critical institutional literature does not seem to offer the same rigorous empiricism as is often claimed for the synthetic approach to thousands of case studies offered by Ostrom's school of work. It can therefore be more easily dismissed as only 'anecdotal', lacking a strong evidence base and therefore not generalizable across contexts.

What would our analysis of institutions look like if we tried to steer a path between the need for complex analyses with a social justice perspective on the one hand and the need for legibility and policy direction on the other? Following Burawoy's categorization of the production of sociological knowledge we might see the need for a project that creates a reflexive public knowledge about institutions and natural resource management (Burawoy, 2005, 2006). Such knowledge would bring the instrumental perspectives beloved of policy-makers into productive engagement with the critical reflection on their underlying concepts and effects favoured by social science academics. This would include scrutiny of taken-for-granted models of human behaviour and of explanations of people/institutions/nature interactions at various levels of analysis (Cleaver and Franks 2008; Franks and Cleaver, 2009). Such reflexive public knowledge could usefully contribute to better understanding the functioning and effects of institutions and point the way towards more socially effective governance of natural resources.

The challenges of framing, scale and focus

Mainstream Institutionalism is largely concerned with the local-level institution as the 'field of action'. Broader scales are dealt with through the concept of institutions nested into layers of linked arrangements. This focus on community management of resources through particular institutions tells us little about their societal 'fit' or their outcomes for 'development' more generally. Unless linked to broader analyses (such as those derived from political economy/ecology or social theory), these narrowly focused cases cannot help explain wider trends in society or recurring patterns in the outcomes of natural resource governance.

For Critical Institutionalists, often concerned with micro-processes of negotiation and resource access enacted through social relationships, the challenge is also to successfully blend a dual focus. Making a similar point, Pauline Peters argues that analyses of land use and property rights that are influenced by post-structuralism correctly emphasize local diversity, adaptability and negotiation and are important in countering over-simplified economic models of tenure. However, in doing so they are in danger of obscuring significant *patterns* of social and political change. Peters suggests the need to balance the focus on local complexities by identifying and tracking those processes (such as commodification, structural adjustment, market liberalization and globalization) that limit the possibilities of negotiation for particular people (Peters, 2004).

Drawing on Peters' insights, I suggest that institutional analysis needs to be able to place local arrangements within wider frames of governance. Examples of attempts to conceptualize such interlinkages include Agrawal's (2004) study of the multi-level nature of forest management as enacted through decentralised government, regulatory communities (villages, forest councils) and environmental subjects (people as forest users). Mollinga (2008) identifies intersecting domains of water politics as including international policy making; negotiations between sovereign states, policy processes within nation states and the everyday politics of water distribution and access. In both these approaches the different domains are not intended as a hierarchy of levels of resource governance; rather, they merge and leak into one another. So the water or forest user at village level may indeed draw on national or international policy ideas in negotiating resource access with their neighbours. It is a tricky task to track the intersection of these different domains, but I suggest that institutions provide an interface at which this happens and can usefully be analyzed as such.

There are considerable challenges of focus posed by trying to capture the complexity of institutional processes and the patterns of outcomes they produce. The purposes, meanings and effects of institutions may not solely be about sustainable natural resource management, even when designed for that purpose. An example is provided by ways in which the state influences natural resource management. Bringing the state back in to analyses of community-level collective action could usefully broaden and deepen institutional analysis, recognizing that in many situations formal state organizations retain responsibility for public goods and for ensuring equity and sustainability. However, literature also suggests that we need to understand ways in which the workings of the state more generally leaks across scales and boundaries. This means that local negotiations over resource access relate both to the workings of the 'informal' or the 'everyday' state and to wider processes of state formation and institutional formalization (Fuller and Benei, 2001; Corbridge, 2005; Sikor and Lund, 2009; Hagmann and Peclard 2010; Titeca and de Herdt 2011).

Linking the material and social

Mainstream Institutional analysis well recognizes the way in which the physical characteristics of natural resources influence institutional arrangements. Critical Institutionalism emphasizes the ways in which material resources are managed through social relationships. Finding a way to combine both perspectives and to include understanding of the ways in which social arrangements also manifest physically (through labour, infrastructure and resource use practices) would significantly strengthen institutional analysis. Institutions are primarily social arrangements, but they shape the ways in which people physically manage and obtain access to material resources.

The resources to be managed through institutions have different material attributes and manifestations (think of the difference between water, which flows, seeps, evaporates, and land, which usually does not [Schlager et al, 1994]). The physical properties of the resource shape human-made arrangements (institutions and infrastructure) and also can be shaped by them. A good example of this is offered by a gravity-fed irrigation system in which the physical infrastructure (gates, canals) and the institutions (including rules about gate opening, water turns, maintenance) are a response to, and also influence, volumetric and seasonal flows of water. Such material arrangements may reinforce or ameliorate socio-spatial inequities, such as those between the water-rich farmers at the head-end of the system and water-poor farmers at the tail-end of the system (Merrey *et al.*, 2007).

The material nature and spatial location of the resource and its management through infrastructure and technology affects rights of access, claims to property and the potential for commodification. So people may claim individual tenure for land they have improved, charges may be levied for a pump or for diesel where charging for water itself is unacceptable. In these ways, investments in creating and maintaining infrastructure, often organized through institutional arrangements, are a material form of creating property rights (a point well articulated by Fleuret, 1985; Mollinga, 2011).

We should not overlook the symbolic importance of natural and human-made material resources. Aspects of the landscape and particular manifestations of natural resources (as in natural springs) may be imbued with significant cultural and affective meaning (Fontein, 2008). Such meaning is also implicated in claims on authority, tradition and on proper social order. For example, Veronica Strang shows how historic struggles over the appropriation of the material culture of water (springs, wells, pumps, fountains) in the Stour Valley in Dorset, England were imbued with *gendered* social meaning. She well illustrates the linking of cosmological ideas with socio-political organization and command over physical and material resources (Strang, 2005).

People access and manage resources through *embodied* practices.

Norms and conventions regarding gendered divisions of labour influence who fetches water or firewood, who pans for gold, goes fishing, does irrigation farming. Command over labour is essential to many aspects of natural resource management including construction (of trenches, canals, bunds, fences), operation of infrastructure (opening weirs and gates) monitoring and patrolling (of grazing areas, forest reserves) for maintenance, and for fee collection.

The focus on inclusive public decision-making in mainstream institutional analysis often overlooks the fact that participation requires physical presence. Such analyses pay scant attention to those physically absent from public decision-making fora – those too old, sick, disabled, poor or discriminated against to participate (Chambers, 1983). Moreover, within public decision-making spaces status, social power and position are physically exhibited in dress and bodily demeanour, which in turn influence outcomes (Bourdieu, 1977, 1985). We also know that those who use, collect and manage the resource in practice (often women and children) are not necessarily the public rule makers, who, by merit of their social position can often delegate the everyday physical tasks of resource appropriation (Karim, 2006; Fonjong, 2008). However, some studies also question whether, if barriers to participation were removed, everyone would *choose* to personally be present in *public* decision-making about resource use (Zwarteveen and Neupane, 1996). So a challenge to analysis is to understand the physical as well as the social dimensions of the interface between agency, institutions and natural resource management.

How does power work?

In the mainstream study of institutions for natural resource management I argue that there is too much emphasis on power exercised by individuals claiming their rights through participation – strategizing and bargaining over the allocation and use of resources. The implied model of power is an instrumental one in which actors can mobilize to influence decision-making to their benefit. Power thus becomes a form of 'capital' which can be created and deployed to secure beneficial outcomes. Critical Institutionalism has the potential to make power and politics more central to the analysis of institutions but does not necessarily do this effectively, partly because of the decentred focus implied in post-structural approaches.

For any analysis of institutions and their effects we need to find a way of examining both the public politics of control over resources *and* of uncovering the 'invisible' operations of power relations (Lukes, 2005; Ribot, 2009). This may seem obvious, particularly to social science academics, but has only recently become an acceptable focus for policy analysis (Hickey, 2009). Colleagues and I were once asked to edit the word 'politics' out of a policy briefing about research on water governance, as, along with conclusions about 'complexity', this was considered off-putting to policy-makers (see the results in ID21 Insights, 2007). The bias against power analysis is not universal and for water governance there is a growing understanding of the need to incorporate a political economy or political sociology perspective (Woodhouse, 2002; Mollinga 2008; O'Meally, 2009). However, the preference for 'technocratic' understandings of relations of authority is strong, often resulting in an emphasis on examining the interests of particular 'stakeholders'. This leads to an explanatory dilemma. For Mainstream Institutionalism too much depends on analyzing publicly visible processes of decision-making, resulting in a sidelining of macro- and micro-level politics. In Critical Institutionalism there is a tendency to focus on examples of the exercise of power by the disadvantaged – a celebration of local instances of resistance or of collective action – without tracking their real and lasting effects on outcomes.

The challenge then is the process tracking of the exercise of power through a plurality of institutions and actors, social practices and everyday encounters – not just through state governance and public spaces. If natural resources are governed through polycentric institutional arrangements, then we need to uncover the workings of power through such overlapping domains and practices. By definition this would involve studying interactions over time, beyond the institutional setting and raises the questions of what the boundaries of institutional analysis should be.

We also need to incorporate awareness of the 'invisible' workings of power into institutional analyses. This refers to the ways in which ideologies, beliefs and norms shape the very nature of decision-making and involves understanding the direct and indirect ways in which power is maintained (Osei-Kufuor, 2010). Why are some institutional arrangements considered appropriate and viable whilst others not even imagined as possible alternatives? Why do those marginalized from decision-making and its benefits so often acquiesce to the inequitable allocation of resources? What configurations of power are reflected in the ways in which people think about their place in the world, their rights of access to resources, their ability to shape institutional arrangements? Analyzing 'invisible' power poses obvious challenges and means moving beyond studying the public spaces of collective action to consider how social structures, ideologies and 'ways of seeing' shape human relations inequitably.

Understanding individual and collective action

An analytic focus on the individual dominates from different conceptual standpoints. We have already noted how Mainstream Institutionalist ideas are underpinned by assumptions about the bounded rationality nature of human behaviour, and are cursory in dealing with the vast array of social motivations that entwine to shape human action. This leads to inadequate exploration, understanding and policy.

Approaches influenced by social theory might usefully enrich such 'thin' models of human agency, and indeed this is one of the promises of Critical Institutionalism. However there are weaknesses in these approaches ranging from too concrete a conceptualization of the social embeddedness of human action (implying that it is fixed in culture, tradition, norms) to the celebration of individualization (as evidenced in instances of resistance to norms, of negotiation of rules, of creating new livelihoods). For Roth (2009), embeddedness may be the source of both coherence and conflict. There is a danger that actor–oriented approaches, in their fascination with the diverse and creative ways in which people navigate social lives and livelihoods, can obscure the real workings of power and inequality.

I have argued above for considering the physical dimensions of human action in institutions and natural resource management. What other factors are key to understanding individual actions? If motivations are not only economic, then what are the elements of more socialized rationalities and how do these shape resource use and management? One significant challenge for institutional analysis here is to better understand the nature of individual actions (in their conscious and non-conscious dimensions) and how these are also shaped by collective identities and allegiances.

In much of the mainstream literature on community-based natural resource management, collective action is seen as the desirable result of boundedly rational individuals cooperating for mutual benefit. The political science literature on governance and social action sees collective action as inherently political – people joining together in social movements to resist oppressive state action, to further progressive change (Hickey and Mohan, 2004; Pearce, 2004). These approaches overlap in their emphasis on the benefits of active participation in decision-making (as resource users or citizens) as a process through which people can individually and collectively improve their lives. In focusing on public/ political manifestations of collective action, neither approach adequately deals with the institutionalized mutual activities of social life – weddings, funerals, rain-making ceremonies, savings clubs, burial societies, place, kin or belief-based networks. As we shall see in the course of this book, these are important as the arenas in which authority is asserted or challenged, joint identities formed and consolidated, norms reproduced or negotiated (Jones, 2009).

Conclusion

In summary, we need to develop richer explanations of how various influences shape human actions and what the effects of socially located institutional processes are for more robust and socially just natural resource management. Specifically, the challenges of institutional analysis are:

- To produce analyses of complex and dynamic institutional processes which are broadly legible to policy and public decision-making.
- To understand community-level natural resource management as located in overlapping domains of action and also patterned by relationships and structures beyond the local.
- To understand the various ways in which institutions as social arrangements manifest in physical practices and material structures.
- To better incorporate power relations into institutional analyses by a combined focus on the public exercise of authority *and* a scrutiny of the offstage, invisible and everyday dynamics of power.
- To develop a pliable concept of embeddedness that allows for meaningful exploration of located individual and collection action. Such analyses would recognize that resource management is patterned but not determined by social structure and would attempt to delineate the 'room for manoeuvre' offered to individuals by institutional arrangements.

This book is an attempt to address some of these challenges. Broadly located within a Critical Institutionalist perspective, it aims to further the more systematic development of this school of thinking through the development of the concept of *institutional bricolage*, elaborated in the following chapters.

Bibliography

Acheson, J. (2006) 'Institutional Failure in Resource Management', *Annual Review of Anthropology* 35, pp. 117–34.

Agrawal, A. (2005) *Environmentality: Technologies of Government and the Making of Subjects*. Durham, NC, Duke University Press.

Agrawal, A. and Chhatre, A. (2007) 'State Involvement and Forest Co-Governance: Evidence from the Indian Himalayas', *Studies in Comparative International Development [SCID]* 42, 1, pp. 67–86.

Agrawal, A. and Gibson, C. (1999) 'Enchantment and Disenchantment: The Role of Community in Natural Resource Conservation', *World Development* 24, 4, pp. 629–49.

—(eds) (2001) *Communities and Nature*. Piscataway, NJ, Rutgers University Press.

Aligica, P. D. and Boettke, P. (2011) 'The Two Social Philosophies of Ostrom's Institutionalism', *Policy Studies Journal*, 39, 1, pp. 29–49.

Andersson, K. and Ostrom, E. (2008) 'Analyzing Decentralized Resource Regimes from a Polycentric Perspective', *Policy Sciences*, 41, 1, pp. 71–93.

Archer, M. (2000) *Being Human: The Problem of Agency*. Cambridge, Cambridge University Press.

Asian Development Bank (1999) *Governance: Sound Development Management*. Manila, ADB.

—(2009) *Kiribati's Political Economy and Capacity Development*. Mandaluyong City, Philippines, ADB.

Beall, J. (2005) 'Decentralizing Government and Decentering Gender: Lessons from Local Government Reform in South Africa', *Politics and Society* 33, 2, pp. 253–76.

Benjaminsen, T. and Lund, C. E. (2002) 'Formalisation and Informalisation of Land and Water Rights in Africa: An Introduction', *European Journal of Development Research*, 14, 2, pp. 1–10.

Berkes, F. (2007) 'Community-Based Conservation in a Globalized World', *Proceedings of the National Academy of Sciences of the United States of America*, 104, 39, pp. 15188–93.

Berry, S. (1994) 'Resource Access and Management as Historical Processes: Conceptual and Methodological Issues', in C. Lund and H. Marcussen (eds) *Access, Control and Management of Natural Resources in Sub-Saharan Africa: Methodological Considerations*, Occasional Paper 13, Roskilde University, Roskilde, pp. 24–45.

—(2005) 'Poverty Counts: Living with Poverty and Poverty Measures', paper presented at the International Conference on the Many Dimensions of Poverty, Carlton Hotel, Brasilia, Brazil, 29–31 August.

Bierschenk, T. and de Sardan, J.-P.-O. (2003) 'Powers in the Village: Rural Benin between Democratisation and Decentralisation', *Africa*, 73, 2, pp. 145–73.

Blaikie, P. (2006) 'Is Small Really Beautiful? Community-Based Natural Resource Management in Malawi and Botswana', *World Development*, 34, 11, pp. 1942–57.

Boelens, R. (2008) *The Rules of the Game and the Game of the Rules: Normalization and Resistance in Andean Water Control*, Wageningen University, Wageningen.

Bourdieu, P. (1977) *Outline of a Theory of Practice*, Cambridge, Cambridge University Press.

—(1985) 'The Market of Symbolic Goods', *Poetics* 14, pp. 13–44.

Bruns, B. (2009) 'Metaphors and Methods for Institutional Synthesis', paper presented at the Water Resource Governance and Design Principles, Workshop in Political Theory and Policy Analysis, Indiana University, Bloomington, June 3–6.

Burawoy, M. (2005) 'For Public Sociology', *American Sociological Review*, 70, pp. 4–28.

—(2006) 'Open the Social Sciences: To Whom and For What?' Address to the Portuguese Sociological Association, 30 March, http://sociology.berkeley.edu/faculty/burawoy/burawoy_pdfburawoy-open_thesocialsciences.pdf.

Campbell, B., Mandondo, A., Nemarundwe, N., Sithole, B., De Jong, W., Luckert, M. and Matose, F. (2001) 'Challenges to Proponents of Common Property Resource Systems: Despairing Voices from the Social Forests of Zimbabwe', *World Development*, 29, 4, pp. 589–600.

Chambers, R. (1983) *Rural Development: Putting the Last First*, Harlow, Pearson Education.

Chase Smith, R., Pinedo, D., Summers, P. M. and Almeyda, A. (2001) 'Tropical Rhythms and Collective Action: Community-Based Fisheries Management in the Face of Amazonian Unpredictability', *IDS Bulletin*, 32, 4, pp. 36–46.

Chhotray, V. (2007) 'The "Anti-Politics Machine" in India: Depoliticisation Through Local Institution Building for Participatory Watershed Development', *Journal of Development Studies*, 43, 6, pp. 1037–56.

Cinner, J. E., Basurto, X., Fidelman, P., Kuange, J., Lahari, R. and Mukminin, A. (2011) 'Institutional Designs of Customary Fisheries Management Arrangements in Indonesia, Papua New Guinea, and Mexico', *Marine Policy*, in press, corrected proof.

Cleaver, Frances (2002) 'Reinventing Institutions: Bricolage and the Social Embeddedness of Natural Resource Management', *European Journal of Development Research*, 14, 2, pp. 11–30.

Cleaver, F. and Franks, T. (2008) 'Distilling or Diluting: Negotiating the Water Research-Policy Interface', *Water Alternatives*, 1, 1, pp. 157–77.

Cleaver, F., Franks, T., Boesten, J. and Kiire, A. (2005) 'Water Governance and Poverty: What Works for the Poor?' Report to DFID, University of Bradford, http://www.splash.bradford.ac.uk/files/PDF%20Water%20Governance%20and%20Poverty%20Final%20Report%2006.05.pdf.

Cleaver, F. and Hamada, K. (2010) '"Good" Water Governance and Gender Equity: A Troubled Relationship', *Gender and Development*, 18, 1, pp. 27–41.

Cleaver, F. and Toner, A. (2006) 'The Evolution of Community Water Governance in Uchira, Tanzania: The Implications for Equality of Access, Sustainability and Effectiveness', *Natural Resources Forum*, 30, 3, pp. 207–18.

Cleveringa, R., Kay, M., Cohen, A. (2009) Synthesis of strategic approaches for enhancing pro-poor investments in water and rural livelihoods. IFAD pp. 1–2, http://www.ifad.org/english/water/innowat/strategic/Chapeau_web.pdf

Cooke, B. and Kothari, U. (eds) (2001) *Participation: The New Tyranny*, London, Zed Books.

Corbridge, S. (2005) *Seeing the State: Governance and Governmentality in India*. Cambridge, Cambridge University Press.

Cornwall, A. (2004) 'New Democratic Spaces', *IDS Bulletin*, 35, 2.

Cox, M., Arnold, G. and Villamayor Tomás, S. (2010) 'A Review of Design Principles for Community-Based Natural Resource Management', *Ecology and Society*, 15, 4, pp. 38–60.

Dikito-Wachtmeister, M. (2000) 'Women's Participation in Decision-Making Processes in Rural Water Projects, Makoni District, Zimbabwe', unpublished PhD thesis, University of Bradford.

Fleuret, P. (1985) 'The Social Organization of Water Control in the Taita Hills, Kenya', *American Ethnologist*, 12, 1, pp. 103–18.

Fonjong, L. N. (2008) 'Gender Roles and Practices in Natural Resource Management in the North West Province of Cameroon', *The International Journal of Justice and Sustainability*, 13, 5, pp. 461–75.

Fontein, J. (2008) 'The Power of Water: Landscape, Water and the State in Southern and Eastern Africa – an Introduction', *Journal of Southern African Studies*, 34, 4, pp. 737–56.

Franks, T. and Cleaver, F. (2009) 'Analysing Water Governance: A Tool for Sustainability', *Engineering Sustainability*, 162, 4, pp. 207–14.

Fuller, C. and Benei, V. (eds) (2001) *The Everyday State and Society in Modern India*, London, C. Hurst & Co.

Goldman, M. (1998) 'Inventing the Commons: Theories and Practices of the Commons' Professional', in M. Goldman (ed.) *Privatizing Nature: Political Struggles for the Global Commons*, London, Pluto Press, pp. 20–53.

Grindle, M. (2007) *Going Local: Decentralization, Democratization, and the Promise of Good Governance*, Woodstock, Princeton University Press.

Hagmann, T and Peclard, D (2010) 'Negotiating Statehood: Dynamics of Power and Domination in Africa', *Development and Change*, 41, 4, pp. 539–62.

Hardin, G. (1968) 'The Tragedy of the Commons', *Science*, 162, pp. 1243–8.

—(1998) 'Extensions of "The Tragedy of the Commons"', *Science*, 280, 5364, pp. 682–3.

Heikkila, T., Schlager, E. and Davis, M. W. (2011) 'The Role of Cross-Scale Institutional Linkages in Common Pool Resource Management: Assessing Interstate River Compact', *Policy Studies Journal*, 39, 1, pp. 121–45.

Hickey, S. (2009) 'The Return of Politics in Development Studies (Part Two): Capturing the Political?', *Progress in Development Studies*, 9, 2, pp. 141–52.

Hickey, S. and Mohan, G. (2004) 'Relocating Participation within a Radical Politics of Development: Critical Modernism and Citizenship', in S. Hickey and G. Mohan (eds) *Participation: From Tyranny to Transformation? Exploring New Approaches to Participation in Development*, London, Zed Books.

House, S. (2003) 'Easier to Say, Harder to Do: Gender, Equity and Water', paper presented at the Alternative Water Forum, University of Bradford, May 1–2.

Houtzager, P. and Lavalle, A. (2009) 'Participatory Governance and the Challenge of Assumed Representation in Brazil', *IDS Working Paper*, 321.

Huppert, Walter (2008) 'Coping with Complexity: Innovative Approaches to an Emerging Issue in Agricultural Water Management', IFAD, www.ifad.org/english/water/innowat/strategic/complexity_web.pdf.

Id21 Insights (2007) 'New Directions for Water Governance', *id21 Insights*, 67.

Inforesources Focus (2010) 'Shaping Institutions for Natural Resources Management', *InfoResouces Focus*, 3/08, Swiss Agency for Development and Cooperation.

Johnson, C. (2004) 'Uncommon Ground: The "Poverty of History" in Common Property Discourse', *Development and Change*, 35, 3, pp. 407–33.

Jones, B. (2009) *Beyond the State in Rural Uganda: Development in Rural Uganda*, Edinburgh, Edinburgh University Press.

Joshi, D., Lloyd, M. and Fawcett, B. (2003) 'Voices from the Village: An Alternative Paper for the Alternative Water Forum,' paper presented at the Alternative Water Forum, Bradford Centre for International Development, University of Bradford, May 1–2.

Karim, K. M. R. (2006) 'Gendered Social Institutions and the Management of Underground Irrigation Water Resources in a Bangladeshi Village', *Gender Technology and Development*, March 10, 1, pp. 13–36.

Lesorogol, C. K. (2010) 'The Impact of Privatization on Land Inheritance among Samburu Pastoralists in Kenya', *Development and Change*, 41, 6, pp. 1091–116.

Lewis, D. (2009) 'International Development and the "Perpetual Present": Anthropological Approaches to the Re-Historicization of Policy', *European Journal of Development Research*, 21, 1, pp. 32–46.

Lukes, S. (2005) *Power: A Radical View*, Basingstoke, Palgrave Macmillan, 2nd edition.

Lund, C. (2006) 'Twilight Institutions: Public Authority and Local Politics in Africa', *Development and Change*, 37, 4, pp. 685–705.

—(2009) 'Recategorizing "Public" and "Private" Property in Ghana', *Development and Change*, 40, 1, pp. 131–48.

McGinnis, M. D. (2010) 'Building a Program for Institutional Analysis of Social-Ecological Systems: A Review of Revisions to the SES Framework', working paper, Workshop in Political Theory and Policy Analysis, Indiana University. http://mypage.iu.edu/~mcginnis/vita.htm#otherpubs.

—(2011) 'An Introduction to IAD and the Language of the Ostrom Workshop: A Simple Guide to a Complex Framework', *Policy Studies Journal*, 39, 1, pp. 169–83.

McGranahan, G. and Satterthwaite, D. (2006) 'Governance and Getting the Private Sector to Provide Better Water and Sanitation Services to the Urban Poor', IIED Human Settlements working paper.

Meagher, K. (2010) *Identity Economics: Social Networks and the Informal Economy in Nigeria*, Woodbridge, Suffolk, James Currey.

Mehta, L., Leach, M. and Scoones, I. (2001) 'Editorial: Environmental Governance in an Uncertain World', *IDS Bulletin*, 32, 4, pp. 1–9.

Meinzen-Dick, R. (2007) 'Beyond Panaceas in Water Institutions', *Proceedings of the National Academy of Sciences of the United States of America*, 104, 39, pp. 15200–205.

Mercer, C., Page, B. and Evans, M. (2008) *Development and the African Diaspora: Place and the Politics of Home*, London, Zed Books.

Merrey, D. J., Meinzen-Dick, R., Mollinga, P. and Karar, E. (2007) 'Policy and Institutional Reform: The Art of the Possible', in D. Molden (ed.) *Water for Food, Water for Life: A Comprehensive Assessment of Water Management in Agriculture*, London, Earthscan, pp. 193–231.

Mizrahi, Y. (2003) *Capacity Enhancement Indicators: Review of the Literature*, Washington, World Bank.

Mollinga, P. (2008) 'Water, Politics and Development: Framing a Political Sociology of Water Resources Management', *Water Alternatives*, 1, 1, pp. 7–23.

—(2011) 'The Material Conditions of a Polarized Discourse: Clamours and Silences in Critical Analysis of Agricultural Water Use in India', *Journal of Agrarian Change*, 10, 3, pp. 414–36.

Morvaridi, B (2008) *Social Justice and Development*, Basingstoke, Palgrave Macmillan.

Mosse, D. (1997) 'The Symbolic Making of a Common Property Resource: History, Ecology and Locality in a Tank-Irrigated Landscape in South India', *Development and Change*, 28, 3, pp. 467–504.

—(2006) 'Collective Action, Common Property, and Social Capital in South India: An Anthropological Commentary', *Economic Development and Cultural Change*, 54, 3, pp. 695–724.

—(2008) 'Epilogue: The Cultural Politics of Water – A Comparative Perspective', *Journal of Southern African Studies*, 34, 4, pp. 939–48.

Mtisi, S. and Nicol, A. (2003) 'Appropriate for Whom? Challenging the Discourse on Decentralisation – Lessons from Zimbabwe', Alternative Water Forum, http://www.splash.bradford.ac.uk/project-six/.

Mumby, D. K. and Putnam, L. (1992) 'The Politics of Emotion: A Feminist Reading of "Bounded Rationality"', *Academy of Management Review*, 17, pp. 465–86.

Neimark, B. (2010) 'Subverting Regulatory Protection of "Natural Commodities": The Prunus Africana in Madagascar', *Development and Change*, 41, 5, pp. 929–54.

Nelson, F. and Agrawal, A. (2008) 'Patronage or Participation? Community-Based Natural Resource Management Reform in Sub-Saharan Africa', *Development and Change*, 39, 4, pp. 557–85.

North, D. (1990) *Institutions, Institutional Change and Economic Performance*, Cambridge, Cambridge University Press.

O'Meally, S. (2009) 'Political Economy, Water and the MDGs', ODI Opinion, http:// simonomeally.wordpress.com/2010/05/02/politcaleconomywaterandmillenium developmentgoal/.

Osei-Kufuor, P. (2010) 'Does Institutionalising Decentralisation Work? Rethinking Agency, Institutions and Authority in Local Governance: A Case Study of Ntonaboma in Kwahu-North District, Ghana', unpublished PhD thesis, University of Bradford.

Ostrom, E. (1990) *Governing the Commons: The Evolution of Institutions for Collective Action*, Cambridge, Cambridge University Press.

—(1992) *Crafting Institutions for Self-Governing Irrigation Systems*, San Francisco, ICS Press.

—(2000) 'Collective Action and the Evolution of Social Norms', *Journal of Economic Perspectives*, 14, 3, pp. 137–58.

—(2005) *Understanding Institutional Diversity*, Princeton, Princeton University Press.

—(2007) 'A Diagnostic Approach for Going Beyond Panaceas', *Proceedings of the National Academy of Sciences of the United States of America*, 104, 39, pp. 15181–7.

—(2008) 'Design Principles of Robust Property-Rights Institutions: What Have We Learned?' paper presented at Land Policies and Property Rights, Lincoln Institute of Land Policy, Cambridge, MA, June 2–3.

—(2009) 'Beyond Markets and States: Polycentric Governance of Complex Economic Systems', Nobel Lecture, 8 December.

—(2010a) 'Nested Externalities and Polycentric Institutions: Must We Wait for Global Solutions to Climate Change Before Taking Actions at Other Scales?' *Economic Theory*, pp. 1–17.

—(2010b) 'A Polycentric Approach for Coping with Climate Change', *Policy Research Working Paper* 5095, background paper to the World Development Report.

Ostrom, E., Janssen, M. and Anderies, J. (2007) 'Going Beyond Panaceas', *Proceedings of the National Academy of Sciences of the United States of America*, 104, 39, pp. 15176–8.

Ostrom, V. (1980) 'Artisanship and Artifact', *Public Administration Review*, 40, pp. 309–17.

Pearce, J. (2004) 'Collective Action or Public Participation?: Complimentary or Contradictory Democratisation Strategies in Latin America', *Bulletin of Latin American Research*, 23, 4, pp. 483–504.

Peters, P. E. (2004) 'Inequality and Social Conflict Over Land in Africa', *Journal of Agrarian Change*, 4, 3, pp. 269–314.

Poteete, A. R. (2009) 'Defining Political Community and Rights to Natural Resources in Botswana', *Development and Change*, 40, 2, pp. 281–305.

Putnam, R. (1994) *Making Democracy Work: Civic Traditions in Modern Italy*, Princeton, Princeton University Press.

Ribot, J. (2001a) 'Decentralized Natural Resource Management: Nature and Democratic Decentralization in Sub-Saharan Africa', summary report prepared for the UNCDF symposium Decentralization Local Government in Africa.

—(2001b) 'Integral Local Development: "Accommodating Multiple Interests" through Entrustment and Accountable Representation', *International Journal of Agricultural Resources, Governance and Ecology*, 1, 3.

Ribot, J. C. (2009) 'Authority over Forests: Empowerment and Subordination in Senegal's Democratic Decentralization', *Development and Change*, 40, 1, pp. 105–29.

Robbins, P. (2004) *Political Ecology: A Critical Introduction*, Oxford, Blackwell.

Rocheleau, D. (2001) 'Complex Communities and Relational Webs Uncertainty, Surprise and Transformation in Machakos', *IDS Bulletin*, 32, 4, pp. 78–87.

Roth, D. (2009) 'Property and Authority in a Migrant Society: Balinese Irrigators in Sulawesi, Indonesia', *Development and Change*, 40, 1, pp. 195–217.

Rudd, M. A. (2004) 'An Institutional Framework for Designing and Monitoring Ecosystem-Based Fisheries Management Policy Experiments', *Ecological Economics*, 48, 1, pp. 109–24.

Sandström, E. (2008) 'Reinventing the Commons: Exploring the Emergence of the Local Natural Resource Management Arrangements', PhD thesis, Swedish University of Agricultural Sciences.

Sayer, A. (2000) *Realism and Social Science*, London, Sage Publications.

Scott W. R. (2008), *Institutions and Organisations: Ideas and Interests*, London, Sage Publications.

Sikor, T. and Lund, C. (2009) 'Access and Property: A Question of Power and Authority', *Development and Change*, 40, 1, pp. 1–22.

Sikor, T., Stahl, J. and Dorondel, S. (2009) 'Negotiating Post-Socialist Property and State: Struggles over Forests in Albania and Romania', *Development and Change*, 40, 1, pp. 171–93.

Schlager, E., Blomquist, W. and Tang, S. Y. (1994) 'Mobile Flows, Storage, and Self-Organized Institutions for Governing Common-Pool Resources', *Land Economics*, 70, pp. 294–317.

Steins, N. A. (2001) 'New Directions in Natural Resource Management: The Offer of Actor–Network Theory', *IDS Bulletin*, 32, 4, pp. 18–25.

Strang, V. (2005) 'Taking the Waters: Cosmology, Gender and Material Culture in the Appropriation of Water Resources', in A. Coles and T. Wallace (eds) *Gender, Water and Development*, Oxford, Oxford, pp. 21–38.

Sturgeon, J. and Sikor, T. (2004) 'Postsocialist Property in Asia and Europe: Variations on "Fuzziness"', *Conservation and Society*, 2, 1, pp. 1–17.

Titeca, K. and de Herdt, T. (2011) Real Governance Beyond the 'Failed State': Negotiating Education in the Democratic Republic of the Congo, African Affairs, vol. 110, no. 439, pp. 213–23.

Tukai, R. (2005) 'Gender and Access in Pastoral Communities: Re-evaluating Community Participation and Gender Empowerment', paper presented at the ESRC seminar Access, Poverty and Social Exclusion, ODI, London, 1 March.

Van Koppen, B., Giordano, M. and Butterworth, J. (eds) (2007) *Community-Based Water Law and Water Resource Management Reform in Developing Countries*, Wallingford, CABI.

Varughese, G. and Ostrom, E. (2001) 'The Contested Role of Heterogeneity in Collective Action: Some Evidence from Community Forestry in Nepal', *World Development*, 29, 5, pp. 747–65.

Vatn, A. (2009) 'Cooperative Behavior and Institutions', *Journal of Socio-Economics*, 38, 1, pp. 188–96.

Wade, R. (1988a) 'The Management of Irrigation Systems: How to Evoke Trust and Avoid Prisoners Dilemma', *World Development*, 16, 4, pp. 489–500.

—(1988b) *Village Republics: Economic Conditions for Collective Action in South India*, Cambridge, Cambridge University Press.

Wardell, D. A. and Lund, C. (2006) 'Governing Access to Forests in Northern Ghana: Micro-Politics and the Rents of Non-Enforcement', *World Development*, 34, 11, pp. 1887–906.

Wong, S. (2009) 'Lessons from a Participatory Transboundary Water Governance Project in West Africa', *Participatory Learning and Action*, vol. 60 – Community Based Adaptation to Climate Change, International Institute for Environment and Development, Chapter 7, pp. 99–106.

—(2010) 'Elite Capture or Capture Elites? Lessons from the "Counter-Elite" and "Co-opt-Elite" Approaches in Bangladesh and Ghana', *UNU-WIDER*, 82.

Woodhouse, P. (2002) 'Natural Resource Management and Chronic Poverty in Sub-Saharan Africa: An Overview Paper', *CPRC Working Paper*, 14.

Wyborn, C. and Bixler, P. (2011) 'Going Up or Going Down? Transferring Approaches to Conservation Across Nested Scales', paper presented at the Colorado Conference on Earth System Governance: Crossing Boundaries and Building Bridges, Colorado State University, May 17–20.

Zwarteveen, M. and Bennett, V. (2005) 'The Connection between Gender and Water Management', in V. Bennett, S. Davila-Poblete and M. N. Rico (eds) *Opposing Currents: The Politics of Water and Gender in Latin America*, Pittsburgh, University of Pittsburgh.

Note

1 The case study of Uchira Water User Association was produced through a research project funded by the ESRC, 'How Participation Evolves: An Exploration of Participation in Community-Based Water Management in Tanzania', (RES-0002200344.) undertaken by Anna Toner and Frances Cleaver. It is elaborated in more detail in Anna Toner's PhD thesis 'Structure, agency and the populist development paradigm: an ethnography of participation in collective village life in Uchira, Tanzania', University of Bradford, 2007.

2 Introducing Bricolage

Introduction

Much contemporary thinking about institutions and natural resource management is influenced by a perceived need to respond to global and local uncertainties. Constant institutional and livelihood adaptation is seen as a desirable response to climatic, political, economic and social change. It is commonly suggested that institutional arrangements must be resilient, implying the need for a good fit with the social milieu and the ecological resource base. In this chapter I advance the concept of institutional bricolage as a tool for understanding just how institutional alteration occurs. Departing from the normative use of terms such as 'adaptation' and 'resilience', I offer ways of analysing how institutions evolve through human action in response to new circumstances, but are shaped with reference to accepted or past arrangements.

Understanding Creativity and Constraint

Bricolage is a French word meaning to make creative and resourceful use of whatever materials are at hand, regardless of their original purpose. The term has achieved a certain contemporary currency in cultural studies, the visual arts and architecture, and in management studies, where it is used to explain innovation and entrepreneurship. In this book, however, I adapt and develop the concept via the formulations of notable anthropologists, using it to explain the combination of practical creativity and constraint in processes of institutional formation. Claude Levi-Strauss developed the concept of *intellectual* bricolage to characterise the ways in which people thought in 'primitive' societies, in particular in the making of myths. Key to Levi-Strauss' concept of bricolage is the idea that people creatively draw on heterogeneous repertoires in their thinking, combining and reordering these, inventing analogies and witty parallels, classifying phenomena. However, these repertoires and their variations are limited by the structures of the society (such as the levels of technology, the divisions of labour) in which they exist. In elaborating how intellectual bricolage works Levi-Strauss drew on the analogy of the bricoleur as a sort of amateur handyman rather than an engineer or craftsman:

> The 'bricoleur' is adept at performing a large number of diverse tasks; but unlike the engineer, he does not subordinate each of them to the availability of raw materials and tools conceived and procured for the purpose of the project. His universe of instruments is closed and the rules of the game are always to make do with 'whatever is at hand', that is to say with a set of tools and materials which is always finite and is also heterogeneous because what it contains bears no relation to the current project, or indeed to any particular project, but is the contingent result of all the occasions there have been to renew or enrich the stock or to maintain it with the remains of previous constructions or destructions. (Levi-Strauss, 2004: 11)

In her book *How Institutions Think* (1987) Mary Douglas took up these ideas, seeing them as relevant to the way people think in 'modern' as well as 'primitive' societies. She developed the concept further as a critique of rational choice assumptions about collective action, showing the ways in which human cognition and individual action is channelled and institutionalised through processes of bricolage.

In this book I further develop the concept of bricolage to explain institutional formation and functioning. Bricolage consists of the adaptive processes by which people imbue configurations of rules, traditions, norms and relationships with meaning and authority. In so doing they modify old arrangements and invent new ones but innovations are always linked authoritatively to acceptable ways of doing things. These refurbished arrangements are everyday responses to changing circumstances. We are all bricoleurs – indeed the conduct of our daily lives consist of much innovation and pragmatic adaptation. (While writing this section I am multi-tasking — helping my son transform some white cloth, an oak stick and a Christmas bauble into a cloak and wand so that he can go to school dressed as a wizard on World Book Day.) But *institutional* bricolage implies more than simply making up and making do. Just any old invention and re-combination will not work as, unlike dressing up clothes, institutions must be legitimised and imbued with authority to have any purchase on the job to be done and to endure over time and space.

How exactly do such processes of innovation, adaptation and

legitimation occur in respect to institutions? In the previous chapter I critically examined some of the explanatory gaps in mainstream institutional analysis, highlighting the need for richer models of human agency and better understandings of ways in which the outcomes of socially constructed institutional processes are patterned. Insights from social theory provide some useful pointers towards addressing these challenges. Such perspectives suggest that human arrangements (such as institutions) are formed in the dynamic interplay of individual action with social structure and that such processes both enable and constrain progressive change in particular ways. However, social theory does not go far enough in suggesting exactly *how* this interplay happens. I argue that the concept of institutional bricolage offers a way of analysing and understanding just how institutions are socially formed and practised.

Structure and agency

Let us return to where we ended the last chapter – by considering how to develop more satisfactory explanations of influences that shape human actions in natural resource management. As previously outlined, I argue that mainstream perspectives tend to over-emphasize strategic individual agency, whilst critical perspectives often over-romanticize the possibilities of agency as negotiation or resistance. Neither is entirely satisfactory in understanding institutional functioning, so let us see how social theory can improve these perspectives.

A key debate in social theory concerns how far individuals can act autonomously and purposefully and how far they unthinkingly follow the well-trodden path of tradition, acting according to societal norms and expectations. Contemporary sociologists often claim that we need to move beyond such dualist understandings of structure and agency, though this is much easier said than done. I argue that one way we can do this is to understand the ways that institutions and everyday social relationships mediate the interface between society and individual behaviour, where each of these has no meaningful existence without the other. As a way of introducing the concept of bricolage, let us pull out some useful insights from the structure/agency debate.

In his elaboration of structuration theory Giddens emphasises that individual action is characterised by the exercise of choice within parameters of constraint (Giddens, 1984). He sets out the argument that individuals are neither conduits of tradition unthinkingly reproducing past practices, nor purely autonomous agents pursuing profit or self-fulfilment. Individual action is a dynamic combination of both these elements. So Giddens, interested in the creative possibility of individual agency, also recognises the structural constraints within which individuals operate in society, the routinized nature of much everyday practice as well as unintended effects of intended actions. For Giddens, the interplay between choice and constraint in individual action is further shaped by the nature of human consciousness. In elaborating structuration theory, Giddens outlined three different types of consciousness: discursive consciousness (where individuals can scrutinise and reflect on what they are doing); practical consciousness (taken-for-granted knowledge of the routinized practices of everyday life not usually subject to discursive scrutiny); and the unconscious (the ways individuals' psyches shape their responses and actions without their conscious control).

These ideas offer a useful insight into individual action in relation to community-based natural resource management. Development interventions tend to emphasise the exercise of a discursive form of agency – expecting people to be able to articulate their needs, strategically reflect on their actions and publicly negotiate these with others. Such approaches often fail to recognise that some social arrangements and practices are so routinized and taken for granted that they are seen as part of the natural order (even when grossly unfair or inefficient), and so are difficult to bring into discursive scrutiny. Furthermore, there is almost no recognition of unconscious and emotional motivations of human action in development interventions – of the responses and behaviours which are shaped for example by feelings (such as of love, fear, mistrust, belonging) and over which people can exercise only partial discursive control (Burkitt, 2012).

Moving beyond an analysis of individual consciousness, Giddens articulates the way in which individuals are both constrained and enabled through the deployment of 'resources' in society. For Giddens, 'resources' are the structured properties of social systems, drawn upon and reproduced by knowledgeable agents in the course of interactions (1984: 15). He distinguishes between the deployment of authoritative resources (implying command over people) and of allocative resources (which relates to command over things). Human individuals make rules that structure the deployment of resources; the patterning of command over resources in turn shapes the actions of agents. Adapted to the management of natural resources, allocative resources might include the patterned distribution and command over natural and physical resources, technology or infrastructure. Authoritative resources relate to decision-making processes and structures such as policies, laws, entitlements and governance arrangements. Together, allocative and authoritative resources shape the institutions, which in turn configure natural resource access. In the management of common property, authoritative resources could include societal discourses about conservation and sustainability, modernisation and development, citizenship and democracy, given material form through allocation (of budgets, people, technology) and through organisation (governance systems, frameworks of rights and legal processes). In Chapter 4 I will elaborate these points through an example of water governance showing how the allocation of societal resources shapes natural resource governance at the local level (see also Figure 2.1 below).

How does the relationship between structure and agency work?

Structuration theory is useful in suggesting both that individuals can adapt, strategise and innovate *and* that such options are constrained by the nature of human consciousness and the patterned distribution of resources in society. However, Giddens' analysis only takes us so far, partly because he developed his structuration theory primarily in relation to 'late-modern societies' – those we might loosely categorise in development terms as belonging to the industrialised global north (Giddens, 1984). So while Giddens recognises that much of everyday practice will be habitual and circumscribed by societal expectations, he is nonetheless rather optimistic about the possibilities of individual agency and has become even more so in his later work, stating for example that 'individualisation has been the main driving force for change in later modern society' (Giddens, 2000: vii). Through 'praxis' – the skilful performance and conduct of everyday life and the creative deployment of resources – he implies that individuals can, to a large extent, overcome societal constraints and shape their own life projects (Greener, 2002). A key concept here is that of 'reflex-ivity' – the ways in which individuals can knowledgeably monitor their own actions, deliberate on the social context and make choices accordingly. This faith in the promise of individualisation has been heavily criticised by sociological commentators similarly writing about late-modern societies. For example, Duncan suggests they fail to account for the ways that individuals shape their actions in relation to meaningful others as well as the enduring effects of structural patterns such as class and gender on people's life chances (Duncan, 2011). Still, Giddens' early structuration theory is useful, but does not really help us to see how the interaction between structure and agency actually works.

In development studies the actor-oriented approach advocated by Norman Long similarly combines a recognition of the constraints of structure with an optimistic outlook on the potential of individuals to shape their life-worlds. For Long, agency, though constrained, is about the ability to choose levels of 'enrolment' in the 'projects' of others and to enrol others on one's own projects (Long, 1992). Actors strategically position themselves in response to conflicting priorities and critical events (Arce and Long, 2000). Long usefully takes us further than Giddens by articulating the idea that there is a permeable social interface between actors and structures (including development interventions). Here the actors' goals and values are reshaped or reinforced but in turn they may adjust and reinterpret aspects of the project or institution. Key questions arise from reading Long. How exactly does this interface work and what are the effects for different people of such interactions? How wide is the scope delineated by particular arrangements for exercising agency? Where resourceful actors are able to create 'room for manoeuvre', do they choose to go along with the collective arrangements or to opt out of them, and what are the outcomes of such choices? Let us now see how far Bourdieu's ideas about habitus help further understanding of structure-agency dynamics.

Habitus and necessary improvisation

In contrast to those social theories optimistic about individual agency, Bourdieu emphasises how strongly people's actions are shaped non-consciously, by *habitus*. Habitus is

> the habitual, patterned ways of understanding, judging, and acting which arise from our particular position as members of one or several social 'fields,' and from our particular trajectory in the social structure (*e.g.*, whether our group is emerging or declining; whether our own position within it is becoming stronger or weaker). The notion asserts that different conditions of existence – different educational backgrounds, social statuses, professions, and regions – all give rise to forms of habitus characterized by internal resemblance within the group (indeed, they are important factors which help it to know itself as a group), and simultaneously by perceptible distinction from the habitus of differing groups. (Bourdieu, 1987: 811)

For Bourdieu, culture, social institutions, habit and routine shape people's practices (Greener, 2002). Their views of the world, ideas about proper behaviour and relationships and their actions are framed by their past experiences, their individual capacities and current social positions; from these they develop a practical sense of orientation that guides them in their actions (Wacquant, 2005). Within particular social fields, people adopt sets of practices without referring to them, and such practices take on the quality of 'rules' or 'norms'. Social structure then becomes embodied in people's practices; such habitus helps to maintain regular social relations by making the actions of individuals intelligible to others. However, people cannot rely simply on the unthinking reproduction of habit. They must also respond to changes in the social fields in which they are situated (Collet, 2009). So, while we all take many of our actions and relationships for granted, everyone is involved in the 'necessary improvisation' of everyday life; habit and creativity co-exist. Drawing on de Certeau, Hall (2010) argues that in going about their daily lives people must constantly manipulate events in order to turn them into opportunities. However, this manipulation is done through 'everyday practices' and it is often difficult to subject these to conscious discursive scrutiny. For Bourdieu, the freedom to innovate is strongly 'conditioned' by social structure and 'conditional' on relations with others (Bourdieu, 1990; 55).

Drawing on Bourdieu, McNay suggests that creative individuals are *sometimes* able to overcome constraint and generate transformational change. She suggests, 'the need for a more precise and varied account of agency to explain the differing motivations and ways in which individuals and groups struggle over, appropriate and transform cultural meaning and resources' (McNay, 2000: 22). These ideas get us a little further in understanding the structure–agency dynamic, but questions remain: what does 'necessary improvisation' mean in practice and how exactly do struggles over meaning and resources co-exist with the acceptance of everyday norms, routines and relationships? I suggest that these processes are mediated through *institutions* as, in their formation and evolution certain innovations, claims and meanings become legitimated, routinized and embedded in social relations (institutionalisation), whilst others are dismissed, marginalised or suffer entropy.

Empowerment and change

I find it useful to further enrich understandings of the relationship between agency and institutions by drawing on gendered theories of empowerment and change. Here it is well recognised that all choices are *not* equal, that all actors are not equally placed to make them and that similar actions produce differing consequences for different people. The extent to which particular societal arrangements offer individuals the possibility of transforming their circumstances or alternatively operate as 'disciplinary' forces is a moot point in gender studies. For example, Jackson, cautioning against overly optimistic expectations of enacting land rights for women in India, argues that women with different subject positions (for example relating to marital status, seniority, caste) perceive the importance of claiming land rights variably and differ in their capacity to effect these rights (Jackson, 2003). Here, relationality matters (and not just for women of course), meaning that people's consciousness and actions are shaped in webs of human connection. Their autonomy is thus conceived of and exercised in relation to significant others. Kabeer (2000) considers not just individuals' ability to act, but how much power they have to make and effect *strategic* decisions that shape their lives. So, for example, a woman may be able to exercise her right to participate in the newly formed water committee or the irrigation association, but this does not necessarily mean that she can act autonomously of the family and marital relationships through which she gains access to land and water. These approaches help to explain the intermittence and unpredictability of change effected through agency.

So again we might ask, what are the actual processes in which struggles over societal resources occur and where are they located? What form does the necessary improvisation of everyday life take and can we distinguish between consciously strategic responses to change on the one hand and practical responses on the other? *How* do these individual responses become part of the taken for granted patterns of relationships in society? To what extent are they able to contribute towards shifting such societal arrangements in new directions?

A critical realist framework for understanding resource governance

Critical realist thinkers offer one explanation by suggesting that the structures (or resources) of society are mediated into effects (events, outcomes) by *mechanisms* (see Sayer, 1992; Archer, 2000). Tom Franks and I have adapted this approach in the formulation of our framework for understanding water governance (which could also be applied to frame analysis of the management of other resources). We define mechanisms as particular context-specific arrangements (in this case for organising access to water). They might include organisational arrangements (water users associations), social arrangements (access to water from a neighbour's well in return for labour on their fields), technology (pumps, pipes etc.), financial arrangements (tariffs, subsidies) or legal arrangements (water rights, contracts, constitutions). In our framework such mechanisms are shaped by the allocation of resources of society and by people's actions. These interactions produce outcomes (for water access, livelihoods, political voice, social inclusion) *channelled* through mechanisms. Mechanisms do not reliably produce the same outcomes for everyone, even in similar contexts.

Mechanisms are not neutral channels but are operationalized through relationships, in changing environments, resulting in a certain variety and unpredictability of outcomes. Inequitable social relations ensure that some individuals, by virtue of their age, class, gender and ethnicity are better able to deploy resources to fashion mechanisms than others.

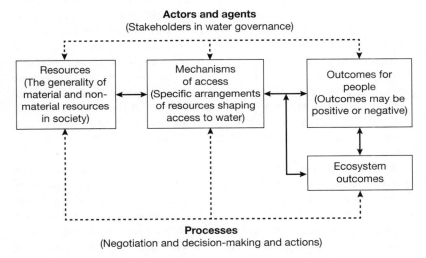

Figure 2.1 Framework for analyzing water governance (Adapted from Franks and Cleaver 2007: 294)

Adopting a governance framework helps us to see that exercising agency and deploying resources is not simply a matter of individual choices or preferences. For example, wider relations of power and authority are implicated in the exercise of agency and shape the ways in which natural resources are governed. For social theorists, power is implicated in the ways that social fields are structured and in people's practices. Bourdieu elaborates the role of symbolic power, which is the capacity to produce and impose legitimate visions of the world, the ability to produce knowledge to shape collective beliefs: 'Symbolic relations of power tend to reproduce and to reinforce power relations that constitute the structure of social space' (Bourdieu, 1989). People are not necessarily aware of the exercise of such power and cannot therefore always select their level of involvement in the projects of others. This conceptualisation comes close to Lukes' (2005) notion of 'invisible power' and is a useful balance to more commonly used ideas about the exercise of power in development, which emphasise the transformatory promise of the individual and collective exercise of agency in public spaces of decision-making (Gaventa, 2006).

One possible way of incorporating a focus on both visible and invisible aspects of power into institutional analyses is through governmentality perspectives. These understand agency, practices and mechanisms as shaped by layers of power, operating through a variety of channels (Dean, 1999; Agrawal, 2005). Drawing heavily on Foucauldian notions of government as the 'conduct of conduct', these approaches see power as exercised in everyday interactions through embodied 'regimes of practice'. Such regimes comprise layers of institutionalised practices – the routine and ritualised ways in which we do things in certain place and at certain times. 'Governmentality' thus refers to the organised practices through which we are governed and through which consciously *and unconsciously* we govern ourselves. From this perspective, institutional arrangements are 'technologies of government' through which access to natural resources, the claiming of rights and relationships of power between people are channelled (Miller and Rose, 1990; Rose and Miller, 1992).

As one example of governmentality work applied to natural resource management, Agrawal's (2005) study of the collective governance of forest resources in India illustrates the linkages between the policies of decentralised local government, the emergence of new localised 'regulatory communities' (village-level forest councils) and the transformation and disciplining of 'environmental subjects' who participate in community decision-making and respond to the regulatory community's claim on the forests. Here the motivations and practices of the individual community members using the forests are re-shaped through the layered exercise of power as well as through their own reflections on changing circumstances and on their relationship to the environment. This approach is a useful attempt to link the actions of interconnected individuals to broader societal governance arrangements, though I suggest it does not adequately theorise the exact processes through which this takes place. Governmentality analyses also emphasise many aspects of plurality: of governing agencies and authorities, of aspects of behaviour to be governed, norms invoked, purposes sought and of effects, outcomes and consequences (Dean, 1999: 19). Such complexity may encompass overlapping scales, arenas and networks within which interactions about governance and self-governance are formed. The concept of plurality finds direct echoes in current thinking in natural resource management and has relevance both for the opportunities and constraints for individual action.

So we have seen that agency is about individual actions undertaken in broader frameworks of authoritative resource allocation, networks of relationships and sedimented layers of practice and meaning. However, the ways in which these factors interact through particular channels and processes requires further elaboration and there is a need for better theorising of such interfaces. In beginning to do this, I now consider the ways in which structure–agency interactions are mediated through institutions.

Institutions and Bricolage

Institutions are the key mechanisms which channel societal resources into outcomes. But institutions are neither inanimate things nor agents – they only exist in relation to people's interactions with one another. It is people, through their behaviour and social relationships, who animate institutions.

While my own formulation of institutional functioning builds upon the literature reviewed above, it is also heavily influenced by the ideas Mary Douglas sets out in her book *How Institutions Think* (Douglas, 1987). Douglas, adapting Levi-Strauss's concept of *intellectual bricolage*, suggests that to a great extent 'institutions do the thinking' on behalf of people. These institutions are constructed through the gathering and applying of analogies and styles of thought that are already part of existing institutions. In this way already existing 'social formulae' are repeatedly used in the construction of institutions, thereby economising on cognitive and social energy by offering easier classification and legitimacy, 'tools' to guide thought and action. So, for example (as we will see in Chapter 3), if a newly introduced village development committee is referred to by leaders as a 'meeting of the people', the legitimacy of a historic tradition of communal decision-making and solidarity is invoked, and particular desirable 'customary' forms of working (through consensus decision-making) are implied. Consequently, there is no need to spend time and effort in explicitly negotiating new ways of establishing and operationalizing institutional arrangements. Social formulae are also implicated in 'institutional leakage' whereby 'sets of rules and classifications of arrangements are metaphorically connected with one another, and allow meaning to leak from one context to another along the formal similarities they show' (Douglas, 1987: 13). Legitimation is often achieved through analogy; for example, the ordering of patriarchal relationships in the living human world may mirror and be linked to the proper ordering of hierarchies in the natural and supernatural worlds, as illustrated in the example of the moral–ecological cosmologies of people in rural Zimbabwe, illustrated in Chapters 3 and 7. Douglas suggests that because of the highly socialised ways in which we think, patterns of authority and precedence are commonly privileged when drawing on analogies and borrowing arrangements (Douglas, 1987). As Bourdieu illustrates, the design of the private and intimate space is in some cultures a microcosm organised according to the same oppositions which are seen to govern the rest of the universe (Hall, 2010).

So bricolage is a sort of institutional 'do-it-yourself' (refurbishment and re-arrangement of existing relationships and classifications) rather than the more explicitly conscious and rational form of institutional engineering or design so often assumed in contemporary literature. This version of bricolage implies that agency involves pragmatic improvisation, deploying pre-existing resources to reconfigure arrangements. Thus the bricoleur 'turns the broken clock into a pipe rack, the broken table into an umbrella stand, the umbrella stand into a lamp, and anything into something else' (Douglas 1987: 66, referring to Levi-Strauss's image of the bricoleur). However, constraint is ever-present and strongly emphasised in Douglas' formulation of bricolage. Structure impedes agency, shaping it in a number of ways. Firstly, as de Koning (2011) points out, the maker of impromptu lamps and umbrella stands is not omnipotent but constrained by available resources and her own capabilities. However competent and innovatory, she is unable to make a space shuttle out of that broken table. Douglas emphasises improvisation within circumscribed limits, thus 'the bricoleur uses everything there is to make transformations *within a stock repertoire of furnishings*' (Douglas, 1987).

Secondly, the limits of human cognition are constraining. For Douglas the processes of adaptation, legitimation, and particularly the leakage of meaning (the borrowing and seeping of symbols, categories, discourses and authority relations from one domain to another) ensure that we are barely aware of many institutional arrangements, taking them for granted as the right or normal way of doing things. For Douglas, institutions maintain the shape and character of past arrangements, even though these might have changed: 'Institutions create shadowed places in which nothing can be seen and no questions asked' (Douglas, 1987: 69). She suggests that it is only through enormous effort that we can bring such taken-for-granted arrangements into discursive scrutiny.

Finally, for Douglas, individuals are not atomised agents selfishly pursuing their own ends. She marvels at the way in which literature drawing on rational choice models of agency presents community-minded or altruistic actions as aberrations rather than normal social behaviour. Additionally, Douglas suggests that people exist in cognitive and institutional worlds in which their own actions and expectations are linked to those of others, to events and phenomena in the natural world and to the supernatural – God, spirits, ancestors. As a result, designed rules are often not necessary to constrain behaviour in socially acceptable ways. Instead, 'The risk of free-riding is controlled by the accounting system. The accounts are audited and debts collected by the way that God or nature furnishes defaulters with disease and death' (Douglas, 1987: 74).

Douglas's ideas encapsulate both the pieced-together nature of institutions and the socially constrained nature of human agency. I see institutional bricolage as often more pragmatically and consciously creative than does Douglas, but I nonetheless find her insights invaluable as an alternative to rational choice models. In her ideas about the leakage of meaning and the use of social formulae Douglas goes some way towards identifying the ways in which structure shapes agency through institutions. In the following sections I suggest additional ways through which this process is articulated.

Key elements of bricolage

So, drawing on the various elements of theory outlined above, I see institutional bricolage as a process in which people consciously and non-consciously draw on existing social formulae (styles of thinking, models of cause and effect, social norms and sanctioned social roles and relationships) to patch or piece together institutions in response to changing situations. These institutions are neither completely new nor completely traditional but rather a dynamic hybrid combining elements of 'modern', 'traditional' and the 'formal' and 'informal'. The institutions produced through bricolage are inevitably uneven in functioning and impact, and are often fuzzy assemblages of meaningful practices, which overlap and serve multiple purposes.

However, leakage of meaning, classification and conferring legitimacy does not just happen – it is undertaken by people consciously and unconsciously navigating the institutional landscape and patching together 'new' arrangements in a dynamic environment. Bricoleurs have varying capacity and opportunities to shape these institutions (although all have the human *potential* to exercise agency) and are differently affected by their functioning. There is then an iterative relationship between bricoleurs and the institutions they shape and are shaped by.

Despite the highly adaptive nature of bricolage, institutional formation is not a seamless, uncontested process. Adapted arrangements must be accepted and validated by other people to become institutionalised – such legitimation then allows repeated use of the arrangement over time. We have seen how leakage of meaning facilitates acceptance of new or adapted arrangements. But there are plenty of instances where the appropriateness of arrangements, their source of authority and legitimacy, *are* publicly subjected to scrutiny by the bricoleurs involved. Negotiation and contestation, involving competing claims to tradition or modernity, or particular sources of authority, is therefore an inevitable part of bricolage.

The following sections summarise some key aspects and elements of bricolage and serve as an introduction to the chapters which substantiate these.

Everyday practice, 'necessary improvisation' and innovation

Institutions are formed in the necessary improvisation of daily practice. People piece together institutional arrangements to address their everyday challenges and to respond to changes in their social milieux. It is by reworking existing institutional arrangements that actors innovate. Such arrangements are therefore a patchwork of the new and the second-hand, and they include:

- Taken-for-granted ways of doing things, which people may ordinarily accept without question (for example, people might regard universal access to water or respecting elders as the 'right way of doing things', which only becomes subject to scrutiny when stresses or shocks shape up the status quo).
- Well-worn and accepted practices adapted to new conditions (for example, 'traditional' meetings of adult men adapted to become 'modern' village assemblies including adult women).
- Organisational arrangements which are invented or cannibalised from elsewhere (for example constitutions or committees 'borrowed' from the bureaucracies of the state).
- New or adapted devices to ensure social applicability (for example exemptions from paying for water, or graded tariffs to reflect local concepts of equity).

Multi-purpose and dynamic institutions

Such pieced-together institutions often have multi-purpose functions. They are rarely organised only according to single purposes, following sectoral divisions, or in relation to particular projects. Even if they begin that way they often evolve to encompass other purposes. So, as we will see in Chapters 3 and 7, in one Zimbabwean village the grazing policemen evolve to become general community policemen and women regulating resource use, acting as village messengers, tracking down criminals and offering advice in cases of domestic strife. A women's burial society, of long standing, becomes the channel through which household contributions to the digging of a dam is organised.

Bricolage is a fundamentally dynamic process characterised by unevenness and temporal intermittence. Institutions formed by bricolage are likely to reflect configurations of social relationships and to have boundaries which vary in their fuzziness or permeability. For example, a waterpoint committee in Zimbabwe nominally comprises representatives of the local user households who contributed to the sinking of the well and who daily draw water there. However, they informally recognise the rights of people from other villages to collect water when their own pumps have broken down. Many of these people are related to the waterpoint users through kinship or marriage. They impose stricter financial conditions on other external users (coming from the nearby town by car to collect water). The rights of these different categories of external users to collect water will vary according to the season and the pressure on the water supplies. Under conditions of scarcity, both rules (e.g. about payments from car users) and negotiations for access at the waterpoint may become more visible and more formalised.

Naturalisation, leakage of meaning, invention of tradition

Bricolage involves the piecing together of old and new to make something different. However key to this process is that the 'something different' must appear familiar, it must work on a routinely accepted logic, it must socially fit. This is because one function of institutions is to economise on cognitive energy – they enable people to go along with arrangements without having to calculate or negotiate every single interaction (although we will see in later chapters that they do not always work in this way). Borrowing well-worn practices, symbols and relationships offers a fast route to weaving new arrangements into the social fabric (rather than relying on repeated interactions over time). There are a number of ways in which new configurations are made to seem familiar and legitimate.

- Tradition is called upon both unconsciously and consciously. Indeed, institutions formed through bricolage are often path dependent – they draw on pre-existing ways of doing things even when these are not the most obviously efficient mechanisms for achieving the desired ends. However, 'tradition' is not a fixed entity, so it is often invented or re-invented in processes of bricolage.

- Meaning leaks from one institutional setting to another. The leakiness of institutions enables the flow of legitimising symbols and discourses across domains. For example, local 'informal' institutions often draw on the legitimising devices of the state to substantiate claims to legitimacy and broader meaning. We will see in later chapters how the use of bureaucratic titles 'chairman' and 'secretary' and the deployment of stamps to legitimise village waterpoint constitutions draw on ideas of state-like authority, even when the state does not functionally reach to that locality.

- Institutional arrangements constructed through bricolage are often 'naturalised' by analogy. This means they are seen as the 'right way of doing things' because they relate to broader views of the nature of cause and effect in the world and the proper place of people within such systems. So, for example, in the case studies from Zimbabwe and Tanzania elaborated in later chapters, consensus decision-making, conflict avoidance and reconciliatory conflict resolution arrangements are considered proper by many local people because they match the pronouncements of ancestral spirits about living cooperatively together. This is significant as it moves us away from the idea that 'tradition' is just a resource to be strategically used to more efficiently craft institutions. Rather, institutions for natural resource management work when they offer 'cognitive fit' with people's worldviews, providing ontological coherence to understandings of individual and collective action, to people–nature relationships.

Conscious and non-conscious action, moral rationalities

Bricoleurs shape institutions both consciously and non-consciously. People devise arrangements of roles and rules for natural resource management, but this is also influenced by routinized everyday practices and conventions (such as the proper ways of collecting water from the well), by moral world views (such as the desirability of living in peace together) and by conscious and non- conscious psychological motivations (for example emotions of belonging, the desire for recognition, the preference for companionship, dislike of conflict and so on).

The ability to exercise agency is thus shaped by people's *social* relationships and circumstances; they do not act purely or even primarily as 'resource appropriators'. A multitude of inter-related factors – their sex, ethnicity, caste or religion, spatial location and physical wellbeing, their wealth, caring responsibilities, politics and aspirations – will all have a bearing on the ways that they shape and engage with institutions. As agency is both 'practical' and 'discursive', some aspects of institutional arrangements are reproduced in routine practice, without scrutiny. Other aspects are subject to negotiation, contestation and justification. As a result no institution can be either unquestioningly replicated over time or fully subject to design. So a feature of bricolage is the blending of both designed and taken-for-granted elements of institutions; the resulting arrangements are then a patchwork of the old and the new, of explicit rules and implicit practices. Although it is possible for people to contest and negotiate these arrangements, they are not all subjected to the same level of discursive scrutiny. Additionally, whilst all bricoleurs have the potential to re-negotiate the institutional rules, they are differently constrained and many are unable to actually do so.

Authoritative processes and unequal outcomes

Bricolage is an authoritative process, shaped by relations of power. The configuring of societal resources shapes the 'institutional stock' from which institutions can be assembled. This stock of resources which might include policies, citizens' entitlements, discourses about rights, development or conservation, is the source of legitimating devices for institutional arrangements. Authoritative resources include moral worldviews – strongly gendered, socially stratified ideas about proper behaviour, living together and the rightful place of individuals with different social identities. Individual bricoleurs are able to exercise different levels of influence over the formation and functioning of institutions, as a result of their social positions. Authority, reputation, status and assets (or the lack of them) all matter when it comes to making and breaking institutional rules.

Power shapes institutional functioning but is often invisible. Hierarchies of authority reinforce one another – for example, elder men may exercise power in the human world, an authority reinforced by their role in mediating with ancestors in the spirit world. Where both human and supernatural authorities emphasise the importance of respect and of living peacefully together (with dire consequences for both individuals and communities for offending these principles), power works invisibly to discourage the public challenging of inequitable access to natural resources.

The taken-for-granted elements of institutions and the need for them to be socially workable ensure the reproduction of social inequalities.

These can be mitigated to a degree by the design of mechanisms which promote fair representation or distribution. However, such arrangements do not function in splendid isolation; they are part of the social world they are intended to modify. The unequal exercise of power and the capture of its benefits are also often an accepted aspect of social relations and so reproduced in institutional formation. So, for example, the constitution of a waterpoint committee is deliberately formulated to promote women's participation. But it is the headman's wife who becomes the chair of the committee, or all the women elected are high caste, or female members exist but decisions continue to be taken by male elders.

Inequalities can be challenged in processes of institutional bricolage, through public negotiation (see the debate over charging the poorest users for water in Chapter 7) and in the daily practical enacting of resource access where endless variations on bending the collective rules are possible. However, neither public spaces nor 'everyday spaces' are neutral, but are sites where power is exercised. The costs to poor or socially marginal individuals of challenging the rules are often disproportionately high, in terms of loss of reputation, goodwill and patronage, payment of fines, time spent resolving disputes and restricted resource access.

Conclusion

In adopting a definition of institutions that is not simply about organisations and formalised public decision-making, then we set a difficult problem of enquiry, for institutions by their very nature are difficult to scrutinise. Woven into long-standing and inequitable social structures and relationships, imbued by social norms and working through taken-for-granted everyday practice, institutions create shadowy places in which the working of power relations can remain hidden. This book argues that whilst such processes of institutional formation and functioning may be complex, multi-layered and negotiable they result in unfair outcomes for many people. The creativity and diversity of institutional design and practice creates room for manoeuvre and new possibilities for some people but simultaneously reproduces and even reinforces social inequalities for others.

What follows in this book is an attempt to contribute to the theorising of structure–agency relations as they articulate through institutional bricolage. In so doing so I aim to embrace complexity and at the same time make visible some of the more opaque aspects of institutions – to shine a light into those shadowy places so as to explore how they work and to what effect.

Bibliography

Agrawal, Arun (2005) *Environmentality: Technologies of Government and the Making of Subjects*, Durham, NC, Duke University Press.

Arce, A. and Long, N. (2000) 'Reconfiguring Modernity and Development from an Anthropological Perspective', in A. Arce and N. Long (eds) *Anthropology, Development and Modernities: Exploring Discourses, Counter-Tendencies and Violence*, London, Routledge, pp. 1–30.

Archer, Margaret (2000) *Being Human: The Problem of Agency*, Cambridge, Cambridge University Press.

Bourdieu, Pierre (1987) 'The Force of Law: Toward a Sociology of the Juridical Field', *Hastings Law Journal* 38, pp. 805–53.

—(1989) 'Social Space and Symbolic Power', *Sociological Theory*, 7, 1, pp. 14–25.

Burkitt, I. (2012) 'Emotional Reflexivity: Feeling, Emotion and Imagination in Reflexive Dialogues, Sociology', published online before print March 15, 2012, http://soc.sagepub.com/content/early/2012/03/14/0038038511422587.abstract.

Collet, Francois (2009) 'Does Habitus Matter? A Comparative Review of Bourdieu's Habitus and Simon's Bounded Rationality with Some Implications for Economic Sociology', *Sociological Theory* 27, 4, pp. 419–34.

de Koning, Jessica (2011) *Reshaping Institutions: Bricolage Processes in Smallholder Forestry in the Amazon*, Wageningen, Wageningen University.

Dean, Mitchell (1999) *Governmentality: Power and Rule in Modern Society*, London, Sage.

Douglas, Mary (1987) *How Institutions Think*, London, Routledge & Kegan Paul.

Franks, T. and Cleaver, F. (2007) 'Water Governance and Poverty: A Framework for Analysis', Progress in Development Studies, 7 (4) pp. 291–306.

Gaventa, John (2006) 'Finding the Spaces for Change: A Power Analysis', *IDS Bulletin* 37, 6, pp. 23–33.

Giddens, Anthony (1984) *The Constitution of Society: Outline of the Theory of Structuration*, Cambridge, Polity Press.

—(1996) 'Affluence, Poverty and the Idea of a Post-Scarcity Society', *Development and Change* 27, 2, pp. 365–77.

Greener, I. (2002) 'Agency, Social Theory and Social Policy', *Critical Social Policy* 22, 4, pp. 688–705.

Hall, Kurt (2010) *The Poverty Construct and Its Resonance with the Experiencing of Deprivation: Social Relations in a Jamaican Community*, unpublished PhD thesis, University of Bradford.

Jackson, C. (2003) 'Gender Analysis of Land: Beyond Land Rights for Women?' *Journal of Agrarian Change* 3, 4, pp. 453–80.

Kabeer, N. (2000) 'Resources, Agency, Achievements: Reflections on the Measurement of Women's Empowerment', in R. Shahra (ed.) *Gendered Poverty and Well-Being*, Oxford, Blackwell.

Levi-Strauss, C. (2004) *The Savage Mind: Nature of Human Society*, Oxford: Oxford University Press.

Long, A. (1992) 'From Paradigm Lost to Paradigm Regained? The Case for an Actor-Oriented Sociology of Development', in N. Long and A. Long (eds)

Battlefields of Knowledge: The Interlocking of Theory and Practice in Social Research and Development, London, Routledge, pp. 16–43.

Lukes, Steven (2005) *Power: A Radical View*, Basingstoke, Palgrave Macmillan, 2nd edition.

McNay, L. (2000) *Gender and Agency: Reconfiguring the Subject in Feminist and Social Theory*, Cambridge, Polity Press.

Merrey, Douglas J., Meinzen-Dick, Ruth, Mollinga, Peter and Karar, Eiman (2007) 'Policy and Institutional Reform: The Art of the Possible', in D. Molden (ed.) *Water for Food, Water for Life: A Comprehensive Assessment of Water Management in Agriculture*, London, Earthscan, pp. 193–231.

Miller, Peter and Rose, Nikolas (1990) 'Governing Economic Life', *Economy and Society* 19, 1, pp. 1–31.

Rose, Nikolas and Miller, Peter (1992) 'Political Power Beyond the State: The Problematics of Government', *British Journal of Sociology* 43, 2, pp. 173–205.

Sayer, Andrew (1992) *Method in Social Science: A Realist Approach*, London, Routledge.

3 The Way We Have Always Done It

Introduction

This chapter adopts an historic and ethnographic approach to understanding the development of institutions for managing natural resources in Zimbabwe. It draws on in-depth research to explore the nature of moral–ecological rationality, which links individual action and collective action to consequences in the supernatural and natural world. The chapter illustrates the tenacity of local principles of conflict avoidance, negotiation and reconciliation in natural resource arrangements and suggests how these sit uncomfortably with the principles underpinning formal designed institutions. It illustrates how institutions are formed and change through conscious design *and* in the practices of everyday life, and how contrived arrangements must be naturalized and legitimized in reference to human and supernatural authorities.

Mainstream institutional thinking directs our gaze to the visible and tangible community efforts to manage natural resources. Functioning committees, formalized rights and public decision-making are commonly identified indicators of community management. But such easily legible evidence of organization is only part of the institutional story – the very tip of the iceberg of interconnecting arrangements, relationships, norms, practices and arrangements by which resources are collectively managed over time. The presence or absence of meetings, elections and written entitlements may indicate little about how institutions actually work.

Ideas about institutional design focus on ways of strengthening the formal arrangements for resource management; in this approach the village water committee can be better crafted to ensure sustainable water use, just as the community forest council can be redesigned to optimize forest management. As we have seen in Chapter 1, various design principles, best practices and lessons inform the crafting of better (that is, resource optimizing) institutions by resource users and policy-makers. From this perspective culture, networks and social norms can contribute to robust arrangements by reducing the 'social overhead costs' of cooperating and helping to ensure compliance.

However, such approaches, with their concern for immediate functionality, can easily overlook the ways in which people access resources through social and cultural relations and how such interactions are themselves patterned around resource dynamics. In this chapter I suggest that there is a need to understand people–natural resource interactions more holistically, in place of analyses which separate out the technical/economic and the political/cultural spheres. Such an approach would locate eco-institutional dynamics in long timescales and in multiple scales and domains, and would conceive of culture as central rather than epi-phenomenal or as an adaptive mechanism to be strategically deployed (Biersack, 1999; Kottak, 1999; Fontein, 2008; Mosse, 2008).

In the case of local water management studied here, a form of moral ecological rationality links individual and collective action to environmental wellbeing and provides a framework within which communal resource management can be understood. This framework for decision-making and action is deeply enmeshed in culture, history and agro–ecological conditions, but is nevertheless susceptible to modification and change. Institutional continuity *and* innovation is generated through everyday livelihood practices and social interactions imbued with cultural meanings *as well as* through purposeful public decision-making. Indeed, these processes are so often interwoven that it is difficult to pick out deliberate institutional crafting as discrete from the interactions of everyday life.

In this chapter I peel away the formal layers of resource management in one village to begin to reveal the complexity of institutional functioning and evolution. I suggest that it is often impossible to disentangle public from private action, formal from informal management and modern arrangements from traditional ones. People's management of natural resources is inseparable from other aspects of their lives, deeply embedded in their everyday livelihood practices over life-courses. The ideal of instrumentally crafting institutions fit for the resource management task is pertinent to development initiatives. However, it needs enriching to reflect the ways in which resource management is enacted through relationships between socially, historically and ecologically located people. Such insights also help us to understand both the potential and limits of negotiability and innovation. The ways in which 'new' institutions are legitimized by reference to existing authorities naturalizes them and invests them with the appearance of being the right way of doing things (Bourdieu and Wacquant, 1992). The inequitable effects of path dependence and authoritative naturalization and the extent to which the 'right way of doing things' can be challenged are further explored in Chapter 4. Here I concentrate on the ways in which people strive (consciously and unconsciously) to generate social continuity and moral order (not just better resource management) through institutions (Karlström, 2004).

To begin to explore these processes, let us consider first this profile of the formal arrangements for managing a well in a village in western Zimbabwe.[1]

Mtswirini Well: 'Formal' Arrangements for Management

Picture Mtswirini well in Eguqeni village, in a dry and little-developed area of western Zimbabwe as it appeared in the dry season of 1992. The well is situated in open scrubby ground. It is fitted with a handpump and has a concrete cover slab, apron, spillway and cattle troughs. The well is surrounded by a fence and a rough gate of thorny branches. Wooden 'shearlegs' stand over the pump – a crude form of scaffolding to facilitate lifting out the pipes for maintenance purposes.

The well is eight years old and was dug by a non-governmental organization with the help of the community, who provided hospitality for the well-sinkers, fetched sand from the Shangani River and dug the first few metres. Before this people used distant sources, including the sandy bed of the Shangani river, forty minutes' walk away.

Mtswirini well normally serves about 15 extended households (150 people), a number which substantially expands during drought. In the dry season, there is a limited supply of water in the well, and restrictions are applied. The pump arm is disabled and only reconnected twice a day, forcing all users to line up and collect at the same time. This way, amounts taken by each user can be monitored.

In line with national policy, the well is managed by a waterpoint committee of three women (as the 'main users' of water) and a male chairman ('for authority'). The chairman is the one who disconnects the pump to operate the 'closer' rule. The committee sees its role as monitoring use of the pump and as the 'eye of the community'. Members report to the village development committee, which conducts decision-making through public meetings, which all adults are entitled to attend.

A number of rules in use regulate access, use of water and preserve the good condition of the well. All households in the immediate vicinity and those who contributed to construction can take water twice a day, others being allowed access after these 'rightful users' have taken water. The water is for domestic purposes, which includes watering goats, sick cattle and sick donkeys. Water can be used for beer brewing but not for vegetable gardening or brick making. All users are expected to participate in maintenance activities. Good condition rules include no banging of or swinging from the pump arm, keeping the surroundings clean and free of animals, no washing of clothes, dirty vessels or bathing at the waterpoint, and the forbidding of use of small-necked vessels and drinking directly from the pump.

Rationing rules are introduced as the dry season progresses. Before water becomes scarce there is no regulation for queuing, people can place as many buckets in line as they can carry, and it is first come, first served. As the drought progresses and water in the well reduces, thirty-litre buckets are banned and only twenty-litre ones allowed. Stricter queuing and rationing is introduced, and each drawer of water can place one bucket in line. When all have drawn one bucket they can queue again until the water is finished.

Despite a severe drought and extreme pressure on the pump, these arrangements seem relatively effective. The pump continues to function throughout the dry season; the well never runs dry. So far, the case broadly confirms mainstream institutional perspectives: the small community (with shared social norms and similar livelihoods) makes collective action easy to organize and distribution relatively uncontroversial. The boundaries of the community and the resource to be managed are relatively clear. Most user households participate in implementation, maintenance and decision-making. The committee monitor arrangements and are accountable both through village meetings and as neighbours and fellow water users.

However, to understand how rules are upheld or broken, how they relate to area-wide resource management, why particular rules evolve and their outcomes, we need to look further than the waterpoint committee and the visible manifestations of management. Let us consider how taking a more socially embedded view of resource management arrangements may be more illuminating.

Embeddedness, Structure and Action

An over-narrow focus on institutional arrangements sidelines factors such as history, politics and geography as 'context' and conceptualizes social relations, culture and norms as a form of institutional glue, deliberating drawn upon to support designed arrangements.

More explanatory power is provided by concepts of embeddedness derived from literature on resource management and from social theory. Pauline Peters (drawing on work on grazing management in Botswana) suggests the need for a complex-embeddedness approach in which the 'definitions of rights, or relative claims, of appropriate uses and users are not only embedded in specific historical sets of political and economic structures but also in cultural systems of meanings symbols and values' (Peters, 1987: 78).

Rather than adhering to the more static ideas of institutional embeddedness as a state of social solidity, we could argue for a definition that allows us to see institutions as embodiments of social process. Granovetter emphasizes a flexible conceptualization of embeddedness involving the importance of networks of personal relations in shaping action (Granovetter, 1992: 92). This brings us close to Douglas's ideas of the interpenetration of meaning in social life (Douglas, 1973) and the need to understand institutions as located social practices. Both Douglas and Giddens see institutions as manifestations of the interaction between structure and individual action:

> The actions of all of us are influenced by the very structural characteristics of the societies in which we are brought up and live, at the same time, we recreate (and also to some extent alter) those structural characteristics in our actions. (Giddens, 1989: 18)

Collective action and institutional formation is no different; institutions cannot be entirely purposively designed, but, as with all human arrangements, also evolve through interactions, some of them shaped by forces and patterns beyond our control. The evolution of resource management institutions do not evolve primarily through the conscious selection of appropriate mechanisms but through a combination of designed measures, everyday relationship interactions, routines and improvised practices.

Examples from Nkayi suggest that institutions are partial, intermittent and often invisible, being located in the daily interactions of ordinary lives. Multiple processes of institutional formation combine conscious and unconscious acts, unintended consequences and significant borrowing from sanctioned social relationships. Institutions so derived survive partly due to the legitimacy bestowed by 'tradition', the moral command of what went before over the present (Giddens, 1984).

In common with much institutionalist literature (Berkes, 1989; Ostrom, 1990; Bromley, 1992) this research supports the importance of practice in shaping use. However, I suggest the need to look carefully at the generation of social, institutional and cultural norms: how are norms generated, legitimized and upheld, how do these shape the rules of water use and how do they evolve and change? Here I illustrate how, by following and analyzing historically and spatially located patterns of social relations, we can enhance our understanding of resource management.

In order to do this we need to expand our focus away from the institution (the Waterpoint Committee) to encompass the local institutional landscape in which people/water interactions are located. Let us begin by exploring some of the less-visible manifestations of institutional arrangements for water management in the same area as the Mtswirini well. We will consider the Shangani River, one of the back-up sources of water for people using the well, forty minutes' walk from that waterpoint. This case illustrates the importance of rules in use and some of the social principles by which cooperation over water resource management and collective action in Nkayi is organized.

Invisible Institutions: Shangani River

Picture now the Shangani River, a dry, sandy river bed strewn with rocks, perhaps fifty metres across. Here and there, close to the river banks, there may be pools of still water and the bed is dotted with shallow 'wells' dug in the sand. Women and girls can be seen washing clothes and carrying buckets of water away, cattle crossing to and fro. Although access is open to all and users of the river bed come from different districts (the river marks the district boundary), there is an accepted system of rules governing resource use there.

Drinking wells are dug in the middle of the river bed where the sand is cleanest and where the water underneath is flowing fastest. Individuals dig the wells, but no one is excluded from using them. The drinking wells are always communal, shared between families partly to minimize the dangers of witchcraft and poisoning between neighbours. Drinking wells commonly have a tin bucket sunk into them to prevent them from collapsing and are covered to protect them from animals. Holes are punched into the bottom of the tin to allow water to filter up into the bucket and branches or pieces of tin are placed over them as lids. Water for gardens, washing clothes and brick making is taken from wells dug at the dirty margins of the river. Again, individuals dig these wells, but anyone can use them. Clothes are washed and soap used at some distance away and the water carried from the well to that spot. There are designated perennial pools for cattle watering and specified sites for men and women to bathe. A special place in the river is reserved for the rain-making ceremonies of spirit mediums or church services to pray for rains. No one is specifically tasked with rule-making or with enforcing this system of management and there is very little non-compliance, the most serious cases reported being children leaving the lids off drinking wells.

Original settlement of the district was along the river banks and we can speculate that the practices of river bed use have a long history. These rules in use are also echoed in institutional arrangements at protected wells and boreholes through the district. They include the norms of:

- General but conditional access: all should have access to water sources in order to meet their basic livelihood needs but such access is conditional on appropriate use.
- Multiple uses of water sources, with a balance between 'domestic' and 'productive' uses, strongly linked with the importance of conflict avoidance between neighbours.
- Preserving quality: the priority given to maintaining the good condition of water, particularly for drinking, shapes many of the rules-in-use.
- Minimal management made possible by general compliance and conflict avoidance: explicit measures are only taken when problems arise; most management is conducted in the ordinary practices of daily life; and is conducted according to flexible perceptions of the 'right way of doing things'.

So we see that management is about more than just committees and is formed in practice by the exigencies of daily lives and livelihoods. But how have these arrangements come about? What are the factors which have shaped both the 'invisible' institutions of river management and the visible management of Mtswirini well? The partial transfer of river practices to protected inland waterpoints may be explained by the political history of planned resettlements in the district and people's experiences of conflict. The patterning and adaptability of such practices can be explained by the concept of 'institutional bricolage' and through the influence of a moral ecological code that provides the framework of interaction between people and with the environment.

To understand the ways in which the past shapes present institutional arrangements and the gestation of norms of water management, a historical perspective is useful (Johnson, 2004). In Nkayi, as elsewhere, political history and ecological dynamics intersect in the practices and institutions of water access (Beinart, 2000; Mosse, 2003).

A Troubled History of Water Access[2]

The history of water resource management in Nkayi is a troubled one. Located in western Zimbabwe, the district is characterized by low rainfall, poor soil, seasonal drought and severe pressure on land and water. A large proportion of the population depend on boreholes, small dams and hand-dug wells. There are two main rivers, the Shangani and the Gweru, and a number of minor ones, but none flows all the year round. In the dry season people dig wells for water in the sand of the river beds.

The history of 'development' interventions in the area could be said to begin in 1894 when the district was designated a Native Reserve by the Land Commission. Originally sparsely populated along the banks of the Shangani river, Ndebele people (including members of the royal family) started moving into the district following the destruction of their state in 1893, gradually displacing the original residents. According to a report of the Native Reserves Commission of 1915:

> It consists of a series of high sandy ridges from three to fifteen miles broad, well covered with a good class of timber, and with narrow valleys holding water ... the long ridges or 'gusu' are quite waterless, and offer but poor grazing. The soil itself is of fair quality, but until water is obtained, this 'gusu' country, though potentially of some value, can carry but a small population. (HMSO, 1917)

Drought was common during the late nineteenth and early twentieth centuries, and to survive people grew a variety of crops, stored and exchanged grain, and relied on assistance from the Native Affairs Department and on wild foods. In 1897 a Native Commissioner noted the failure of the rains: 'on the banks of the Shangani river there are a good many people who are living on the pith of palm trees' (Iliffe, 1990: 26).

Water supplies were developed to enable the reserve to carry a larger population (freeing land elsewhere for European agriculture) and to develop the cattle trade (enabling the African population to pay taxes). Boreholes were drilled in the inland areas away from the main river banks in the 1920s and 1930s. As early as 1915 a cost recovery policy was introduced: new residents were expected to make a lump sum payment for the capital cost of water supplies and to pay an annual water tax for maintenance costs. By the 1920s government had resigned itself to paying the capital costs, but maintenance fees were collected by headmen, and used to pay a technician from the district headquarters when borehole repairs were required.

Until the 1940s the administrators complained that development of infrastructure was constrained by the 'reluctance of the natives themselves to provide labour' and they considered the district unhealthy, conservative and backward: 'The past year has been very much like the rest, nothing of importance to remark upon, but a steady battle against the odds to develop a backward district' (Shangani District Native Reserve, 1951). Older residents recall both hardship and abundance; natural resources (game animals, thatching and grazing grass) were plentiful; but demands on the people to provide community labour and pay taxes were onerous, particularly given the frequent droughts. They remember 'forced' labour used to develop infrastructure. One informant recalled, 'In 1934 I was arrested for running away with a young girl and taken prisoner at Nkayi. My sentence was to do community service under Mr Cupboard, which was helping in the drilling of Manyabe Borehole' (Cleaver, 1996: 94).

In the 1940s and 1950s there was a major forced resettlement of people into the district from land designated for 'European' farming in other districts. An associated borehole drilling programme was executed to facilitate this but was seen by both the Native Commissioners and residents as inadequate. People remember being 'dumped' in the forest, somewhere near a borehole, and expected to reconstruct their livelihoods. In 1947 the district suffered major drought, the effects magnified by the disruption of the forced in-migration.

Political activity intensified in the 1960s and developed into guerrilla war in the mid 1970s. During this period struggles for control over water were defining features of people's everyday lives. Water collection journeys were hazardous, as women and children ran the risk of encountering soldiers or guerrillas. The guerrillas prevented people from using the dip tanks near boreholes and many people survived during this time on unprotected sources – filtering water through the sandy riverbeds or using seasonal pools. One District Commissioner[3] of the 1960s disconnected boreholes as a form of collective punishment for political activity:

> what happened was that ... They were refusing to dip their cattle or some bloody thing, so I disconnected all the boreholes, there was no water for them, which was highly effective ... When it collapsed, of course, I put all the parts back and everything was OK again.

By the 1970s the security situation meant that boreholes were not being mended.

Nkayi district was peaceful for only three years after Zimbabwe's independence in 1980. From 1983 onwards it became a centre of an operation by the Fifth Brigade of the Zimbabwean army (known locally as the 'Gukhurahundi') to suppress political dissidents through the intimidation of the civilian population. The terror tactics of the Fifth Brigade severely disrupted people's daily lives, development activities faltered, houses were burnt and many people 'disappeared', were beaten or killed during this time. Local administrative structures and official leadership effectively ceased to function (Catholic Commission for Justice and Peace, 1999).

Following the end of hostilities and a national amnesty in 1988 an Integrated Water Supply and Sanitation Project became the major development activity in the district. A policy of resettling people into 'lines' to ensure efficient land use planning and the centralized provision of development infrastructure was pursued, though with very slow progress.

Let us pause at this significant moment in Zimbabwean history, as in Chapter 7 we will return to Nkayi and consider the evolution of water institutions over the following two decades of state governance crisis.

Path Dependence and the Evolution of Norms

Many strands of this historic experience can be tracked through into 'modern' institutional arrangements. The troubled political history and ambivalent relationship of Nkayi people with the state constrains their willingness to provide collective labour, to volunteer for positions of authority, to invest time and effort in management arrangements. Experience of political conflict and its dire consequences means that people have deeply embedded preferences for avoiding confrontations with neighbours and public expressions of dissent. Long experience of drought has emphasized the importance of people maintaining access to a variety of sources and being extremely careful about the amounts of water they use. The history of in-migration into the district means that to a certain extent 'tradition' is invented (Hobsbawm and Ranger, 1992) – resettled people piece together ways of living together derived from past experience and current circumstances (so confirming historical ecological approaches).

So we can see how institutions are shaped by past practices and experiences. Douglas highlights the strength of forces which tend to reinforce inertia, resulting in institutions maintaining the shape and character determined by past events and circumstances, even though these might have changed (Douglas, 1987: 69). The prevalence of norms of access derived from historic uses of the river bed as the primary water supply during the early period of settlement in the district is an example. However, there is no need to be over-deterministic here. Institutions and social relations are path dependent in the sense that they are shaped, rather than determined by, what went before. The Nkayi case well demonstrates that path dependence is modified by negotiation and practice – people do not always and automatically accept what went before as a guide to future arrangements, as illustrated below by reference to water access, management arrangements and the role of authority.

Evidence from Nkayi illustrates both how the existence of strong social norms *and* their negotiation have shaped access to water and the balance achieved between competing uses of water. Thus universal access to water in Nkayi is seen by most as a 'natural' and desirable principle, despite the fact that most people no longer live along the main river beds and the increasing challenges of maintaining universal access to protected waterpoints of limited capacity. In suggesting negotiability as a counter to over-deterministic explanations of people–resource interactions I am not suggesting that such arrangements are always strategically crafted. Rather, I see water practices as imbued with a plethora of values and meanings and as markers of place-based identity and social status (Strang, 2004). Other studies from Zimbabwe suggest that the dynamics of water access defy dichotomous classification into 'traditional and modern' understandings or 'formal and informal' arrangements and well illustrate how 'custom' accommodates change (Derman, 2003; Nemarundwe and Kozanayi, 2003). In the case of Mtswirini well in Eguqeni village, access rights are applied with varying degrees of flexibility (shaped by social identity), and 'customary' decision-making arrangements blend with 'modern' ones.

Social Relations of Access

The boundaries of the Mtswirini pump-user community were both fuzzy and permeable. Whilst interviewees asserted the 'traditional' norm that no one should be excluded from taking water, as the dry season drought progressed, arguments for exclusion became stronger. Many of the regular users said that they allowed anyone whose water supply had failed to collect from the Mtswirini well. However, some users explicitly said, 'There is not enough water for all comers. They [the committee] should be restricting it to those whom it is supposed to serve ... People must stick to their own waterpoints.' Users from outside the village were observed being refused access by the committee chairman, who then called them back and allowed them to take water when everyone else had finished. These users were distantly related by marriage to the chairman. Workers upgrading a nearby road were unable to access the pump and had to ask at nearby households for a cup of water when they needed it. 'Conditional' users from other villages spoke about how precarious their rights of access were – they were only able to 'squeeze in' and pump one bucket of water after everyone else has finished, if they were lucky. 'Traditional' (and possibly mythical) ideas about open access were contested, modified and re-negotiated by people explicitly drawing on development-inspired messages about community 'ownership' in which rights of access are secured by participation in implementation and through payments. Access rights were also asserted both publicly and in practice by claims based on proximity of residence, calls on kin and social relations, and equal citizenship of the modern Zimbabwean state.

Although general compliance was normal, people felt able to break rules of access and partitioning if they were perceived as unreasonably onerous. In Eguqeni village Mrs P. Nyoni was observed persistently using the pump at closed times, apparently without incurring punishment, or even disapproval. Villagers suggested that this was acceptable in her case as she had a large number of young children and lived far from the pump; making it difficult for her to collect enough water for her basic needs within pump opening times. This generous interpretation of the rules was a conscious modification of the norm of compliance and a recognition of the specific structural constraints, livelihood and social identity of the non-complier. Mrs Nyoni's reputation for hard work and her relationship to the dominant family in the village were also significant in her being allowed to bend the rules.

Significantly, these examples suggest that it is not just water access that is being negotiated in these interactions, but notions of authority, rights and citizenship, the governance milieu which frames people's daily livelihood activities. Such negotiations do not always occur in spaces of public debate but in the very practices of collecting water, gendered divisions of labour and in conversations at the waterpoint, in households and beerhalls.

Practices of Management and Decision-Making

Arrangements for management were minimal and transaction costs at the waterpoint itself kept to a minimum, but considerable effort was put into generating general consensus about community decisions. The 'closer' rule ensured that everyone took water at the same time. Compliance was general, although the rule was only symbolically enforced – any child could reconnect the pump arm by inserting a stick in place of the missing part. The chairman, who lived nearby, was responsible for disconnection but the ways in which he did this did not go unquestioned. He and his family were said to occasionally break the 'closer' rule and to fetch water for their vegetable patch and goats. Women water collectors grumbled when the chairman was inconsistent in opening the pump, was absent at a funeral or left his grandchildren to do it for him at unpredictable times. On one occasion such grumbling resulted in a modification of the opening arrangements.

The committee had a very simple strategy for ensuring that there was compliance with collective decisions. On one occasion they decided to reinforce the fence around the pump to prevent animals from getting in. A notice was posted on the shearlegs to the effect that all 'drawers' must participate. No one would be allowed to draw afternoon water until the work was done. Twelve adults appeared to fix the fence, representing most of the regular user households, and the work was duly completed.

Although a waterpoint committee existed, decisions were generally made on the basis of whole-community meetings. Membership of different local committees overlapped and a common record book was kept at village level. The villagers made public decisions through meetings of the people, nominally held under the auspices of the multi-purpose village development committee (VIDCO). All adult members of the community were entitled to attend such meetings, which some saw as in the tradition of the meetings of adult men under the nineteenth-century Ndebele state. Minutes of meetings often did not identify particular committees but merely said 'We had a meeting to discuss the following.' Over a year this village discussed a range of subjects at meetings, including disputes over sale of a house, warnings to grazing scheme offenders to pay up, preservation of grazing lands, organization of Food for Work projects and distribution of food, registration of elderly people for social welfare, the effectiveness of the councillor, the possibility of contributing money for waterpoints, the district council's ban on beer brewing (the community's objections) and registration of pre-school children (Eguqeni VIDCO Minutes, 1992).

Whilst management was minimal and all efforts were made to economize on transaction costs (the 'closer' rule being an example of this), considerable time and effort was spent on inclusive decision-making and securing agreement in meetings. The Nkayi model of decision-making was high on transaction costs – meetings were lengthy and decisions only taken on the achievement of consensus, after hearing all who wished to speak. Thus instead of designed rules being backed up by graduated sanctions, publicly applied (as suggested in Mainstream Institutionalism, Ostrom, 2008), compliance is sought rather through lengthy, sometimes opaque and non-confrontational negotiation. In Nkayi district such processes could stretch over a number of meetings, sometimes extending over several months. A single village meeting which I attended lasted for twelve hours (sitting under a tree) with little being concluded, some contentious issues being aired and others left for another time. Such a laborious decision-making process is part of the conscious forging of a common base of understanding, of a consensus which not only contributes to a generalized community solidarity but also lessens the subsequent need for monitoring and sanctions. People are well aware that maintaining public culture of respect and cooperation needs working at. Thus the agenda for one village meeting read:

Box 3.1 Village Development Committee Agenda

---

1. To round up the year (or) plan for next year.
2. Advantages and disadvantages to be seen.
3. How to work together as a cooperative village – as the backbone of the village.
4. How to respect each other at meetings.
5. How we receive and deliver the message to the people.
6. How we punish (one) who disobeys.
7. Things for next year (plan).
8. To see those tired of their duties or to vote to replace.
E.T.C.
(*The document is signed by the secretary to the Eguqeni Village Development Committee*)

Whilst high on initial transaction costs, such a model may be considered effective in ensuring compliance with decisions made. This well demonstrates the need to look beyond the functional arrangements for water management to wider patterns of decision-making, social interaction and the generation of norms. There is a danger here in over-romaticizing such processes. In fact, consensus was often achieved by overlooking or downplaying differences and inequalities, agreement secured because less-powerful community members were unable or unwilling to express dissent. The outcomes of such decision-making were not necessarily equitable; an issue that will be addressed further in Chapter 7. People who were not present at meetings where collective decisions were made often grumbled about them and felt less committed to abide by them. In Nkayi meetings were often held on Wednesday (the '*izilo*' day, when people don't work in the fields out of respect for the spirits). Anyone with paid work could not attend on a Wednesday, but if the people tried to hold meetings on Saturdays the Seventh Day Adventists complained, and on Sundays those who went to other churches could not attend.

Thus we see resource use and decision-making based on deeply embedded social norms and on the conscious modification of these.

The Nature of Authority

Much literature suggests that a robust system for common property resource management requires clear structures of authority to rigorously impose a series of graduated sanctions against those who cheat and free-ride (Ostrom, 1992: 71). Conversely, there is a common assumption that the dictates of social norms will be so strongly internalized by each individual as to mostly ensure unquestioning compliance (Wade, 1988a, 1988b). The Nkayi case offers data to query both assumptions.

Few claims to authority and tradition in the district can be taken for granted. As we have seen, the social and political history of the area has been one of repeated disruption, resettlement of population and changing of boundaries and authority structures. In Douglas's terms, the categories of political discourse, the cognitive base of the social order, are being constantly negotiated, though often not in immediately obvious ways. Much of this negotiation is hidden or implicit as 'new' arrangements are often invested with older meaning. Such naturalization is important in processes of bricolage:

> There needs to be an analogy by which the formal structure of a crucial set of social relations is found in the physical world, or in the supernatural world, or in eternity, or anywhere, so long as it is not seen as a socially contrived arrangement. (Douglas, 1987: 29)

Key, then, to the crafting of institutions through conscious discussion over time are socially embedded concepts of appropriate or legitimate authority.

In Nkayi, debate tended to revolve around the 'right way of doing things' shaped by history, agro-ecology, claims to tradition and everyday livelihood demands. 'Traditional' systems (based on the chiefly system and headmen at various levels) and 'modern' systems of authority (based on ward, village and district chairmen) existed side by side, both partially discredited during the war years. Development initiatives introduced new players (teachers, nurses, extension workers) whose authority derives from their professional knowledge and status. The supernatural world also provided an overarching system of authority, which will be elaborated upon below. People in Nkayi were eclectic in their reference to various human authority figures in resolving problematic issues; often their main concern was to keep disputes at the lowest possible level, without reference to 'higher' authority. Different authority figures were invoked according to the nature of the problem, the perceived competence of the individual and perceptions of the right way of doing things. The authority situation was complicated by the fact that during the war years very old or obviously incompetent people were nominated for local leadership positions, on the assumption that they could not be considered political targets. (Similarly, people had the habit of not using real names for places, to confuse hostile authorities and visiting researchers!) So whilst individual authority figures are interesting, we need to look more carefully at the ways in which more general ideas about authority work to secure compliance with community norms.

In the 1990's formal authority structures in the Eguqeni village and wider area were considered by government and development officials to be 'weak'. Authority to make and enforce rules was exercised through family, traditional and modern structures. At the end of the twentieth century the village was dominated by one prominent family – three brothers in their late seventies and eighties held the position of VIDCO chairman (modern leader), Sobhuko (traditional leader) and chairman of waterpoint committee. Squabbles about the authority to make and enforce rules occurred between the three old men (the sons of different mothers), with the VIDCO chairman claiming the right of veto and the importance of being able to brief government on village activities. The chief was a 'boy' in his twenties who had inherited the position from his older brother. The elected ward councillor (who represented the local villages on the district council) was complained about both by the villagers and by people in authority for his absence from meetings and alleged selling of Food for Work maize. Despite the supposed weakness of local authority structures, broad compliance with rules (as well as their negotiation) was noted. To explain this, we look beyond the formal village structures of decision-making and authority to understand the disciplining effects of habit, routine and precedent and the wider cosmological framework within which everyday water practices, collective and individual action took place.

Mainstream Institutional theory holds both that pursuing similar livelihoods in close proximity generates trust, that the chance of securing cooperative behaviour in transactions is enhanced by face-to-face talk and that there may be a need to supplement these norms and processes with explicit rules and sanctions (Ostrom, 2008; Poteete, Janssen and Ostrom, 2010; Cinner *et al.*, 2011; Mehring *et al.*, 2011). Here I demonstrate how solidarity and cooperation is consciously worked at (as well as being unconsciously generated in everyday interactions) and how general adherence to wider, shared cosmological understandings of cause and effect may be preferred to instrumental rules and human-made sanctions. This does not render collective action apolitical, nor does it imply that cooperation is achieved without the exercise of authority. Rather, I suggest that our focus should be broadened from the immediate scrutiny of transactions to include the way that worldviews shape constructions of authority, and thus individual and collective behaviours. Indeed, many studies of African society emphasize the deeply rooted concepts of power which merge the ecological, religious and political (Ellis and Ter Haar, 1998; Bernard 2003; Chabal 2009) and frame the ways in which authority is conceived and exercised.

In drawing on past practices to legitimize current arrangements, people often invoke a previous 'golden age' of cooperation. However, such solidarity is also perceived as something that is difficult to achieve, requiring considerable effort on the part of the cooperators. Generalized notions of solidarity often substitute for clear authority structures and sanctions, but are not automatically generated by living together. We have already seen that people prefer to spend more time negotiating consensus than establishing and imposing sanctions. Cooperation is not only about agreeing over the mechanisms of water resource management, but also about maintaining good relations in the wider interactions of everyday life (Berry 1989; Solway 1994). Solidarity is perceived both as functionally advisable (for example in gaining access to donor resources) as well as morally desirable and critically necessary for the maintenance of the social and natural order. People in Nkayi often referred to the Liberation War as a time when cooperation was critical to survival and disputes between neighbours could be fatal:

> During the war many people ran away, so the few who were left really stuck together or we would all be dead. We warned each other if the soldiers were coming, then we would run away and spend the night in the forest together and help each other with food. We loved each other then. If that had continued we would be God's own people. (Cleaver 1995: 328)

This very positive memory of solidarity overlooks the incidences of inter-community conflicts that also occurred during times of struggle, but nonetheless reflects a recurring theme in the way that people in Nkayi talk about their survival in a difficult political and physical environment (Alexander, McGregor and Ranger, 2000). It wasn't just because of the painful experiences of the war years that cooperative relations were favoured. People in Nkayi commonly attributed unexpected death or misfortune to stress or witchcraft resulting from conflict between neighbours. The ability to live peacefully together with others and not cause disputes were expected attributes of leaders. Both Douglas and Giddens assert the importance of a psychological sense of wellbeing, of ontological security in shaping people's perceptions and actions, and yet this is rarely referred to in the modelling of incentives in common property resource management literature. It is clear from the history of Nkayi why people should find the prospect of conflict so distressing, but it also relates to a wider explanation of a world order, to perceptions of the moral ecological framework within which their lives are conducted. Solidarity and cooperation play key parts in moral–ecological explanations of environment and change in Nkayi, as the following section shows.

Moral–Ecological Framework

One way of avoiding over-instrumental understandings of culture in institutional formation is to pay attention to the moral meanings and values attached to human–environment interactions and the exercise of power. Ideas about moral community and moral personhood are fundamental in orienting human action and yet little accommodated in many institutional analyses (Karlström, 2004; Hyden, 2006). The exercise of power is often legitimized or challenged within moral rather than functional frames of reference (Chabal, 2009), processes which are observable in everyday practices and negotiations over access to resources. Common to many African societies is an ecological ethic embedded in physical, spiritual and social landscapes (Bernard, 2003; Impey, 2009). Here, human action and the exercise of power are linked to the supernatural world of God, ancestral spirits and guardians. The effects of such actions are felt both by individuals in terms of their health, economic and social wellbeing and in natural phenomena – the falling of rain, flowing of rivers, fertility of land, incidence of pests and disease. In the Zimbabwean case power and ownership is invested in ancestral spirits embodied in the landscape and where this is acknowledged by human agents all should go well (Mazarire, 2008). The fundamental importance of such understandings is illustrated by recent and contemporary contestations over political power, land and development initiatives in which contested claims are often reinforced by various parties with reference to the spirits (Lan, 1985; Ranger, 1999; Spierenburg, 2004; Chikozho and Latham, 2005; Cox, 2007).

The example of a rain-making ceremony in Nkayi illustrates such beliefs and their adaptation. In October 1992 Nkayi was in the midst of a deep and terrible drought; the crops had failed the previous year and when it was time to prepare the field for planting in anticipation of new season rain the ground was rock hard and most of the draught cattle were dead. Just near the village where I was living a spirit medium (*hosana*) from the Njelele rain shrine was invited to stay in the village and dance for the rains.[4] Over the three weeks of the rain-making ceremony we heard the drums playing every night and a steady stream of people passing by to make their offerings of black and white cloth or maize meal. The medium from the Njelele shrine, Sikore, was called by the local medium to help summon up the rains. Sikore's reputation preceded her. She was a short, round woman with no front teeth. Dressed in black and wearing a string of red beads around her wrist, she was renowned for her hyper-fertility – people in the village passed round a crumpled and indistinct photo allegedly showing the two sets of quads she had given birth to ('Two pregnancies, eight kids!' village women commented in awe).

The rain-making took place on the stamped ground around the big old Mtolo tree; there was dancing and drumming there every night. Members of my host family participated by playing the drums, sending dishes of white maize for the hosana and brewing beer. The hosana told me that she was teaching people that the drought was due to the fact that they were no longer keeping the traditional ways.

At the end of three weeks there was a big neighbourhood gathering. On the day of the big dance everyone gathered at the Mtolo site. People were there from the whole neighbourhood, not just the village. The medium was facing the people when we arrived, already possessed by the Njelele spirit. She was crouched down with her head to the ground and speaking instructions that could not be heard by the audience. Naison Nyoni, son of the headman and a local spirit medium himself, transmitted what she said to the crowd and passed their questions on to her. Through the medium the Njelele spirit said the following:

- People were stingy and not bringing enough snuff (as an offering).
- The rule that they should not sweep their floors with grass brushes[5] was false: they should continue to do so.
- People must not sell wild fruits or vegetables.
- They must not plough the fields the day after the rains.

- They must observe Wednesday as a rest day.
- They must plants seeds in a way that the hosana would demonstrate afterwards.
- It was untrue that people had to bring marijuana, cows, corn and money to Njelele.

After giving these instructions and prohibitions the spirit asked for evidence of what people had seen at the Mtolo site that day. One person had seen a tshongololo (a large millipede). This was interpreted as evidence that the spirit was serious and there would be rain, as such creatures were only seen in the rainy season. Another person said they had seen a tiny scarlet velvet spider – the ones that are common when it rains.

At this the ceremony was over and everyone walked across the fields to the nearby compound of the headman. There people gathered in groups for dancing and beer drinking and this went on all night. The spirit medium stayed in a hut and carried out healing ceremonies of people brought to her, including a member of my host family terminally ill with tuberculosis. The next day the ladies of the Catholic choir also came to sing and pray for her in a Christian healing ceremony. At around this time many people who had participated in the Njelele ceremony also prayed for rain in their churches; the Lutheran church held prayers for rain at the site also used for 'traditional' spirit ceremonies in the dry river bed.

Invention of Tradition and the Naturalization of Institutions

The rain-making ceremony outlined above suggests that tradition is constantly being invented and re-invented, but that so is everyday life. Just as people diversify their livelihood activities, they seek rain making and healing from the spirit medium as well as from the hospital, the Lutherans and the Catholic choir. But this is not to suggest that anything goes; that any new arrangement can be taken up. The need to naturalize, legitimize and gain the approbation of existing authorities means that institutions formed through bricolage, the piecing together of new arrangements from resources at hand, will result in arrangements which refer to the past, to accepted ways of doing things.

As we have already seen, Douglas writes convincingly of the need for credible social institutions to be attributed some natural or supernatural legitimacy rather than being perceived as contrived arrangements (Douglas, 1987: 48). Giddens (1984: 25–6) echoes this point in highlighting the role of ideology in the reification of social relations and the discursive naturalization of human action. The moral ecological framework in Nkayi generates, legitimizes and reinforces social relations of authority, norms of respect and conflict avoidance by linking them to the natural and supernatural worlds. It is no accident that human hierarchies follow similar patterns to hierarchies in the spirit world, and indeed the two inter-relate.

The desirability of conflict avoidance, the requirement to behave respectfully to authority figures and to do things the right way is deeply embedded in the moral–ecological and solidarity models. Conflicts are perceived as deeply threatening to communities and disputes between people and a failure to live together are likely to incur the wrath of the ancestors and result in punishment through lack of rain, disease and crop failure. Amos Nyoni, the village chairman, illustrated this point:

> In the 1950s there was plenty of rain but from the start of the liberation struggle the rains started to decline. 1967 was the last year that we had good thatching grass around here … The lack of rains is due to the bad deeds by the people who are no longer following the traditional ways. There is too much fighting and too much blood being shed. The other problem is that long back the hosanas [spirit mediums] were respected. They would come without being asked and they were really respected. Now little respect is shown. (Cleaver, 2000: 378)

Conflict avoidance as the 'right way of doing things' becomes part of a wider system which reinforces human authority structures with supernatural legitimacy and combines the concepts of rationality and morality with respect for authority.

However, the dictates of tradition and the spirit world are, like human arrangements subject to negotiation, reshaping and approximate compliance. For example, observance of Wednesday as the izilo day, when people do not work in the fields (in respect for the spirits), was general and reinforced at ceremonies, as we have seen. However, people were very flexible in their application of this 'rule'. People often excluded picking food for that day's meal from the prohibition on field work and would often 'take a walk' in the fields to check on the progress on their crops on izilo days.

The flexible, pragmatic and evolving nature of people's beliefs is well illustrated by Amos Nyoni's explanation of the effectiveness of rain-making ceremonies. Like other older men in positions of authority, he emphasized the need for respect in maintaining the natural order. He suggested that belief in the Njelele rain shrines was one adopted by the

Eguqeni people when they settled in Nkayi. He claimed they participate fully in the ceremonies because these things can definitely work if everyone believes in them and joins in. His daughter-in-law, a teacher and active Christian, said 'these ceremonies have been known to work if everyone believes wholeheartedly' (Cleaver, 2000: 379).

The moral ecological framework has the authority of tradition but this does not mean that all aspects of it are automatically accepted. People discursively reflect on the legitimacy of authority figures and the efficacy of collective and individual actions. In a visit two years after the rain-making ceremony I found doubts were being expressed about the legitimacy of the medium. She had given up rain-making in favour of healing, in which she was renowned (and which was more lucrative). She had come under suspicion when one woman died after treatment and another turned yellow. People suspected that she was either a fake or being punished by the spirits for some mistake. They thought it suspicious that she operated largely alone and did not go to ceremonies with other mediums.

So, in the rain-making ceremony, we have participation in a form of collective action in which the actors are not blindly following habit or social norms but can discursively justify their participation and consciously construct the 'tradition'. However, they value inclusiveness – a deeply embedded principle of living together. Such ceremonies, with participants coming from a neighbourhood wider than simply that of the village, helped to maintain social solidarity and to retain the idea of a broad community. Indirectly, this facilitated access to water outside the immediate area and across administrative boundaries. We can then see boundaries of resource use and authority in a dynamic relationship with overlapping and interactive networks.

Moral–Ecological Understandings and Bricolage

The moral ecological framework helps to illustrate the concept of institutional bricolage. The concept of the crafting of institutions suggests that specific institutions are deliberately developed for particular functions. This model can be queried on a number of grounds. Institutions for resource management may be multi-purpose; management may be both intermittent *and* robust, an integral part of social relations *and* subject to negotiation. Evidence from Nkayi suggests that institutional formation through processes of bricolage are less purposeful, more partial, ad hoc, historically embedded and morally framed than those suggested by common ideas about institutional design.

In this Nkayi case, arrangements for water resource management were borrowed or constructed from existing institutions, styles of thinking and sanctioned social relationships. For example, principles of water use derived from living by the river were applied to inland artificial water sources for which they were less suitable and thus subject to contestation and change. Under the impact of war and modernization 'meetings of the people', derived from meetings of male elders in the nineteenth-century Ndebele state, were adapted to include (in principle) all adults in a community. The experience of conflict and war, when solidarity was perceived as critical to survival, had reinforced norms of inclusiveness, cooperation and conflict avoidance in everyday relations. The form that institutions for cooperation took, however, was also strongly influenced by development messages, linking responsibility to ownership and collective action to payment. Desirable community relations were modelled on the ideal of family relations whilst appeals to the Njelele rain spirits, to the Christian God and to proper behaviour on the part of the people all had their part to play in resource management.

Moreover, there were numerous instances where institutions purposefully established to manage one resource are adapted for others. For example, a 'general community purse' was established in a village to finance hospitality for visitors and then extended to fund water supply maintenance and the construction of fencing for the pre-school. Resource management in Nkayi was not based simply on structures of authority manifested in particular leaders but on a wider system of authority based on the collective norms of the 'right way of doing things', linking human action with the natural and supernatural environments.

Conclusion

Let us return to some observations as to why these insights from Nkayi are significant in understanding institutions. The material from Nkayi suggest that institutions are partial, intermittent and indeed often invisible, being located in the daily interactions of ordinary lives. Collective action is frequently ad hoc, variable and not necessarily output-optimizing.

Firstly, institutions are formed from and reproduced through the interactions of daily life. This in fact ensures both continuity and change in institutional form. Following Bourdieu, it is the necessary improvisations of everyday life, the seemingly unimportant blurring of boundaries, compromises and bending of rules that enable institutions both to survive and change. Water resource management in Nkayi would be impossible within rigid boundaries, strictly enforced rules and strict procedures for imposing sanctions. Case studies cited throughout this book similarly demonstrate the fuzziness of boundaries, the flexible application of local rules, norms and sanctions and the shaping of individual and collective action in wider frameworks of meaning. It is the embeddedness in everyday life and in broader cosmologies that allow institutions to be 'naturalized'. Thus new or adapted arrangements become seen as the 'right way of doing things'; invested with the authority of routine, precedent and proper approbation of human and supernatural authorities.

In this way culture and tradition becomes enmeshed with authoritative relations, with power and politics. Whilst the Mainstream Institutionalists uphold a model of institutions broadly compatible with Weberian bureaucracy and contemporary good governance agendas; Africans themselves often see the sources of power and authority in institutions, linked to living patrons and to the spirit world. The moral framing of human actions in relation to natural resources deeply imbues taken-for-granted notions of the 'right way of doing things'. This shapes the ways in which institutions evolve as well as everyday practices.

We have noted above how institutional arrangements may be legitimized by claims to tradition or to modern development messages by reference to the rights of citizens. The authoritative nature of claims to tradition and modernity also shape the institutions through which governance is exercised, citizenship constructed and through which the everyday state manifests.

I suggest that an understanding of moral–ecological rationality is important because it is one of the ways in which people make sense of change and bring order to uncertainty. Moral motives are central to the exercise of human agency and so shape institutions in particular ways (a theme we will return to in Chapter 5). Whilst there are plenty of studies focusing on the fascinating manifestations of moral–ecological beliefs on community dynamics and institutional formation (for example, see the literature on sacred groves and the local management of forests: Nyamweru and Sheridan, 2008; Roth, 2009; Katani 2010), I see the need to ensure that we retain a focus on their outcomes. In the following chapter I will explore themes relating to the equity effects of institutional formation, the extent to which individuals can reshape institutions and their effects and the remaking of institutions and moral community in changing conditions.

Bibliography

Alexander, J., McGregor, J., Ranger, T. (2000) 'Violence and Memory: One Hundred Years in the "Dark Forests" of Matabeleland', Oxford, James Currey.

Beinart, W. (2000) 'African History and Environmental History', *African Affairs* 99, pp. 269–302.

Berkes, F. (1989) *Common Property Resources: Ecology and Community-Based Sustainable Development*, London, Belhaven Press.

Bernard, P. S. (2003) 'Ecological Implications of Water Spirit Beliefs in Southern Africa: The Need to Protect Knowledge, Nature and Resource Rights', in A. Watson and J. Sproull (eds), *Science and Stewardship to Protect and Sustain Wilderness Values: Seventh World Wilderness Congress Symposium 2001 November 2–8 Proceedings*, South Africa, Port Elizabeth.

Biersack, A. (1999) 'Introduction: From the "New Ecology" to the New Ecologies', *American Anthropologist* 101, 1, pp. 5–18.

Bourdieu, P. and Wacquant, L. (1992) *An Invitation to Reflexive Sociology*, Oxford, Polity Press.

Bromley, D. (ed.) (1992) *Making the Commons Work: Theory, Practice, and Policy*, San Francisco, ICS Press.

Catholic Commission for Justice and Peace (1999) *Breaking the Silence, Building True Peace: A Report on the Disturbances in Matabeleland and the Midlands 1980–1988*, Harare, Zimbabwe, Catholic Commission for Justice and Peace/Legal Resources Foundation.

Chabal, P. (2009) *Africa: The Politics of Suffering and Smiling*, London, Zed Books.

Chikozho, C. and Latham, J. (2005) 'Shona Customary Practices in the Context of Water Sector Reforms in Zimbabwe', paper presented at the International Workshop on African Laws: Plural Legislative Framework for Rural Water Management in Africa, Johannesburg, South Africa, 26–28 January.

Cinner, J. E., Basurto, X., Fidelman, P., Kuange, J., Lahari, R. and Mukminin, A. (2011) 'Institutional Designs of Customary Fisheries Management Arrangements in Indonesia, Papua New Guinea, and Mexico', *Marine Policy*, in press, corrected proof.

Cleaver, F. (1996) 'Cost Recovery in the Water Sector', *Development Research Insights*
—(2000) 'Moral Ecological Rationality, Institutions and the Management of Common Property Resources', *Development and Change* 31, 2, pp. 361–83.

Cox, J. (2007) *From Primitive to Indigenous: The Academic Study of Indigenous Religions*, Aldershot, Ashgate.

Derman, W. (2003) 'Cultures of Development and Indigenous Knowledge: The Erosion of Traditional Boundaries', *Africa Today* 50, 2, pp. 67–85.

Douglas, M. (1973) *Rules and Meanings*, Harmondsworth, Penguin.
—(1987) *How Institutions Think*, London, Routledge & Kegan Paul.

Ellis, S. and Ter Haar, G. (1998) 'Religion and Politics in Sub-Saharan Africa', *The Journal of Modern African Studies* 36, 2, pp. 175–201.

Fontein, J. (2008) 'The Power of Water: Landscape, Water and the State in Southern and Eastern Africa: An Introduction', *Journal of Southern African Studies* 34, 4, pp. 737–56.

Giddens, A. (1984) *The Constitution of Society: Outline of the Theory of Structuration*, Cambridge, Polity Press.
—(1989) *Sociology*, Cambridge, Polity Press.

Granovetter, M. (1992) 'Economic Action and Social Structure: the Problem of Embeddedness', in M. Granovetter and R. Swedberg (eds) *The Sociology Of Economic Life*, Oxford, Westview Press.

HMSO (1917) *Papers Relating to Southern Rhodesia Native Reserves Commission*, London, HMSO.

Hobsbawm, E. and Ranger, T. (eds) (1992) *The Invention of Tradition*, Cambridge, Cambridge University Press.

Hyden, G. (2006) 'Introduction and Overview to the Special Issue on Africa's Moral and Affective Economy', *African Studies Quarterly* 9, 1 & 2, pp. 1–8.

Iliffe, J. (1990) *Famine in Zimbabwe 1890–1960*, Gweru, Mambo Press.

Impey, A. (2009) 'Songs of Mobility and Belonging: Gender, Spatiality and the Local in Southern Africa's Transfrontier Conservation Development', paper presented at 54th Society for Ethnomusicology Conference, November 19–22, Mexico City.

Johnson, C. (2004) 'Uncommon Ground: The "Poverty of History" in Common Property Discourse', *Development and Change* 35, 3, pp. 407–33.

Karlström, M. (2004) 'Modernity and its Aspirants: Moral Community and Developmental Eutopianism in Buganda', *Current Anthropology* 45, 5, pp. 595–619.

Katani, J. Z. (2010) 'The Role of Multiple Institutions in the Management of Micro Spring Forests in Ukerewe, Tanzania', PhD thesis, Wageningen, University of Wageningen.

Kottak, C. (1999) 'The New Ecological Anthropology', *American Anthropologist* 101, 1, pp. 23–55.

Lan, D. (1985) *Guns and Rain: Guerrillas and Spirit Mediums in Zimbabwe*, Oxford, James Curry.

Mazarire, G. C. (2008) '"The Chishanga Waters have their Owners": Water Politics and Development in Southern Zimbabwe', *Journal of Southern African Studies* 34, 4, pp. 757–84.

Mehring, M., Seeberg-Elverfeldt, C., Koch, S., Barkmann, J., Schwarze, S. and Stoll-Kleemann, S. (2011) 'Local Institutions: Regulation and Valuation of Forest Use – Evidence from Central Sulawesi, Indonesia', *Land Use Policy* 28, 4, pp. 736–47.

Mosse, D. (2003) *The Rule of Water: Statecraft, Ecology and Collective Action in South India*, Oxford, Oxford University Press.

—(2008) 'Epilogue: The Cultural Politics of Water – A Comparative Perspective', *Journal of Southern African Studies* 34, 4, pp. 939–48.

Nemarundwe, N. and Kozanayi, W. (2003) 'Institutional Arrangements for Water Resource Use: A Case Study from Southern Zimbabwe', *Journal of Southern African Studies* 29, 1, pp. 193–206.

Nyamweru, C. and Sheridan, M. (2008) 'Introduction', in C. Nyamweru and M. Sheridan (eds) *African Sacred Groves: Ecological Dynamics and Social Change*, Ohio, Ohio University Press, pp. 2–8.

Ostrom, E. (1990) *Governing the Commons: The Evolution of Institutions for Collective Action*. Cambridge, Cambridge University Press.

—(1992) *Crafting Institutions for Self-Governing Irrigation Systems*, San Francisco, ICS Press.

—(2008) 'Design Principles of Robust Property-Rights Institutions: What Have We Learned?' paper presented at Land Policies and Property Rights, Lincoln Institute of Land Policy, Cambridge, MA, June 2–3.

Peters, P. E. (1987) 'Embedded Systems and Rooted Models', in B. J. McCay and J. M. Acheson (eds) *The Question of the Commons: The Culture and Ecology of Communal Resources*, Tuscon, University of Arizona Press, pp.171–93.

Poteete, A. Janssen, M. A. and Ostrom, E. (2010) 'Working Together: Collective Action, the Commons and Multiple Methods in Practice', Woodstock, Oxfordshire, Princeton University Press.

Ranger, T. (1999) *Voices from the Rocks: Nature, Culture and History in the Matopos Hills of Zimbabwe*, Bloomington. Indiana University Press.

Roth, D. (2009) 'Property and Authority in a Migrant Society: Balinese Irrigators in Sulawesi, Indonesia', *Development and Change* 40, 1, pp. 195–217.

Spierenburg, M. (2004) *Strangers, Spirits and Land Reforms: Conflicts about Land in Dande, Northern Zimbabwe*, Leiden, Brill.

Strang, V. (2004) *The Meaning of Water*, Oxford, Berg.

Wade, R. (1988a) 'The Management of Irrigation Systems: How to Evoke Trust and Avoid Prisoners' Dilemma', *World Development* 16, 4, pp. 489–500.

—(1988b) *Village Republics: Economic Conditions for Collective Action in South India*, Cambridge, Cambridge University Press.

Notes

1 The case is drawn from research conducted in 1992 and 1994, funded by a Leverhulme Trust research grant . In Chapter 7 research conducted in the same village in 2010 is presented. Material here is drawn from my thesis, 'Community Management of Rural Water Supply in Zimbabe', University of East Anglia, 1996, and builds on my previous papers using this work, for example (2000) 'Moral Ecological Rationality, Institutions and the Management of Common Property Resources', *Development and Change* 31, 2, pp. 361–83.

2 An elaboration of the political dynamics of water supply in Nkayi during the twentieth century can be found in my (1995) 'Water as a Weapon: The History of Water Supply Development in Nkayi District, Zimbabwe', *Environment and History* 1, pp. 313–33.

3 Nkayi District Commissioner NA Hunt 1865–1868 Oral/240, pp. 60–1, 80–1, National Archive of Zimbabwe, Harare.

4 The Njelele rain shrine is based in the Matobo hills in Matabeleland south and is one of several cave shrines of the High God, Mwali. Rain shrine beliefs are generally associated with peace and fertility and with the linking of 'bad deeds' to dire environmental consequences. The dictates of Mwali are made known through mediums when possessed.

5 This prohibition was allegedly a government-given measure aimed at preserving supplies of thatching grass.

4 Plural Institutions: New Arrangements, Old Inequalities?

Introduction

In the previous chapter we have seen how institutions are produced in everyday practices and framed with reference to wider schemes of meaning. Let us now turn to a case study from Tanzania to further explore institutional plurality and the ways bricoleurs navigate such arrangements. Here we will see how plurality manifests through the diverse interests of multiple stakeholders, overlapping regimes of governance (traditional and modern) and varying values and uses of the resource. Plurality is also evident in the ways in which people improvise and borrow through different channels to form resource management institutions. Bricolage helps people to make sense of such complexity, blending and bestowing legitimacy on assembled arrangements.

In this chapter I suggest that institutional plurality is more socially dispersed than suggested in much literature on polycentric environmental governance, which focuses on decentralized but largely formalized units of decision-making and management. I raise questions about how far institutional plurality builds social capital and how far it reinforces and reproduces social inequities. To illustrate that there is no normative superiority of institutions formed through 'bricolage' or through 'design', I explore the 'dark side' of institutional formation and functioning – the deployment of authority, rules and norms to reinforce and reproduce social inequalities and resource exclusion. Plural institutional processes are presented here as authoritative, often reproducing structural inequalities whilst simultaneously offering chances for some to reshape them.

Plural, Complex or Polycentric Resource Governance?

There is a growing consensus in natural resource management literature about the need to work with a variety of stakeholders; laws, rules and procedures; uses and values (Merrey *et al.*, 2007: 212). Recognizing such diversity is seen as a necessary antidote to unsuccessful over-centralized models of environmental management. From a complexity perspective, dilemmas of natural resource management are 'wicked' problems which are perceived differently by a variety of stakeholders, are socially complex in nature, defy clear boundaries and have no obvious end point (Rittel and Weber, 1973; Franks and Cleaver, 2009). Such issues are unlikely to be resolved by uni-dimensional solutions such as a technical fix or a rigidly applied management blueprint. Rather, various 'adaptive pathways' to achieving good resource governance, involving strong stakeholder representation, are seen as more viable and effective (Ramalingam *et al.*, 2008).

Mainstream Institutional theory has been increasingly concerned with the concept of polycentric governance, particularly in relation to adaptation to climate change (Ostrom, 2010). The concept of polycentric governance is often applied to understanding how small- and medium-scale institutions can be 'nested' into wider governance arrangements. So, for example, in a Tanzanian case considered in this chapter, different irrigator associations in the same sub-catchment manage water through making and enforcing rules and drawing on local norms and practices. They also 'nest' under an apex or umbrella organization where their representatives negotiate water allocation between their schemes and with higher levels of authority (such as the whole river basin office). Both vertical and horizontal dynamics are implied in these concepts in which networks of polycentric institutions are nested into hierarchies of governance arrangements at various scales (Wyborn and Bixler, 2011). So theoretically, while decentralization deals with local-level collective action problems, nesting enables these to also be tackled at scale. From this perspective, governance takes place through multiple layers of nested enterprises – a diverse mosaic of linked subunits with no one dominating authority (Andersson and Ostrom, 2008) and resource users are able to 'switch back and forth between levels' (Ostrom, 1990: 46). Such slotting together of various levels of management activity is thought to combine the benefits of adaptive management and democratic governance:

> A polycentric governance regime with strong stakeholder partici-pation and a balance between bottom-up and top-down processes is assumed to be more adaptive than a centralised regime with hierar-chical top-down control. (Pahl-Wostl *et al.*, 2011: 304)

There seems to be a certain amount of congruence between Mainstream and Critical Institutional thinking in terms of embracing polycentric governance arrangements. For example, in relation to water governance, Lankford and Hepworth (2010) draw on a lively analogy of the 'cathedral and bazaar' to outline the differences between monocentric and polycentric approaches to river basin management. For them, the 'cathedral' represents centralized (monocentric) control of water, often focused at the river basin level, delivered by government and expert professionals, drawing on legislated water rights and addressing the need to transfer water between sectors. By contrast, the 'bazaar' represents a polycentric model of water management that focuses on smaller management units within the river basin (water user associations and the like), where local policy is developed by groups of users, crucially involving the *negotiation* of customary rights and 'lived law'. Exploring the intersection between 'customary' and 'modern' water governance in Southern Africa, Maganga (2003) suggests that the promotion of nested governance arrangements might include water user groups, chieftaincies and their hierarchies, governmental and parastatal water agencies, local administrative and other relevant government departments.

However, let us approach such ideas with some caution. Analyses of polycentricity still largely focus on public and visible institutional arrangements (Merrey *et al.*, 2007; Lankford and Hepworth, 2010). Ideas about polycentric governance are part of the 'deliberative turn' in natural resource management and there is a tendency to assume that such plural arrangements create significant 'room for manoeuvre' for a broad variety on non-state actors (Neef, 2009). Such ideas are often based on rather optimistic models of communicative action which underplay inequalities in people's ability to influence decision-making, and which assume 'ethno-romantic' conceptualizations of communities, their traditions and norms (Ribot *et al.*, 2006; Neef, 2009; Neimark, 2010; Wong, 2010). Such optimism is tempered by views which suggest that plural systems may multiply disadvantage for certain people while expanding opportunities for elite others (Odgaard, 2002; Boelens *et al.*, 2007). The unevenness in plural governance regimes can be exacerbated by tensions at the interface between different types of arrangements, by the broader political and historical legacies which shape institutions and by variable levels of resources and capacities at community level (Sokile *et al.*, 2005; Falk *et al.*, 2009). Such tensions are explored, for example, in studies of legal pluralism, which consider the processes of hybridization and transformation of state institutions, laws and norms of equity and justice that occur in everyday social and political life (Von Benda-Beckman, 2002; Von Benda-Beckman and Von Benda-Beckman, 2006).

Social Capital as a Resource for Polycentric Governance

Underlying ideas about polycentric resource governance are assumptions that diversity and richness of associational relations constitute an institutional resource. Mainstream Institutionalists tend to see decentralized and polycentric arrangements as both drawing on and contributing to stocks of social capital in a virtuous cycle of association, participation and good governance. From this perspective institutions must be appropriately embedded in the social milieu from which the norms to support purposive decision-making can be drawn (Ostrom, 1990). Traditions, cultural norms and relations of association constitute the social cement which can be utilized to strengthen institutions and reduce the transaction costs of cooperation. People, as social entrepreneurs, consciously invest in relationships of trust and the creation of norms in anticipation of reciprocity and tangible benefits (Ahn *et al.*, 2003).

These views of social relations as an institutional resource dovetail nicely with concepts of social capital. A version of this concept became popular in development thinking in the 1990s because it seemingly specified an asset to be mobilized to further sustainable livelihoods, supported the effective management of common property resources and contributed to the proper workings of democracy (Putnam, 1994; Grootaert 1998; Wong, 2003; Cleaver, 2005). Social capital, in the form of cooperation and trust embodied in associational relationships (such as membership of clubs and societies), allegedly makes institutions work better. It does this by generating improvements in transactions and facilitating learnt cooperation: associated individuals have access to more information, enabling them to coordinate activities for mutual benefit; repeated interaction generates trust and reduces opportunistic behaviour (Dasgupta, 1988). Through repeated social association people are thought to develop the habits necessary to democracy, learning to exercise voice in public fora and to hold decision-makers to account. Mainstream social capitalists have argued that it may be useful to distinguish between 'bonding' and 'bridging' social capital. 'Bonding' refers to relationships within homogeneous social groups which may be restrictive and exclusionary, even anti-social, and 'Bridging' to associational links made across social categories from which the main beneficial effects of social capital are thought to derive (Woolcock, 2001).

Critics, however, suggest that the concept of social capital is too often used to sidestep issues of injustice and inequality, overlooking evidence of the negative aspects of social life, the dark side of networks which build antisocial norms and exclude people with particular identities (Levi, 1996). Further critiques concern the mainstream treatment of social capital as an asset, much like money or property, that can be stored, traded or substituted according to need (Fine, 2001). Such depoliticized social capital analyses struggle to account for persistent structural inequalities in society such as those around gender, and there is a danger of blaming individuals for their own lack of social capital and marginalization (Edwards *et al.*, 2003; Schuurman, 2003; Wong, 2003). Despite these critiques, the idea of social capital both as a building block and a product of institutional arrangements retains significant purchase, particularly in policy approaches to natural resource governance.

So in mainstream views institutions are embedded in two ways; firstly, through the nesting which locates decentralized institutions in scaled configurations and, secondly, in social relations, particularly in the medium of social capital within which they operate. Such concepts of dual embedding, whilst intending to capture the plural and dynamic nature of resource governance, nonetheless have a tendency in practice to be reduced and solidified; polycentric, nested arrangements are perceived as to complex hierarchies (made acceptable by some bottom-up dynamics); social relations are seen as an asset to be deployed in building enduring institutions.

Plurality and Social Embeddedness

How far do ideas about polycentricity and social capital help us to understand how institutions actually work and how outcomes are shaped? How can we improve on ideas about polycentric governance? I suggest that we need to further decentre the dominant model in which horizontally and vertically interlinked formal institutions are the sites in which social capital is purposefully generated and used. A more 'complex-embedded' perspective would analyze the multiple overlapping processes and practices of social life and layers of meaning in which institutional arrangements form, as I began to illustrate in Chapter 3. This allows better understanding of the ways in which resource governance is shaped beyond the boundaries of visible institutional arrangements. It also allows us to refocus on the ways that people who engage with institutions are located in multiple and overlapping networks and invested with rich social identities.

In complex-embedded approaches networks of personal relations are located in wider social and historical dynamics, individual choices and social relations shaped by larger frameworks of meaning and action (Long, 1992, 2001). Drawing on such approaches, we could reconceive social capital more as configurations of relationships and networks which are patterned over time, but cannot easily be constructed and stored like other assets. Institutions are embodiments of such processes which both enable and constrain individual actions and may reproduce structural inequalities of class, caste, gender and generation (Beall, 2001, 2005).

Of course, this implies a broader concept of institutions than that commonly assumed in writing about polycentric governance. In this more decentred view plural institutions are not only 'units' or 'subunits' (as in water user associations or village assemblies) but are also arrangements of meaningful relationships that recur over time and space (as in kinship connections, or commonly held cosmological beliefs). Exploring such plural and socially embedded institutional arrangements means focusing on people's *situated practices*, which blend strategic behaviour, social values and norms, conscious and non-conscious behaviour, and which embody social structure (Bourdieu, 1990; Odgaard, 2002).

Material presented here queries the extent to which polycentric arrangements offer opportunity or constraint, especially for poor people. If institutions as embodiments of social processes ensure that things are done the 'right way' locally, they may also confirm dominant world views, uphold existing relations of authority and channel routinized everyday actions to reproduce inequalities. Social theorists often celebrate the creative ways in which individuals navigate the adverse terms of social life by deploying the everyday 'weapons of the weak', which variously involve accommodating, negotiating or resisting unequal relations (Scott, 1985; Arce and Long, 2000). I argue that this emphasis on the possibilities for the weak to exert influence, to evade and resist oppression often underplays the enduring and crippling constraints experienced by many poor and marginalized people. Of course, such people possess the human *potential* to exercise agency, but their ability to influence resource governance is constantly and routinely frustrated by the constraining effects of inequitable relationships and institutional processes.

The concept of bricolage helps us to examine the complex nature of natural resource management and the dynamic ways in which institutions, livelihood networks, a plurality of practices and meanings are enmeshed. In the rest of chapter I draw on data from natural resource governance in the Usangu plains, Tanzania,[1] to illustrate three key points:

- The plurality of institutional arrangements and the improvisation involved in these.
- The varying ability of actors of different identities to negotiate these arrangements to their advantage.
- The potential and limits of institutionalized collective action and its outcomes.

Natural Resource Management in the Usangu Plains

The case study material presented here is derived from two projects studying the management of natural resources in the Usangu Plains, situated in the Great Ruaha river basin in Tanzania. The projects were undertaken over a decade apart (from 1999–2001 and in 2011) and so offer an opportunity to track some of the processes of institutional evolution.[1]

Planners and policy-makers have long perceived the Usangu plains, situated in the Great Ruaha river basin in south-west Tanzania, as facing critical problems of degradation and depletion of grazing land and water. Competition over natural resources is of constant concern because water flows impact on biodiversity (especially in the *ihefu* – the perennial swamp and surrounding seasonally flooded grasslands at the centre of the plains), on irrigated agriculture, on the wildlife tourism potential of the Ruaha National Park and on hydro-electric power generation downstream.

Usangu is characterized by a long history of in-migration of Baluchis from Iran, Masaai and Sukuma pastoralists from the north of Tanzania and agriculturalists from neighbouring areas. Despite a plurality of competing groups of resource users in the Usangu plains, there is a dominant political discourse highlighting conflicts between sedentary agriculturalists (of 'indigenous' Sangu and in-migrant Nyakusa and Hehe ethnic groups) and itinerant pastoralists (predominantly Il Parakuyu Masai and Sukuma). Notably, 'ethnic' agriculturalists predominate in local political and administrative structures. Policy discussions often assume a developmental struggle between entrepreneurial 'modernizing' agriculturalists and intransigently 'backward' pastoralists (Walsh, 2006).

At the end of the 1990s a project funded by the British Department for International Development aimed to analyze the natural resource dynamics of Usangu and to develop local capacity to manage these. Professionals diagnosed natural resources in the area as 'fragile' and 'depleted', a situation caused by open access, conflicts and population pressure. There was a perceived management deficit in terms of the organization of collective action and the apparently unregulated use of natural resources. Local public institutions were characterized as ineffectual or corrupt; for example, village councils were seen as badly organized, poorly informed and ill equipped, lacking transparency and often dominated by a few powerful people. Traditional resource management arrangements were largely unrecognized or thought to have been seriously eroded, in need of strengthening and harmonizing with 'formal' structures (SMUWC, 1999, 2001a).

Despite the 'incompetence, conflict and corruption' analysis of existing institutions, policy and project documents asserted the 'natural' basis of cooperation latent in village life and placed great faith in the efficacy of a range of *new* formal institutional arrangements to support community-based resource management (SMUWC, 2001c). These included proposed village land and natural resource management committees (subsequently implemented as environment committees) and water user associations, epitomizing principles of mainstream institutional theory. These institutions were intended to operate in a formal and transparent way to promote effectiveness and public confidence. They were to assess land and water use trends, introduce land registration, formulate village land use plans, allocate and monitor land and water rights, draft bye-laws, and identify and resolve conflicts. The various committees were to be nested into other layers of resource management through their constitution as part of village government and through interaction with district level natural resource management teams (SMUWC, 1999). The formalized water user associations were to nest under a newly created 'apex body' whose role was to with broader issues of water allocation in the same catchment area.

The evolution and effectiveness of such newly designed institutions is a story told elsewhere (see Cleaver and Franks, 2005). Here I concentrate on illustrating what the analysis diagnosing an 'institutional deficit', to be solved by 'institutional design', missed. The focus on formalized, transparent and representative institutions overlooked a plurality of socially embedded arrangements for collective action.

Plurality, Improvisation and Overlapping Logics

Institutional plurality manifests in diverse ways. Firstly, institutions, established for one purpose, often evolve through bricolage to be multi-functional. Mainstream Institutionalist ideas about 'crafting' suggest that specific institutions are deliberately developed for particular functions (Alexander, 2002). Thus, as in this case, an irrigation committee may be intentionally designed to regulate the distribution of water and maintenance of furrows and a grazing association to co-ordinate the use of grasslands. However, in the improvised and dynamic evolution of institutions, existing decision-making arrangements and relations of cooperation may be coopted for new purposes. Such adapted, multi-purpose institutions abound in Usangu. For example, evangelical church choirs are some of the most vibrant forms of associational life, with membership crossing ethnic, gender and livelihood divides. As well as singing in church, members might join together as rotating credit groups, collective labour groups (also working as hired labour

Table 4.1 Institutions and stakeholders involved in irrigation and pastoralism in Usangu

Institution	Key interest
Water user groups at different levels	Water management. Protecting crops from livestock
Pastoralist groups at different scales	Access to land and water, pastoralist rights
Meetings of elders	Resource management and conflict resolution
Traditional leaders and ceremonies	Wellbeing of people and environment
Work groups	Maintenance of infrastructure, self-defence, cultivation, herding
Cultural groups	Dancing, singing, socializing, collective work
Village councils	Allocating land resources within the village.
District council	Raising taxes from agriculture and livestock
District livestock development officer	Supporting livestock production
District irrigation officer	Supporting irrigation development
District natural resources officer	Monitoring grazing, forest and other land resources
Local government at various levels	Village plans aggregated at ward level. District plans formulated within regional/ national frameworks
Rufiji basin water office	Allocating water resources within the basin. Collecting water fees
Zonal irrigation office	Development of irrigation in the basin
Usangu Game Reserve	Exclusion of pastoralism from the Usangu Game Reserve/National Park
District administration	Mediating resource management, Implementing National Policy in favour of irrigation
Magistrate's court	Adjudicating resource management conflicts
NGOs	Interests in environment, often opposed to pastoralism
The media	A continuing interest on water availability and pastoralism in Usangu
Ruaha National Park	Water availability downstream
Mtera hydroelectric system	Water availability downstream
Development projects, development agencies and their institutions	Participatory forest management, natural resource management, irrigation management

Source: adapted from Cleaver and Franks, 2005

gangs on village works) and as performers at 'traditional' social ceremonies and functions. In research in 2011 we found a community offering rent-free irrigated land to a choir master to come and settle in the village and lead the church choir. Such embedded relationships combine productive and social functions and draw on both traditional and modern forms of interaction.

Secondly, polycentric governance arrangements encompass diverse types of institutions and stakeholders, operating at different scales and levels of formality, with variable interests in the management of natural resources and differing access to institutions. Sketching out the institutional landscape during the SMUWC project of 1999–2001 it soon became clear that improvements in the management of water and grazing land would not be achieved only by strengthening water user or pastoralist associations. Indeed, while these institutions *were* important in shaping the use of resources, local-level governance was also formed through a variety of formal and informal arrangements, some more obviously linked to natural resource management than others, as illustrated in Table 4.1 above (adapted from Cleaver and Franks, 2005).

Notably, different groups of actors attributed varying importance to formal and informal institutions in their local area, and many of those who relied on water for their livelihoods did not engage in water user associations. For example, in 2011 a focus group of women of varying ages gave prime importance to *social* networks and institutions, as Figure 4.1, below, shows. Women's associational life was largely organized around families, neighbours, the church and informal savings and credit associations. The women further emphasized the importance of the drinking water supply (managed by the Nyaugenge Water User Association) and welfare services such as the school and dispensary. Although they were all irrigation farmers in their own right, they took little part in the water user association managing their scheme (the Mbuyuni Intake Association) partly because they thought they could exert little influence over the powerful men (mostly head-end farmers) dominating the association. They only included village government in the diagram when prompted by researchers, and said they had little time to attend meetings and preferred to hear about village matters and water issues from their neighbours 'on the street'.

By contrast, a group of young men identified the institutions and networks with which they engaged quite differently, as illustrated in Figure 4.2. For them, trying to establish themselves as adults and set up their own households from the proceeds of rice farming, the irrigators' association (Mbuyuni Intake Association) along with the

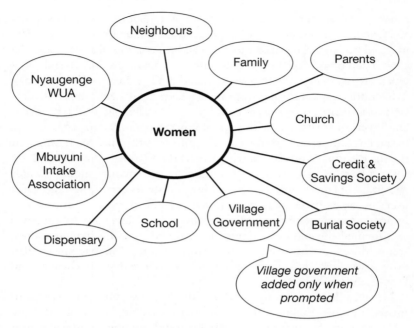

Figure 4.1 Institutional networks: women's focus group[3]

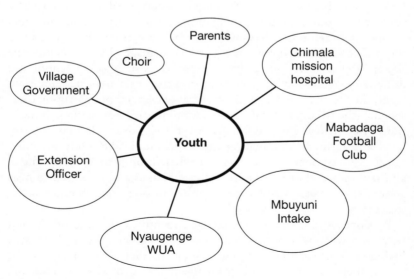

Figure 4.2 Institutional networks: youth focus group

district agricultural extension officer were of prime interest. However, as 'youth' holding very small quantities of irrigated land, they were sceptical about their ability to influence the decisions taken either in the water user association or by the village government. For them, the football club and the choir were important institutions through which they formed friendships and allegiances.

Thirdly, institutions, formed through bricolage and shaped by social and livelihood practices, combine and blend logics (Scott, 2008). The example of evolving arrangements for the management of smallholder irrigation systems illustrates this point (Scott, 2008). For example, at the end of the 1990s farmers in Usangu would commonly refer to 'traditional' smallholder rice irrigation systems (differentiating these from government-run large schemes). However, this 'tradition' had a mixed and partly exotic provenance. Rice growing probably started in the mid nineteenth century, introduced by members of Arab trading caravans, whilst the irrigated gardens of the indigenous Sangu were observed by early explorers.[4] 'Modern' rice irrigation was introduced into Usangu by Baluchi immigrants from Iran in the 1940s. 'Traditional' smallholder irrigation management drew on adapted committee structures introduced under government and NGO development projects and on 'indigenous' collective labour arrangements. Whilst water cooperatives and associations were in some cases established in the past in order to formally claim water rights, many of these are were non-functional by the 1990s, farmers perceiving them as unnecessarily bureaucratic (Gillingham, 1999). However, roles such as 'chairman' established under such projects often remained. Under such 'traditional' arrangements conflicts over irrigation water were generally resolved between irrigators themselves, by reference to 'traditional' elders and (Sangu) customs. Only if unresolvable were they referred to the village government and to ward tribunals for further attempts at reconciliation. Baluchis resolve disputes through reference to Islamic law or statutory rights (Maganga and Juma, 1999; Maganga, 2003).

Let us see how these different dimensions of plurality manifested in local-level institutional arrangements for water governance. By 2011, due to project interventions, new policies and new legislation, considerable attempts had been made to formalize irrigation water management at the local level. For example, in the Kimani sub-catchment three small-holder irrigation schemes depended on water from the same river. In attempts to regulate the quantities and times when water was drawn from the river, water user associations representing land owners in each of the schemes had been formally constituted and legally registered, with assistance from local non-governmental organizations. A pastoralist association and a water user association for the drinking water supply were similarly formalized. In a classic case of designed governance, they were linked to a new apex organization (MAMREMA), whose remit was to deal with overall water allocation issues. The water user associations and the apex body had functioning committees, constitutions, bye-laws and bi-annual general meetings of members. They collected fees, attempted to resolve conflicts, managed water distribution, conducted some scheme maintenance and lobbied the river basin office for increased allocations. In terms of production, the irrigation schemes were seen as highly successful.

However, the newly formalized water user associations and the designed governance arrangements in which they were to operate were not the whole story of water management. Firstly, the formalized water user association superceded, or was superimposed upon, previous arrangements. As a result, overlapping and unequal rights and claims to land and water in the schemes remained, many based on history, precedent and social authority. A farmer could obtain fields in irrigated areas through allocation from the village council (although by 2011 this route to obtaining land was almost closed) through inheritance, buying the land or hiring it from existing owners. Only people who owned the land were eligible for membership of the water user association, and they constituted a minority of farmers in the schemes. Fields were often hired out through social networks. With large farmers and scheme leaders dominating at the head-ends of the schemes, down-streamers found it difficult to break into this market. The families of farmers who had founded the schemes by digging furrows (referred to as the 'elders' of the schemes) controlled large quantities of land, had canals named after them and seemed to exercise certain preferential rights to water according to the 'first in time, first in right' principle.

Additionally, whilst one role of the associations was to deal with water conflicts, in practice conflict resolution was more dispersed with a variety of routes to resolution described by farmers for particular cases. Generally, the associations exercised the right to fine people for breaking rules (taking water out of turn, allowing animals to graze in the scheme) if this could not be dealt with at furrow (sub-canal) level. However, the bad behaviour (verbal and physical abuse) associated with rule-breaking was referred to village councils, advised by elders. The apex body, the police and the primary courts were less often involved, and this partially depended on the severity of the conflict and the social identities of the protagonists.

Finally, although allocation of water between and within schemes through the formally constituted WUAs was important, beliefs about the influence of supernatural powers on rainfall, water flows and abundance of crops remained significant. In early 2011, the rains had faltered, there was insufficient water in the canals to operate the designed rotations effectively and the young rice plants were severely stressed. At the request of residents, one village council financed the council of elders to organize a traditional rain-making ceremony, paying for the necessary offerings and for transport to the ceremonial site. The village council additionally invited the churches of the village (Christian and Muslim) to hold joint prayers for rain. The different ceremonies took place, rain followed, water flowed through the canals and inclusive thanksgiving ceremonies were duly held. Whilst a number of younger modernizing decision-makers in the village council and water user associations expressed scepticism about the rain being caused by such ceremonies, they also emphasized that it was important to show respect to the elders by supporting them.

Borrowing, Invention and Legitimation

We have already seen in Chapter 3 that the ubiquity of processes of blending and adaptation of the old and the new, the formal and informal, does not mean that any arrangement is possible or acceptable. New arrangements generally have to be awarded some social legitimacy. To this end, people consciously and non-consciously draw on legitimizing symbols (derived from the state, from culture and tradition, from the natural world) to cognitively anchor new institutional and social arrangements (Douglas, 1987). In processes of borrowing and adaptation the distinction between what is modern and what is traditional becomes blurred and tradition becomes reinvented. Additionally, the line between formal organization, the workings of the state and socially and culturally embedded networks become fuzzy. Such blurring is neither necessarily good nor bad, as the example of adapted cattle militias well shows.

During work mapping rural livelihoods for the SMUWC project (1999–2001 SMUWC, 2001d), the research team visited pastoralist families who periodically sent their boys and young men to camp in the rich grasslands surrounding the swamp for seasonal grazing. We found an active network of *Sungusungu* linking the home villages and the seasonal camps. At first sight this seemed to be a traditional Sukuma (pastoralist) cattle-guarding militia comprised of young men. However, these militia had evolved through bricolage in ways which retained elements of this traditional form, but also incorporated new roles and ways of functioning. In the villages studied, Sungusungu had either replaced or supplemented official village defence committees. The fear of cattle theft, the need to resolve potential competition over grazing and lack of confidence in government institutions had led to the semi-official legitimizing of the Sungusungu, borrowed from Sukuma customary defence organizations. Such institutions had become cross-ethnic, with ethnic Sangu (agriculturalists) and Masaai as well as Sukuma operating as 'commanders'.

The Sungusungu was made responsible by village consensus for cattle security and keeping order in the seasonal grazing lands. It operated on a basis of demarcation of roles between elders and youth, a practice common to all ethnic groups, with the youth acting as the foot-soldiers and the elders acting as advisors on tactics, bestowers of charms and medicines, and dispensers of justice. This unofficial militia was considered by members to be formally accountable to (modern) village government, whilst the practices of its operation were largely based on socially embedded principles of reconciliation and conflict minimization.

The Sungusungu, like many institutions formed through processes of bricolage, was multi-purpose. Villagers reported how they called on Sungusungu when facing problems requiring collective action, such as searching for a lost child, and used Sungusungu communication channels to disseminate messages around the village. One of the Sungusungu operating amongst seasonal grazing camps at the ihefu organized the different camps of young men (from widely dispersed villages) into units. The commander collected from them a cash subscription and this was used as a common welfare fund to pay for a bus or bicycle to transfer a sick herder to his home area.

This case well illustrates how processes of institutional bricolage (invention, borrowing, legitimation) cross scales and domains. The adapted SunguSungu was not unique to Usangu, but an institutional form that had spread through Tanzania as a form of vigilantism from the 1980s in response to problems of law and order and the lack of police in rural areas. After initial opposition from the police and judiciary, the ruling party gave Sungusungu quasi-legal status under the people's militia laws in 1989. Compulsory membership was required of adult men, but this proved unpopular and was cancelled at the 1995 elections. The institution developed unevenly across the country, but often thrived in remote rural areas where state administration was weak. In this hybrid form remnants of tradition (such as the blowing of a wooden whistle or horn to call assistance and the involvement of diviners to identify thieves) existed side by side with modern committee structures and the exercise of local state administrative and judicial power. The apparently benign nature of the Sungusungu that we found in Usangu at the turn of the twenty-first century is in contrast to more violent vigilante groups documented elsewhere in Tanzania and in Kenya (Abrahams, 1987; Fleisher, 2000, 2002; Heald, 2002, 2007a, 2007b).

By 2011, the form and functions of the Sungusungu in Usangu had further evolved, following a period when the pastoralists had been forcibly, and some report violently (Walsh, 2008), evicted by government from the grazing lands, ostensibly to allow for the extension of the Ruaha National Park. Many pastoralists with large herds of cattle were now relocated to other areas of Tanzania, but remnants of their families remained grazing smaller herds around villages, some turning increasingly to agriculture. During 2011 local government officials announced further restrictions – cattle herds were to be limited to twenty animals. Although some influential pastoralists held positions on the village council and on the formalized pastoralists association, many were marginalized and felt alienated from the formal institutions of local decision-making. In our study area the Sungusungu now was functioning more covertly, meeting secretly in the bush, apparently to discuss pastoralist welfare issues and to ensure pastoralist security. The diversity of institutional forms and purposes all going under the name Sungusungu further illustrates processes of bricolage and constant adaptation of 'traditional' arrangements to new purposes.

Conflict and Cooperation

It is often claimed in institutional theory that drawing on social capital in institutions economizes on transaction costs as people can draw on common norms in formulating collective arrangements (Mehta *et al.*, 2001). However, whilst calling on familiar symbols and devices offers a sort of cognitive shorthand, it does not necessarily constitute a *shortcut* to formulating legitimate institutions. In processes of institutional bricolage 'the categories of political discourse, the cognitive base of the social order are being constantly negotiated' (Douglas, 1987: 29). Collective consensus decision-making, forging and renegotiating norms, maintaining social networks, reputations and relations of trust are not easy processes, and require inputs of considerable time and energy. An example is seen in the priority given to avoiding or resolving conflicts, in constructing institutional mechanisms which emphasize reconciliation and forgiveness. Evidence from Usangu suggests that conflict is both an integral part of normal life and something to be avoided or underplayed whenever possible.

Project and policy approaches tend to see conflict as undesirable, as a breakdown in normal relations, something to be avoided or resolved as quickly as possible and optimistically insist on perceiving cooperation as the norm and as 'the basis of village life' (Devitt, 1999;

SMUWC, 2001a). Perversely, bureaucratic institutional arrangements often draw on an adversarial logic, emphasizing the need for public confrontation of difference, the speedy, strict and impartial penalization of non-conformers (Ostrom, 1990, 1992; SMUWC, 2001a, 2001c; Maganga, 2003).

We have already seen how, even when the functions of water user associations were formalized, conflict resolution was conducted through a number of channels. A basic psychological dislike of conflict was illustrated by interviewees who identify the occasional disagreements with neighbours and kin as major (if intermittent) source of stress in their lives, especially when associated with witchcraft. In Usangu, herding and farming families are networked through labour exchange, the use of draught power and by intermarriage as well as by church and club membership. However, an overemphasis on direct and instrumental reciprocity is misplaced. Relations of cooperation may be indirect and function across lifecourses, generations and localities; they may be valued for contributing to pleasure and wellbeing rather than just livelihood productivity. Values of social respect and conflict avoidance are deeply embedded in moral–ecological worldviews, as outlined in Chapter 3.

Norms of conflict avoidance are common to all types of resource users in Usangu. Despite the rhetoric of high levels of conflict in Usangu and supposed irreconcilability of different cultures, Maganga (SMUWC, 2001b) found very few cases of conflicts over resources reaching court, partly reflecting a strong desire amongst people to resolve these at the lowest possible level, and particularly to avoid falling out with neighbours. Values emphasizing deference to elders were common to all social groups (if not always adhered to), but interviewees suggested that leaders who inherited their positions still had to *earn* respect through their ability to resolve conflicts and encourage harmonious relations within communities.

The imperative towards emphasizing cooperation is strong. Evidence of potential conflict being minimized and turned towards cooperation instead is illustrated in accounts from Usangu and elsewhere in Tanzania (Maseruli, 2000; Mnzava, 2000). These illustrate how communities (often hamlets and villages) may impose fines or penalties on those repeatedly offending against communal rules or failing to cooperate in communal work. Such penalties are not imposed impartially but take into account the social situation of the offender; a certain amount of 'social riding' being permitted. When extenuating circumstances are not taken into account, fines may be contested. In the relatively uncommon event of fines being levied then the proceeds (money, livestock, household goods) are used to fund a celebration (a beer drink or feast) for those who did participate in the communal activity *as well as the offender.* According to informants, one of the purposes of this occasion is to 'celebrate forgiveness'.

It would be naive, of course, to present too rosy a picture of conflict avoidance and reconciliation. We found plenty of examples of mistrust between people (particularly over the management of funds) and norms of reconciliation may not benefit all, as we will see in examples of women trying to claim property and marital rights in Chapter 5. Some people expressed relief that the newly introduced formal rules of the water user associations depersonalized their conflicts with neighbours, or could provide the justification for requiring the omnipotent big landowner to pay his water fees. So how far can different people navigate these various institutional norms? If resources are managed through polycentric plural arrangements, how much room for manoeuvre does this offer to people with different social identities and relationships? Can all be meaningfully involved in crafting new institutions and in the improvisation and reshaping integral to bricolage?

Plurality, Social Identity and Room for Manoeuvre

A key element of further decentering ideas about plural resource governance is the recognition that resource users have complex and overlapping social identities belying simple classifications such as 'pastoralist' or 'irrigator'. The privileging of single aspects of people's identities ill reflects the complexity of motivations derived from plural livelihoods, overlapping social networks and the ways these change over time. For example, in Usangu people's interests rarely fit easily into the agriculturalist/pastoralist divide; many pastoralists are semi-sedentarized and engaged in cultivation, whilst young pastoralist men migrate or mine gold in order to establish themselves economically. Similarly, as agriculturalist families generate surplus over time, they may invest in cattle, and use these to marry, support extended families and diversify into business. Such complexity of social identity adds another dimension of plurality to the dynamics of polycentric resource governance (a theme explored further in Chapter 5).

An example of overlapping identities, norms and networks crossing scales and shaped by wider social factors is provided by one Usangu household. In 1999 and 2000 we interviewed 'Karim', a farmer of irrigated rice, rain-fed maize and groundnuts. A relatively wealthy man with two wives, he could hire workers (usually neighbours with money problems) to cultivate his fields and used the surpluses to diversify into business, trading beyond his village in rice and charcoal. He was chairman of his hamlet, a member of the village council and chairman of the water committee, so well placed to shape the norms and rules of resource use.

A Sangu by ethnic origin, Karim had in-migrated to Usangu from the nearest big town. As well as farming, he was a traditional herbalist, having 'inherited' his knowledge and skill from his grandfather. He could treat conditions ranging from heart problems and diabetes to venereal diseases, craziness and problem love affairs. He also had the ability to counter diseases caused by witchcraft. Through his herbalist skills he had extensive networks; he was one of five representatives from Tanzania who attended a conference in Malawi discussing herbal medicines and their powers with scientists. As a result, he maintained contact with other herbalists in Tanzania, Malawi and the Congo.

He and his family followed Sangu traditions and ceremonies, travelling to the site of a big tree near his home area with his family to make offerings of sheep, hens and beer and to pray for safeguarding against calamity. As a Muslim, he also hosted Islamic prayers at his house, attended gatherings for Islamic traditions and festivals and undertook the circumcision of children. Later in the chapter we return to Karim's household to consider how its interests and institutional engagements evolved over time, and to what effects.

Institutional theory as translated into policy and practice implies that representatives on committees and in associations directly represent the resource users by translating community norms into more regularized institutional arrangements (SMUWC, 2001a, 2001c). However, as we have seen above, norms and practices, and the relationships of trust and cooperation which underlie them, are often generated and negotiated outside the formalized institutions. Polycentric resource governance, then, takes place in a wider social arena than that defined by visible bureaucratic resource management institutions.

Social identity and institutional engagement are recursively linked, as we have seen in the case of the well-off Karim above. Karim's identity and networks were pan-African as well as local and regional. His role on committees and councils meant that he was well placed to shape resource management arrangements. But he was also a traditionalist with spiritual and material interests in particular configurations of the natural and social order. We might well ask which aspects of his identity predominated; which interests he furthered when acting as a representative of others in institutional arrangements. What does this overlapping of interests, networks and identities mean for poor people and their chances of shaping and benefitting from plural resource governance arrangements? There is the possibility that designed formal institutions can further equity, for example by specifying quotas for representation of marginalized people, or exempting then communal labour. There is also the possibility that socially embedded arrangements are underpinned by strong norms of a place and a living for all. Too often, though, poor people are multipally disadvantaged by plural institutional configurations. A variety of interlocking factors constrain both their public engagement and their social networks.

A rural livelihoods study conducted in Usangu in 1999–2000 characterized chronically poor families as both highly dependent on natural resources and severely constrained in accessing them. They often lived in small households with high dependency ratios, suffering from poor health and nutrition and frequently caring for those with chronic diseases. Such families depended on their own labour (including of children) for subsistence farming and piecework on other people's fields. Social relationships with kin and neighbours were characterized by patchy and unequal exchanges. For example, poor people might labour for wealthier villagers in exchange for food or credit. They routinely had to resort to supplication to secure assistance, such as sending a sick child to ask for help with medication from the neighbours. To many, even the most basic of activities which defined social personhood, such as attending or hosting funerals, were seen as a burden they could barely meet. Families who suffered numerous bereavements, particularly of children, were often suspected of witchcraft and treated with suspicion (SMUWC, 2001d).

Whilst kinship and neighbourliness is central to people's livelihoods, close ties can also create vulnerabilities and tensions (over inheritance, witchcraft) and can preclude people from wider social engagement by emphasizing constraining norms of gender and generation (Republic of Tanzania, 2002; Koda, 2000; Cleaver, 2000; Beall, 2001). The social choices available to people in these circumstances severely limited their livelihoods, resulting in further contraction of social networks. A thumbnail sketch of one chronically poor household (interviewed in 2000 and 2001 and detailed in SMUWC, 2001d) illustrates how their lives were constrained by the daily struggle for existence, poor social networks and a lack of institutional engagement.

The Multiple Dimensions of Institutional Disengagement

The household consisted of a couple perhaps in their late fifties and their granddaughter, Shida, aged about fifteen. Shida's mother had died and her father was unknown. The family lived in poor housing and suffered considerable ill-health and disability. The family farmed less than an acre of rice, had no livestock and were food insecure. Shida helped secure their daily food by selling fruits, labouring on neighbours' rice fields and collecting and selling bundles of firewood.

Neither of the grandparents was fluent in the national language, Swahili, and this constrained their participation in public decision-making. The grandfather attended burials in the village and went to hamlet and village meetings to listen, but never to contribute. He had one friend to talk to who once lent him 200 shillings for household needs. The grandmother hardly left the house. They had stopped attending the Moravian church due to ill health. They thought of switching to the Roman Catholic church to get more assistance but took no action. Their immediate neighbours, both widows, occasionally helped them with salt and relish but felt that their own poverty precluded them from making a difference to the household's chronic problems.

Shida attended the Moravian Sunday school but she never went to other church celebrations or activities, being unable to contribute to the collection. She paid her own school fees (for Primary Six) by selling her labour and selling firewood. She wrote to an uncle asking for help with school fees but he refused. She did most of the household manual work, including collecting of water and firewood and farming.

The poverty suffered by this family crippled their associational life and institutional engagement. This case (elaborated in Cleaver, 2004) well illustrates the fragility of social networks for poor people and the ways this limits their institutional engagement.

The sections above have illustrated numerous dimensions of the plurality of institutional arrangements, including the diverse sources and sites for the generation of norms. They have also shown how poor people are often ill-placed to shape social relationships and norms to their advantage. What are the implications, then, for navigating the interface between social relationships and institutional engagement in natural resource management?

We have already seen how ideas about polycentric governance are underpinned by assumptions that social relations of trust and cooperation can be drawn upon to strengthen institutional functioning. Repeated association (especially through collective action) is thought to generate trust (Uphoff and Wijayaratna, 2000; Ahn *et al.*, 2003), although this view is partly challenged by studies which illustrate the ad hoc and intermittent nature of cooperative endeavour and the exclusionary and well as inclusive processes involved (Mehta *et al.*, 2001; Benjaminsen and Lund, 2002). Several studies illustrate the inability of local groups and associational activities to compensate for the activities of failed governments or to operate equitably in inequitable communities (Stewart, 1996; La Ferrara, 2000). The faith placed in collective action arrangements which stress voluntarism, bargaining, accommodation and persuasion through face-to-face interactions (Uphoff, 1993: 609) is highly enticing, but possibly over-optimistic. In the next section I examine a spectrum of collective action arrangements and the variable opportunities they offer for people of different social identities.

Collective Labour, Clubs and Societies

In Usangu, agricultural livelihoods were critically dependent on the timely supply of labour (for preparing fields, planting, bird scaring, weeding, transplanting, harvesting and threshing). 'Traditional' arrangements involved collective labour undertaken by family, neighbours and friends in return for food and beer, and the loose expectation of reciprocation. Some households were able to regularize such arrangements over time, to use such labour to mitigate climate-related risks and successfully expand the land under their cultivation.

However poor households rarely hosted collective labour days because of the costs of supplying food and drink and the difficulties of attracting volunteers from their restricted social networks. For labour-scarce poor families, the opportunity costs of such voluntary labour were high if it involved forgoing a day of paid work. They were also often perceived by others as unreliable, and peak labour demand occurred at times of seasonal livelihood stress when food supplies were low, diseases rife and taxes due to be paid.

Adapted collective labour arrangements are drawn upon in development activities as visible manifestations of community participation. In Tanzania, people are expected to provide collective labour to support village development by repairing roads, constructing schools and clinics, and digging wells or pipelines. Additionally, members of water user schemes may be required to clean canals and provide labour and materials for rehabilitation. Such collective action is thought to generate an increased sense of community 'ownership' over such facilities. Such labour is organized at the hamlet (sub-village) level, where exemptions are decided, but the village can fine non-contributors. Wealthy households often choose to pay a fee in lieu of labour contribution, or send a hired worker, poor relative or neighbour as proxy. Collective labour arrangements disadvantage the chronically poor, who have to meet their labour obligations at the expense of meeting daily basic needs. Exemptions are primarily granted for bereavement. When unable to attend or pay the fine, poor people sometimes forfeit basic household goods such as pots and pans or stools.

So while wealthier, better-connected households are able to bend the rules, secure exemptions from collective labour or primarily rely on hired labour, the participation of poor people is disproportionately costly to them. Although cooperation and reciprocation is also negotiated for wealthier people, the arrangements established are more reliable, the social transaction costs lower, the outcomes less risky. The social and material benefits secured through such collective efforts are unevenly spread.

Associational life in Usangu ranged from small, informal savings groups or drinking circles of immediate neighbours and kin to more formalized associations and clubs, often established in response to some development initiative (these included irrigators associations, pastoralists associations, goat rearing clubs etc). Ethnically based cultural groups existed for singing and dancing at public events and ceremonies and for facilitating livelihood activities such as livestock rearing. The entry fees for formal clubs and societies could be high, but an ability to pay them could secure access to denser social and productive networks.

> Mr SM is a member of the Mbange Milk Goats Group, set up under an IFAD and Ministry of Agriculture project. The first person to be offered a goat had to pay 5000 shillings to IFAD, then the first kid produced was given to another member and so on, until all had a goat. The group meets twice a month to talk about goat husbandry. They also make contributions of 1000 shillings each so that they can get credit from the Ward Bank for rice cultivation. Last year they borrowed 60,000 shillings. Mr SM says that being in the group is an advantage because you can also make personal lending and borrowing arrangements with group members.
>
> Mr SM is also chair of the Motombaya Irrigation Scheme, established by FAO and consisting of about 214 members. Some of these own fields and some hire fields to others. They meet weekly and in past years have contributed 5000 shillings as a one off 'entry fee' and 1000 shillings subscription. The scheme ensures that furrows are well kept, that claims to furrows are legitimate and that no-one steals water from others (SMUWC, 2001d).

We heard numerous accounts of poor people initially being allowed to join such groups, having managed to scrape together the entry fee (or an installment of it). However, their inability to make regular contributions, or to reliably attend meetings, ensured that they were soon excluded. A group of women interviewed in 2011, several of them lone parents heading households, specified how they only joined groups and activated their credit circles when circumstances allowed – after a good harvest, for example.

Cultural forms of association are not necessarily more accessible to the poor, often requiring contributions in kind, or particular uniforms, which are beyond the means of the poorest to buy or maintain. Such informal exclusion is significant, as Odgaard shows how engagement with both the formalized institutions of the state *and* the less bureaucratic social and cultural institutions can contribute to the double safeguarding of rights and access to resources (Odgaard, 2002). Conversely, an inability to secure such access and rights undermines the sustainability of livelihoods and may result in double institutional exclusion.

Participation, Articulation and Access to Institutions

Mainstream Institutional theory, social capital theory and development policy overlap in emphasizing the mutually beneficial relationship between social norms of cooperation and public participation in governance (Narayan *et al.*, 2000; Republic of Tanzania, 2003). In this section I consider how gendered social norms shape participation in public institutions. I show how institutional plurality can offer opportunities as well as reinforce power relations.

Gendered norms of articulation run as common threads through social relationships and institutional encounters. In Usangu, people with grievances (inheritance or marriage disputes, cattle theft, water diversion) against family or neighbours were faced with two options for public resolution. One was to pursue their complaints through local, 'traditional' institutions – usually meetings of male elders. These often overlapped with village government structures. Adopting a preferred principle of reconciliatory conflict resolution, such authorities usually tried to achieve some sort of negotiated accommodation between the parties in dispute.

An alternative strategy to reconciliation was to pursue disputes, grievances and the claiming of rights through the formal court system (primary courts). Although nominally free, such systems were known to be costly, 'fees' often being required for speedy resolution of conflicts. Life history accounts of poor people specified how the costs of pursuing cases in court had crippled them, or how they had withdrawn their cases when fees threatened. Interestingly, the primary courts heard a high proportion of divorce cases where the woman was suing for a share of land, livestock or custody of children.

Let us return to the household of 'Karim', the successful farmer, herbalist and maintainer of Sangu and Muslim traditions, first studied for the SMUWC project 1999–2001. Returning to the household in 2011, we found that Karim had passed away in 2003, but we were able to interview his second wife, Mrs M. After becoming a widow, she had moved away from her marital home to a neighbouring village, to be nearer to her natal family. She had struggled to retain the irrigated rice fields she inherited through marriage. Her brother-in-law had tried to reclaim these for Karim's family by taking out a case in the primary court. Although the court had found in Mrs M's favour, in practice she had found it difficult to 'scramble over water with the powerful ones' in order to farm these downstream fields. So at the time of interview she was renting out her marital fields and using the rent to hire fields to cultivate (fewer acres) in her natal village.

Despite the court ruling, the brother-in-law, aided by Mrs M's own uncle, continued to lobby influential men in the village government to reallocate the fields, asserting that Karim had cultivated those fields *before* marrying Mrs M. As owner of the marital fields, Mrs M paid the requisite fees to the water user association, but rarely attended meetings. For the land she now hired in her village of residence (located in another irrigation scheme), she had no obligation to pay the water fees, this being the responsibility of the land*owner*.

In this example, Mrs M asserted her rights through the primary court, but she had to work hard to make these rights real in opposition to powerful men both in her extended family, in the village government and the water user association. Her claims on water and land, her rights to participate and be represented in institutions of governance, crossed boundaries of villages and irrigation schemes, and her family networks were similarly complex. Mrs M had resources of cash, time and the ability to articulate, which enabled her to mitigate some of the discriminatory processes she faced, but this was stressful and costly to her, and such strategies were not available to poor people.

Conclusion

An understanding of the plural institutional channels through which people conduct their livelihoods and secure access natural resources is critical to an understanding of outcomes. Institutions can both include and exclude, and social relationships can reinforce or ameliorate such impacts. Understanding the interaction between agency and norms is critical, as even apparently benign and social desirable institutional principles (such as negotiated reconciliations over competing interests)

Actors and agents

for example

Resources for water governance	Mechanisms of access	Outcomes (gendered, positive and negative)
Institutional resources. Policies	Formal institutions (village government, River Basin Office, water user, pastoralist groups)	Access to basic supplies
Social structures		Livelihoods (crops, fishing, livestock, forestry) Enabled or constrained
Rights and entitlements, legislation	Associational groups (choirs, women's groups, savings clubs)	Social inclusion and exclusion. Cohesion and capacity for collective action
Financial resources	Family relationships, kinship groups	
Technology	Cultural ceremonies, groups	Political voice and representation by different groups
Natural environment	Customary and modern land and water rights	
Human capabilities	Formal Water rights, informal water claims	
	Payments in cash or labour to maintain infrastructure	
	Water control structures, access points to seasonal surface flows	

Ecosystem outcomes

Pattern of flows and levels in the catchment and downstream

The poor are constrained from influencing these processes through physical weakness, labour demands, lack of participation and other factors of embodiment and voice

Processes of management practice

(such as operational; procedures, turns, queues, rotations, maintenance activities, channel clearance, fund collection, communal labour etc)

Figure 4.3 Polycentric water governance in Kimani sub-catchment

Source: adapted from Franks and Cleaver, 2007 p. 299

may operate to the disadvantage of those with few resources and little status. It seems to me to be critical to understand plural institutional configurations as shaped by the broader structures of society as this helps to explain the patterning of these arrangements and the outcomes they produce. So, elaborating on the water governance framework introduced in Chapter 2, we could attempt to map some of the plural institutional arrangements (mechanisms) that we have considered in this chapter in relation both to societal resources and to the outcomes produced for different groups of people, as in Figure 4.3.

In recognizing the complexity of plural governance arrangements we should beware of normatively attributing value either to institutional plurality or to particular types of arrangement. Plurality has the *potential* to create opportunity; processes of bricolage, of borrowing, of institutional improvisation may also create spaces for negotiation, and contestation, for different voices to be heard. It is *possible* that the plasticity of human-made arrangements could shape distribution of resources in emancipatory directions (Berry, 1994). However, questions about how far institutions drawing on different logics create inequalities or undermine relations of trust and cooperation remains. A major challenge then to those concerned with building institutions for the management of natural resources is to avoid reproducing socially and historically embedded injustices (Falk *et al.*, 2009). Where natural resource management requires strengthening, we need interventions based on an understanding of the content, the underlying principles and social effects of institutions, not merely on their visible form. A bricolage perspective can contribute to this sort of understanding. In the next chapter I explore further the nature of individual agency and its relation to collective action and institutional bricolage.

Bibliography

Abrahams, R. (1987) 'Sungusungu: Village Vigilante Groups in Tanzania', *African Affairs* 86, 343, pp. 179–96.

Ahn, T. K., Ostrom, E. and Walker, J. M. (2003) 'Heterogeneous Preferences and Collective Action', *Public Choice* 117, 3, pp. 295–314.

Alexander, E. R. (2002) 'Acting Together: From Planning to Institutional Design', Mimeo, University of Wisconsin-Milwaukee, School of Architecture and Urban Planning.

Andersson, K. and Ostrom, E. (2008) 'Analyzing Decentralized Resource Regimes from a Polycentric Perspective', *Policy Sciences* 41, 1, pp. 71–93.

Arce, A. and Long, N. (2000) 'Reconfiguring Modernity and Development from an Anthropological Perspective', in A. Arce and N. Long (eds) *Anthropology,*

Development and Modernities: Exploring Discourses, Counter-Tendencies and Violence, London, Routledge, pp. 1–30.

Beall, J. (2001) 'Valuing Social Resources or Capitalising On Them? Limits to Pro-Poor Urban Governance in Nine Cities of the South', *International Planning Studies* 6, 4, pp. 357–75.

—(2005) 'Decentralizing Government and Decentering Gender: Lessons from Local Government Reform in South Africa', *Politics and Society,* 33, 2, pp. 253–76.

Benjaminsen, T. and Lund, C. E. (2002) 'Securing Land Rights in Africa', *European Journal of Development Research* 14, 2.

Boelens, R., Bustamante, R. and de Vos, H. (2007) 'Legal Pluralism and the Politics of Inclusion: Recognition and Contestation of Local Water Rights', in B. Van Koppen, M. Giordano and J. Butterworth (eds) *Community-Based Water Law and Water Resource Management Reform in Developing Countries,* Wallingford, CABI, pp. 96–113.

Bourdieu, P. (1990) *The Logic of Practice,* Cambridge, Polity Press.

Cleaver, F. (2000) 'Moral Ecological Rationality, Institutions and the Management of Common Property Resources', *Development and Change* 31, 2, pp. 361.

—(2005) 'The Inequality of Social Capital and the Reproduction of Chronic Poverty', *World Development* 33, 6, pp. 893–906.

Cleaver, F. and Franks, T. (2005) 'How Institutions Elude Design: River Basin Management and Sustainable Livelihoods', BCID Research Paper, www.bradford. ac.uk/acad/bcid/research/papers/ResearchPaper12CleaverFranks.pdf.

Dasgupta, P. (1988) 'Trust as a Commodity', in D. Gambetta (ed.) *Trust: Making and Breaking Cooperative Relations,* London, Blackwell, pp. 49–72.

Devitt, P. (1999) *Community Engagement Programme Report,* SMUWC, Rujewa, Tanzania.

Douglas, M. (1987) *How Institutions Think,* London, Routledge and Kegan Paul.

Edwards, R., Franklin, J. and Holland, J. (2003) 'Families and Social Capital: Exploring the Issues', *Families and Social Capital Research Group Working Papers* 1, London, South Bank University.

Falk, T., Bock, B. and Kirk, M. (2009) 'Polycentrism and Poverty: Experiences of Rural Water Supply Reform in Namibia', *Water Alternatives* 2, 1, pp. 115–37.

Fine, B. (2001) *Social Capital versus Social Theory: Political Economy and Social Science at the Turn of the Millennium,* London, Routledge.

Fleisher, M. (2000) 'Sungusungu: State-Sponsored Village Vigilante Groups Among the Kuria of Tanzania', *Africa* 70, 2, pp. 209–28.

Fleisher, M. (2002) '"War is Good for Thieving!" The Symbiosis of Crime and Warfare among the Kuria of Tanzania', *Africa* 72, 1, pp. 131–49.

Franks, T. and Cleaver, F. (2009) 'Analysing Water Governance: A Tool for Sustainability', *Engineering Sustainability,* 162, 4, pp. 207–14.

Gillingham, P. (1999) *Community Management of Irrigation in the Usangu Wetlands and their Catchment,* SMUWC, Rujewa, Tanzania.

Heald, S. (2002) 'Domesticating Leviathan: Sungusungu Groups in Tanzania', *Crisis States Research Centre Working Papers Series* 1, 16.

—(2007a) 'Controlling Crime and Corruption from Below: Sungusungu in Kenya', *International Relations* 21, 2, pp. 183–99.

—(2007b) 'Making Law in Rural East Africa: SunguSungu in Kenya', *Crisis States Research Centre Working Papers Series* 2, 12.

Koda, B. (2000) 'Democratisation of Social Relations at the Household Level: The Participation of Children and Youth in Tanzania', in C. Creighton and C. K. Omari (eds) *Gender, Family and Work in Tanzania*, Aldershot, Ashgate.

La Ferrara, E. (2000) 'Unequal Access to Social Capital? Evidence from Tanzania', *Development Research Insights* 34, Brighton, University of Sussex.

Lankford, B. and Hepworth, N. (2010) 'The Cathedral and the Bazaar: Monocentric and Polycentric River Basin Management', *Water Alternatives* 3, 1, pp. 82–101.

Levi, M. (1996) 'Social and Unsocial Capital: A Review Essay of Robert Putnam's Making Democracy Work', *Politics and Society* 24, 1, pp. 45–55.

Long, A. (1992) 'From Paradigm Lost to Paradigm Regained? The Case for an Actor-Oriented Sociology of Development', in N. Long and A. Long (eds) *Battlefields of Knowledge: The Interlocking of Theory and Practice in Social Research and Development*, London, Routledge, pp. 16–43.

Long, N. (2001) *Development Sociology: Actor Perspectives*, London, Routledge.

Maganga, F. (2003) 'Customary Systems and Water Governance: Insights from Southern Africa', Seminar 5 on Splash Water Governance Research website, University of Bradford, http://www.splash.bradford.ac.uk/project-four/.

Maganga, F. and Juma, I. (1999) *From Customary to Statutory Systems: Changes in Land and Water Management in Irrigated Areas of Tanzania – A Study of Local Resource Management Systems in Usangu Plains*, a report submitted to ENRECA, Dar es Salaam.

Maseruli, B. (2000) 'Local Institutions and the Management of Natural Resources', unpublished field notes, College of African Wildlife Management, Mweka, Tanzania.

Mehta, L., Leach, M. and Scoones, I. (2001) 'Editorial: Environmental Governance in an Uncertain World', *IDS Bulletin* 32, 4, pp. 1–9.

Merrey, D. J., Meinzen-Dick, R., Mollinga, P. and Karar, E. (2007) 'Policy and Institutional Reform: The Art of the Possible', in D. Molden (ed.) *Water for Food, Water for Life: A Comprehensive Assessment of Water Management in Agriculture*, London, Earthscan, pp. 193–231.

Mnzava, D. (2000) 'How Modern Water Resources Management Conflicts with Traditional/Indigenous Management: The Case of Arusha Water Project', unpublished working paper, University of Bradford.

Narayan, D., Chambers, R., Shah, M. and Petesch, P. (2000) *Voices of the Poor: Crying Out for Change*, Oxford, Oxford University Press for the World Bank.

Neef, A. (2009) 'Transforming Rural Water Governance: Towards Deliberative and Polycentric Models?' *Water Alternatives* 2, 1, pp. 53–60.

Neimark, B. (2010) 'Subverting Regulatory Protection of "Natural Commodities": The Prunus Africana in Madagascar', *Development and Change* 41, 5, pp. 929–54.

Odgaard, R. (2002) 'Scrambling for Land in Tanzania: Processes of Formalisation and Legitimisation of Land Rights', *The European Journal of Development Research* 14, 2, pp. 71–88.

Ostrom, E. (1990) *Governing the Commons: The Evolution of Institutions for Collective Action*, Cambridge, Cambridge University Press.

—(1992) *Crafting Institutions for Self-Governing Irrigation Systems*, San Francisco, ICS Press.

—(2010) 'Polycentric Systems for Coping with Collective Action and Global Environmental Change', *Global Environmental Change* 20, 4, pp. 550–57.

Pahl-Wostl, C., Jeffrey, P. and Sendzimir, J. (2011) 'Adaptive and Integrated Management of Water Resources', in R. Grafton and K. Hussey (eds) *Water Resources Planning and Management*, Cambridge, Cambridge University Press, pp. 292–310.

Putnam, R. (1994) *Making Democracy Work: Civic Traditions in Modern Italy*, Princeton, Princeton University Press.

Ramalingam, B., Jones, H., Reba, T. and Young, J. (2008) 'Exploring the Science of Complexity: Ideas and Implications for Development and Humanitarian Efforts', Overseas Development Institute Working Paper 285.

Republic of Tanzania (2002) *The 2002/3 Tanzania Participatory Poverty Assessment, Site Report for Nzanza Village, Meatu District, Shinyanga Region*, Dar es Salaam, Economic and Social Research Foundation.

—(2003) *Poverty Reduction Strategy: The Second Progress Report*, Dar es Salaam.

Ribot, J. C., Agrawal, A. and Larson, A. M. (2006) 'Recentralizing While Decentralizing: How National Governments Reappropriate Forest Resources', *World Development* 34, 11, pp. 1864–86.

Rittel, H. and Webber, M. (1973) 'Dilemmas in a General Theory of Planning', *Policy Sciences* 4, 2, pp. 155–69.

Schuurman, F. (2003) 'Social Capital: The Politico-Emancipatory Potential of a Disputed Concept', *Third World Quarterly* 34, 6, pp. 991–1010.

Scott, J. (1985) *Weapons of the Weak: Everyday Forms of Peasant Resistance*, London, Yale University Press.

Scott, W. (2008) *Institutions and Organisations: Ideas and Interests*, London, Sage.

SMUWC (1999) *Management of Village Land and Natural Resources Document*, Rujewa, Tanzania, SMUWC.

—(2001a) 'SMUWC Final Report: Community Engagement Programme', http://www.usangu.org/reports/cep.pdf.

—(2001b) 'SMUWC Final Report: Conflicts', http://www.usangu.org/reports/conflicts.pdf.

—(2001c) 'SMUWC Final Report: Sub-Catchment Resource Management Programme', http://www.usangu.org/reports/srmp.pdf.

—(2001d) 'SMUWC Final Report: Rural Livelihoods', http://www.usangu.org/reports/rural.pdf

Sokile, C., Mwaruvanda, W. and Van Koppen, B. (2005) 'Integrated Water Resource Management in Tanzania: Interface Between Formal and Informal Institutions', paper presented at the International Workshop on African Water Laws: Plural Legislative Frameworks for Rural Water Management in Africa, Johannesburg, South Africa, 26–28 January.

Stewart, F. (1996) 'Groups for Good or Ill', *Oxford Development Studies* 24, 1, pp. 9–24.

Uphoff, N. (1993) 'Between State, Markets and Households: A Neoinstitutional Analysis of Local Organisations and Institutions', *World Development* 21, 4, pp. 623–32.

Uphoff, N. and Wijayaratna, C. (2000) 'Demonstrated Benefits from Social Capital: The Productivity of Farmer Organisations in Gal Oya, Sri Lanka', *World Development* 28, 11.

Von Benda-Beckman, F. (2002) 'Who's Afraid of Legal Pluralism?' *Journal of Legal Pluralism* 47, pp. 37–83.

Von Benda-Beckman, F. and Von Benda-Beckman, K. (2006) 'The Dynamics of Change and Continuity in Plural Legal Orders', *Journal of Legal Pluralism* 53–4, pp. 1–44.

Walsh, M. (2006) 'Conservation Myths, Political Realities, and the Proliferation of Protected Areas', paper presented at the African Environments Lecture, African Environments Programme, Oxford University Centre for the Environment, University of Oxford, 24 November.

Walsh, Martin (2008) 'Study on the Options for Pastoralists to Secure Their Livelihoods: Pastoralism and Policy Process in Tanzania – Mbarali Case Study', Report Submitted to TNRF.

Wong, K.-F. (2003) 'Empowerment as a Panacea for Poverty: Old Wine in New Bottles? Reflections on the World Bank's Conception of Power', *Progress in Development Studies* 3, 4, pp. 307–22.

Wong, S. (2010) 'Elite Capture or Capture Elites? Lessons from the "Counter-Elite" and 'Co-Opt-Elite" Approaches in Bangladesh and Ghana', *UNU- WIDER* 82.

Woolcock, M. (2001) 'The Place of Social Capital in Understanding Social and Economic Outcomes', *Canadian Journal of Policy Research* 2, 1, pp. 1–17.

Wyborn, C. and Bixler, P. (2011) 'Going Up or Going Down? Transferring Approaches to Conservation across Nested Scales', paper presented at the Colorado Conference on Earth System Governance: Crossing Boundaries and Building Bridges, Colorado State University, May 17–20.

Notes

1 Much of the material presented here was gathered during a DFID-funded project (Sustainable Management of the Usangu Wetland and its Catchment, or SMUWC, 1999–2001), the aim of which was to investigate the causes of resource depletion in Usangu and developing local capacity to collectively manage the natural environment. This material and analysis has been updated with preliminary data gathered for a British Academy research project 'Understanding Water Governance in Challenging Environments: How Institutions Adapt to Change' being undertaken at the time of writing. This project is jointly conducted with Tom Franks, Faustin Maganga and Sikitiko Kapile, on whose insights I gratefully draw. The chapter also draws on and elaborates material from previously published papers by the author (2002, 2004), Cleaver and Franks (2005) and Franks and Cleaver (2007).

2 Two focus group sessions were conducted for each group, in February and in September of 2011. Discussion was centred around participatory Venn diagrams.

In the second round of sessions the original diagram was reviewed and modified. Of course, this process produced composite diagrams for the group, but the researchers also endeavoured to draw out individual differences and nuances, which were recorded in the discussion.

3 Personal comment from Rie Odgaard.

5 Continuity and Change: Gendered Agency and Bricolage

Introduction

This chapter builds understanding of the authoritative nature of bricolage by critically considering how individuals shape institutions and are shaped by them. Here I explore the ways in which people act as 'bricoleurs', consciously and unconsciously putting together arrangements for natural resource management. In challenging dominant 'bounded rationality' models of agency, I consider how much room for manoeuvre different individuals have in shaping institutions and engendering change. Proposing a model of agency that is situated, relational and embodied, I outline a number of factors which shape people's identities, motivations and behaviours. Institutional bricolage is a process animated by human agents: this chapter explores interactions at the interface between people and institutions and considers how these might both challenge and reinforce inequalities.

Women's Involvement in Forest Management in a Swedish Village

Let us begin by hearing one woman's reflection on her participation in a village association concerned with community-based forest management.

> Old habits persist ... women are quiet in big groups. Women don't get much of a chance to talk at the meetings. I know two women who stopped going to the association because they felt that they were always expected to make coffee and tea and bake buns for the meetings. I refuse to do that. The forest has always been the men's domain and many [women] think that it is not really their concern, that they don't understand what is going on. I wanted to find out

myself what is going on regarding the forest. Now I know. But it takes so much energy. I have been strong and continued, but not everyone can do that. I don't have any small children at home so I can spend time on that.

This extract is taken from Seema Arora-Jonsson's (2005) study of women's involvement in forest management in a Swedish village. The woman quoted above raises a number of significant points about the exercise of agency in formalized public institutions. She points to the tenacity of historic divisions of labour and gendered norms of public articulation; she highlights the effort and costs involved in participation and the constraining effects of social relationships on some women. Here she examines women's ability to exercise agency and engage in public institutions in the context of a society that is regarded as one of the most gender equal in the world. I deliberately begin with this illustrative material from the global north in an attempt to unpick what is universal about the exercise of agency and what is contextual. The case well illustrates how collective action and institutional engagement are shaped both by the actions of gendered individuals and by wider discourses, structures and social norms.

The case concerns the village of Drevdagen in the north of Sweden, where a village association was formed in the 1990s in the context of the community's struggle to gain management rights over the forest. The village association became involved with a number of national and international networks, successfully opposed the sale of surrounding forests and developing projects for forest co-management. Although the village association was intended to be inclusive, women quickly dropped out of it, alienated by formal protocol, its increasingly extraverted focus (towards bureaucrats, politicians, forest company officials and external networks) and its dominance by a minority of older village men. As one woman reported:

at the meetings, the agenda and so on takes a lot of time and at the end, when one wants to discuss important questions ... the other questions ... then it is time to go home.

Another woman pointed out how, even when she participated, her contribution was not valued:

If I happened to make a suggestion at the association, nobody said anything. About 15 minutes later when Leo said the same thing, it was discussed with great enthusiasm (Arora-Jonsson, 2005: 245)

Many women found that the type of forest management being proposed and the focus on grandiose plans had little relevance to their day-to-day lives. Some women attempted to influence the workings of the village association through their husbands and informally on social occasions. Others dropped out, but did not disengage from associational life. Instead, these women participated in a loose network of overlapping groups (including a cattle grazing association and cow cooperative, a sports association and a spiritual group) which better reflected their priorities and through which their voices could be better heard. With the help of a university researcher, some women established a women's forum in the village, which they strove to keep as an open and inclusive space. Meetings were informal and sociable and the forum developed as a way of strengthening village life, both socially and economically. In the forum, women shared life stories and visions of future development.

In Drevdagen women's gendered positions in the household and community shaped their motivations and associational actions. According to Arora-Jonsson's analysis, rather than being solely concerned with forest resource appropriation, these women were motivated by concerns of 'having, loving and being' – of securing the wellbeing of selves, family and community in the local environment. For some women, the spirituality group offered an alternative way of relating to the forest and of being close to nature – an affective connection they found lacking in the formal association and its activities. In furthering their visions of local development through the women's forum, women told stories of their past lives in the village, often cast in reference to a longer historical memory. Prominent in these stories was a notion of a golden age of past solidarity and sociability, linked to the traditional crafts and pastimes, and connected to the forest and the natural world (the revival of cattle farming, a 'traditional' occupation of women, was cast in this light).

Both men and women in Drevdagen drew on experience of the previous struggle by the community against the authorities over the fate of the village school to characterize themselves as both oppressed and strong. Men also referred to 'tradition' to justify contemporary gendered divisions of labour in associational life. Influenced by the alternative route taken by the women's forum, the village association then began to broaden its' own focus to situate forest management in the context of wider village development, nicely illustrating the leakage of meaning and legitimacy between institutions. With the help of university and activist networks, the village association organized a conference including participants from community forest management projects in Scotland and India. For one woman at least, the international experience added grander meaning to their local action:

Imagine, it really makes you think and gives you strength when you see that the struggle against the state for your forests isn't something only in Drevdagen or Sweden but is actually a global phenomenon ... That one can now try and struggle for our environment together. (Arora-Jonsson, 2005: 149)

The effects of women exercising agency through alternative institutions was mixed. Organizing informally had advantages in that it allowed for more inclusion and for the airing of different voices and visions of village development. However, the disadvantages were that informality rendered it largely illegible (and insignificant) to those outside it. Arora-Jonsson suggests that by organizing less formally, women drew attention to existing power structures in ways that many men found threatening. Senior men in the village were rather dismissive of the women's activities, seeing them as peripheral and domestic, compared to the men's involvement in the 'bigger' work of forest management. For some women, their engagement with the forum inspired them sufficiently to reinvigorate their participation in other more long-established local institutions such as the village association and the village newsletter. When a woman subsequently became chair of the village association and deeply involved in forest management issues she was criticized by men for being 'too strong' and 'not like other women'. Some of the previously dominant men in the association tried to undermine her by calling meetings with other villagers and not informing her.

Is Individual Action Rational or Social?

The case sketched out above serves to introduce some of the key aspects of agency explored further in this chapter. These include the way different people exercise voice in formal and informal institutions; the influence of affective attachments (between people and the environment); the impact of everyday livelihoods on people's institutional engagement; and the way deliberate individual action is also shaped by societal norms.

The concept of agency is central to understanding how institutions work, but mainstream concepts of agency, focusing on individual strategizing and deliberative public decision-making, are unhelpfully narrow. We need to pay more attention to the ways in which people shape institutions, collective action and natural resource management in the social interactions of their daily lives. Drawing on actor-oriented perspectives (Long, 1992; Arce and Long, 2000; Long, 2001), I nonetheless caution against over-emphasizing the transformatory possibilities of individual action (in the form of resistance, creative adaptation and entrepreneurship). From a bricolage perspective, agency is both enabled *and* constrained through institutions, the effects produced are uneven due to the patterning of social structure *and* the dynamism and unpredictability of inter-connected human actions (McNay, 2000).

Assumptions about the nature of individual agency underlie policy-making and shape its effectiveness (Greener, 2002). International development policy, strongly influenced by liberal concepts of individual capacities and rights, sees institutions as the channels through which these can be enhanced or secured. In this view, purposeful individual actions to secure livelihood interests are aggregated through institutions to produce collectively useful and empowering outcomes. Local institutions, such as the village association in Drevdagen, supposedly facilitate the articulation of needs and allow 'stakeholders' with different interests (or their representatives) to negotiate rules of resource use.

This 'bounded rationality' model of human agency, strongly influenced by economics and game theory, is founded on the three key assumptions of methodological individualism, utility-maximizing behaviour and exogenous preferences (Bardhan and Ray, 2006). Here individuals (in whom agency and autonomy reside) are assumed to strategize about resource appropriation in their own interests. Such self-regarding strategies are 'bounded' by the limited human capacity to access and process all necessary information. People's tastes and preferences may be shaped by 'endogenous variables' and by norms generated through repeated and multiple individual acts. Nonetheless, mainstream institutionalism explains people's actions *primarily* as individual responses to incentives, rules and sanctions. For Ostrom (2005), the question is the extent to which people behave as 'rational egoists' or 'conditional cooperators', the assumption being that individuals tend to revert to 'free-riding' or cheating in the absence of rules or norms. In mainstream views individuals cleverly *calculate* their engagement and compliance with rules and *use* social norms to maximize their access to natural resources. Their participation in public decision-making is assumed to positively influence their compliance with the rules made. Within this school of thought various attempts have been made to develop ideas about the ways in which institutions shape people's preferences (through creating norms) and structure the decision-making environments by defining logics to be applied. Though there are numerous variations in the ways that mainstream theorists account for collective action, they all tend to be grounded in assumptions of methodological individualism in which utility-based explanations account for the social aspects of people's choices (Vatn, 2009: 190).

Bounded rationality models of agency have been criticized for their over-simplification, abstraction and rationalization of human behaviour. Such critiques concern the ways in which such second-generation rational choice models still explain collective outcomes by examining individual behaviour, implying that people can distance themselves from social relationships in their decision-making. Critics suggest that the role of cognition, emotion and ideology is often underplayed, resulting in impoverished understandings of human subjectivity and motivation – thus people's behaviour is dichotomized broadly as either 'selfish' or 'altruistic'. Cause–effect relationships between individual actions and their effects are also oversimplified, based on the assumption that people's actions are primarily intentional and performed in knowledge of their consequences. Mainstream institutionalism is primarily concerned with agency-as-decision-making, with the choices people make rather than their ability to make them. Equity of outcome is not a major concern, the emphasis being on optimization of resource management, which is thought to work best when all those affected by the rules are involved in decision-making (Johnson, 2004; Agrawal, 2005; Wong 2009).

So how can we enrich this 'thin' model of human agency and invest the rather abstract individuals of mainstream institutionalism with meaningful socially located personhood (Ballet *et al.*, 2007)? In the following sections I will draw on insights from social and political theory and from feminist studies to explore the multi-faceted, inherently social nature of individual action, and the ways it is both enabled and constrained by institutions. In the following sections three inter-related debates concerned with 'thick' models of human agency are considered: (1) the extent to which the actions of individual are enabled or constrained by their social embeddedness; (2) the ways in which power relations shape individual participation in resource governance; and (3) how we understand the *effects* of exercising agency.

Enablement and Constraint

In the opening chapters of this book we considered ideas about whether the social embeddedness of individuals offers more constraint than opportunity. Positions taken on this issue significantly shape our expectations of the outcome of institutional processes (Granovetter, 1985; Bardhan and Ray, 2006). In social theory agency is seen as the capability, or power, to be the originator of acts and a distinguishing feature of being human. Reflexivity and the ability to act purposively commonly feature in definitions of agency. For example, Weber characterized human action as shaped by a rationality consisting of self-consciousness, reflection, intention, purpose and meaning (Rapport and Overing, 2000). Agency is commonly conceptualized as relational; it does not exist in a vacuum but is exercised in a social world in which structure shapes the opportunities and resources available to individuals, in which appropriate ways of being and behaving are not simply a matter of individual choice. Whilst most social theorists recognize the relationship between individuality and relationality, their interpretations differ mainly in two areas. Firstly, they diverge as to how far individual agency can generate empowerment and social change, and secondly, as to how far it is constrained by inequitable social arrangements and norms.

Earlier we have seen that the agency-as-enabling argument is well represented by the later work of Anthony Giddens. Writing of contemporary 'late-modern' societies, in which the decline of tradition supposedly makes personal identities more important than social ones, Giddens emphasizes the ability of agents to navigate societal challenges, to confront and deal with risk. In this sense individuals 'create their own biographies' (Giddens, 1996; Greener, 2002; Gross, 2005). Development thinking tends towards the optimistic late-Giddenesque version of agency, emphasizing the instrumental, empowering and transformatory effects of conscious individual strategizing actions. These assumptions are prominent for example in applications of sustainable livelihoods approaches in development and polices promoting the use of social capital by the poor to substitute for their lack of other resources.

The simplifications and reifications involved in translating these thin concepts of agency into policy *are* subjected to critical scrutiny, for example by those who demonstrate the complex motivations and factors that shape people's environment/livelihood interactions (Ahlers and Zwarteveen, 2009; Van Hecken and Bastiaensen, 2010). Additionally, development thinking includes very useful attempts to locate individuals in multi-faceted lifeworlds. For example, Norman Long is concerned with understanding how people's multiple identities and motivations mean that they are only ever 'partially enrolled' in the projects of others (Long, 2001). Other scholars attempt to enrich Sen's dominant capabilities approach (1999), with its emphasis on freedom and individual agency, by showing how the exercise of human capabilities also involves *collective* actions, overlapping allegiances and multiple identities (Ibrahim, 2006; De Herdt and Abega, 2007; Deneulin and De Herdt, 2007).

Fascinating though these insights are, there is, as I have already argued, a tendency to emphasize enablement rather than constraint and to celebrate the empowering aspects of the exercise of agency. Let me briefly recap this argument for the purposes of this chapter. For example, 'post-tyranny' thinking about participation, critical of over-simplified and instrumental models, nonetheless assumes that agency is the range of socio-political practices through which people can *increase* control over resources and *extend* their status, primarily by their active engagement in public spaces (Cornwall, 2004; Hickey and Mohan, 2004; Kesby, 2005; Osei-Kufuor, 2010). Similarly, Long, whilst recognizing structural constraint, suggests that agency is about the ability to devise ways of coping with life, to *choose* levels of enrolment in the project of others and to enrol others in one's own projects (Long, 1992: 22, italics added; Arce and Long, 2000: 3).

As we saw in Chapter 2, Bourdieu (1977) offers a more constrained view of individual agency where he emphasizes how strongly habitus (a set of societally formed preferences and habits that incline agents to act and react in particular ways) shapes agency and the ways in which hegemonic elites shape habitus. For him, individuals possess agency, but its nature is partially prescribed by the culture in which they are situated. So, according to Bourdieu, agency is not simply comprised of conscious reflexive action but also by unreflexive practice; habitus orients preferences and actions without determining them, providing a practical sense of what action is appropriate in particular circumstances (Greener, 2002: 691–2).

In such 'thick' models of agency, debates about the nature of cognition and reflexivity are significant. To what extent are people able to bring their knowledge of the world and their own behaviour into conscious scrutiny and to use this reflection to plan strategic action (see for example Archer, 2000; Giddens, 1984)? How far do the human limits of cognition and computation predispose us to make decisions and institutions based on approximations, patterns, re-arrangements, rather than on empirically detailed deductions? (Levi, 1996). And how far is the 'social fit' of such arrangements shaped not just by 'rationality' but also by our feelings and how we think others feel about us (Douglas, 1987; Burkitt, 2012)?

Despite different emphases on the balance between enablement and constraint, social theorists tend to agree that whilst individuals are embedded in social life they are not totally submerged in it – structures, rules, norms and relationships are all mediated by human agency. In this sense people are both creative agents *and* subjected individuals and this duality goes some way to explain the variability, intermittence and unpredictable consequences of the exercise of agency in institutions (Henriques *et al*, 1984; McNay, 2000; Agrawal, 2005).

The individual exercise of agency is tied into relations of power and authority. For Giddens, individuals may exercise agency-as-power by deploying material and authoritative resources. Therefore, he contends that such resources 'are the media through which power is exercised' and these resources are themselves 'structured properties of social systems, drawn upon and reproduced by knowledgeable agents in the course of interaction' (Giddens, 1984: 15). Human agents make rules which structure the deployment of resources; thus the patterning of command over resources in turn shapes the actions of agents. This raises questions about who is able to command material and non-material resources to the benefit or detriment of others, whose agency is mediated through the actions of others, and to what effects (Hickey and Bracking, 2004)?

For Bourdieu (unlike Giddens), securing individual empowerment through the creative exercise of agency is difficult partly because social status is *embodied* in a person's dress, demeanour and actions, and partly because of the role of non-reflexive behaviour in human action. In Bourdieu's model, non-elite actors are further constrained by the hegemonic power of state, cultural, economic and political elites to shape the habitus of society. Power is relational and poor and marginalized people must make arrangements with the powerful to be able to function. Individuals may seem powerless to escape from difficult circumstances because their constrained situation is so ingrained in overlapping perceptions and practices that it seems normal; lack of opportunity seems natural and inevitable (Hoggett, 2001). Here individuals are constrained by hegemonic power, trapped by its third dimension in which the psychological and ideological boundaries of action are 'invisibly' shaped by the working of dominant ideologies and societal norms (Lukes, 2005). Such invisible power shapes the ways in which people consciously and non-consciously conceptualize their place in the world – it limits their 'imagined autonomy' and therefore their exercise of agency.

The insidious workings of power in relation to agency also feature in governmentality analyses, drawing on Foucauldian ideas about the organized practices through which we are governed and (consciously and unconsciously) govern ourselves (Dean, 1999; Agrawal 2005). Here power is often exercised through taken-for-granted everyday interactions, through embodied 'regimes of practice'. Such governmentality analyses see dispersal of power in multiple localities, an approach which is highly compatible with the notion of plural institutions formed through processes of bricolage. As we have seen in Chapter 4, opinions differ substantially about the extent to which institutional pluralism provides individuals with more room for manoeuvre, increased opportunities for the negotiation and flexing of arrangements (Odgaard, 2002; Maganga, 2003; Cornwall, 2004; Kesby, 2005; Ostrom, 2005; Merrey *et al.*, 2007).

Effects of Exercising Agency

So the workings of power through plural institutional settings shapes the exercise of agency, the ability of individuals to effect significant difference in their lives.

Power may be exercised and accepted both consciously and unconsciously and be reproduced through everyday acts and relationships. We have already seen that whilst social constraint is recognized there is a tendency in development and natural resource management literature to focus on agency as choice and resistance. Thus reflexive agents supposedly can *question* norms, *challenge* inequitable distribution of resources, *claim* and *extend* their rights. From this point of view agency is empowering, although as McNay notes, the individual and innovative ways in which individuals respond may hinder as well as catalyze social change (McNay, 2000: 5).

However, not all choices are equal, not all people are equally placed to make them, and similar actions may have very different outcomes. Agrawal, in his study of community-based forest management in India, shows how apparently equitable forest rules have unequal impact on different people whose responses to them vary because of their subject positions. In the communities he studied the forest guards detected and reported women and *harijans* most frequently for violating the forest rules; such offenders were not only more frequently detected but they paid their fines more promptly than offending high-caste neighbours. In this case we could speculate that discriminatory perceptions of the women and harijans by rule enforcers and the skewed dependence of the marginalized on good reputation and relations of patronage shaped the actors' rule-following and sanctioning behaviour.

For Kabeer the issue is not so much whether individuals can choose to act in a particular circumstance but about how much control they have to make *strategic* decisions which shape their lives. She distinguishes between first- and second-order choices; the former referring to decisions fundamental to the shape of a person's life, the second to choices which affect quality of life but do not constitute its defining parameters (Kabeer, 2000: 28). Importantly for Kabeer, the exercise of agency is not just about *potential* ability to exercise choice but about the real *effects* these choices can have. In participatory natural resource management, the participation of individuals *in itself* is assumed to lead to benefits to them, although this is demonstrably often not the case.

Exercising agency to secure better access to natural resources can come at significant social cost. For example, Delgado and Zwarteveen (2007) document the experience of 'Lupe', a Peruvian woman who separated from (but did not divorce) her alcoholic husband. Following the separation she diligently maintained a prominent role in both formal and informal arrangements for the regulation of irrigation water and fulfilled all the community water work expected of the household. Despite this, she struggled to get her name officially registered with the communal land board and to become an official member of the irrigation committee in place of her husband. This struggle involved gaining the approval of the male members of the irrigation administration and a statement by a judge about her marital separation. Lupe eventually obtained her irrigation control card, allowing her membership of the water users association. The right to control land and water was won at considerable social cost, though – most other water users did not approve or support her, accusing her of being a '*machista*' (behaving – inappropriately – like a man).

So we can see that neither the exercise of agency nor societal structures *determine* outcomes – they are rather shaped in the interaction between the two. Human agency is not exercised in moment-by-moment calculations in accordance with obtaining a fixed goal. Rather it manifests in the dynamic interplay between, habit, structured creativity and pragmatic subjectivity unfolding in different locations over time. However, the exercise of agency is an unequal process often leading to inequitable outcomes. In the following sections I outline factors to consider in developing a 'thicker' understanding of human agency in institutions and natural resource management, emphasizing the ways that this is often constrained for poor and marginalized people.

Moral Worldviews

Given the instrumental focus and neo-liberal framing of developmental initiatives it is unsurprising that people's agency is conceptualized as primarily exercised through markets and meetings. But all of us frame our actions within certain understandings of the world and our place in it, of cause–effect relationships and accepted ideas of order, proper behaviour and what is fair or right. Such worldviews are at least as important in shaping agency as utility-maximizing ones; rationality is shaped by belief as well as calculation and both shape social behaviour, political expectations and understanding of the social order.

We have seen in Chapters 3 and 4 how, in Zimbabwe and Tanzania, a form of moral–ecological rationality links people's perceptions of their own actions with consequences in the natural and supernatural worlds, an analysis supported by work from other regions (Adams *et al.*, 1997; Mosse, 1997; Boelens, 2008). These often-unspoken cosmological assumptions influence individuals' willingness to abide by collective decisions and to comply with unwritten norms of resource use. Moral worldviews often include strongly gendered and socially stratified ideas about proper behaviour (as in showing respect to elders) and the 'rightful' place of individuals in the social order.

Such beliefs do not exist in a realm separate from designed institutions or from 'modern' forms of governance. Worldviews are not simply about arcane cultural beliefs inevitably eroding in conditions of modernization. As several writers point out, worldviews reflexively shape agency and socio-political organization more generally (Strang, 2004; Osei-Kufuor, 2010). In his study of water control in the Andes, Rutgeerd Boelens (2008) shows how elements of Andean cosmological beliefs persist even in the most marketized of communities, emerging more strongly in times of crisis. Such myths and cosmologies can be used to legitimize the actions of particular interest groups and they are built into everyday behaviour, social relationships and water control (von Benda-Beckman and von Benda-Beckman, 2006).

So worldviews play a part in shaping the political and social order and in delineating the room for manoeuvre for different actors within it. In her work in India, Deepa Joshi analyses access to water to show how caste beliefs in Hindu society help to reproduce the *gendered* social order of water management (Joshi and Fawcett, 2001; Joshi *et al.*, 2003). Such worldviews, reinforced by political power, shape people's everyday behaviour (such as food consumption and water use practices) and their ability to participate in formal decision-making through the water committee. One woman explained the consequences for her agency of a social order in which certain water sources are 'prohibited' to those defined as 'untouchable'. She highlighted the meaning of a daily life spent dealing with socially created water scarcity:

> It is to wait for someone from the (high caste) house to give us water from their *naula* [spring]. It is to walk up and down their path, calling a little, waiting a little, hearing them say they are too busy and helplessly remembering our own tasks at home. It is to steal water stealthily, taking care not to spill any on the concrete floor for fear of being suspected; feeling the guilt of stealing. It is all this and much more; being obliged *physically, socially and morally* for the water they give us ... (Joshi and Fawcett, 2005: 53, italics added)

Cosmological beliefs may be routinized and naturalized so that they are difficult for people to examine or question; they seem like the right way of doing things. But this is not always the case; reflexive agents can also subject such views to scrutiny and to manipulation. Mercy Dikito-Wachtmeister (2000) studied the dynamics of women's participation in village water committees in Zimbabwe. She noted that belief in witch-craft shaped some women's willingness to speak out or to disagree on matters of water management. As one respondent said:

> I prefer to keep quiet because there are people here who use lots of witchcraft. If you exchange words with these people it makes their magic work on you. The best thing is to keep quiet, and not give them a chance. (Dikito-Wachtmeister 2000: 219)

However, Dikito-Wachtmeister also suspected some of strategically using this belief to excuse themselves from onerous and time-consuming public decision-making. So another respondent said of the water committee members:

> I think some of them will want to pretend that the reason they do not do their duties is because of fear of witchcraft, when they are either lazy, or can't because of other responsibilities. Witchcraft has become an excuse for everything ... They use it to explain everything that has not worked out well or to justify their lack of participation in community things. (Dikito-Wachtmeister, 2000: 219)

While cosmological beliefs are important in shaping agency, it is often unclear where the boundaries of reflexivity are; when and to what extent people can choose to negotiate the norms. At these rather blurred boundaries there may be room for creative adaptation to occur, struggle to appropriate resources and meaning also occur here. However, the Indian case cited above illustrates that the awareness of discriminatory norms, the ability to reflect on them, does not necessarily translate into the ability to reshape them. So cultural beliefs may be accepted by many, partially negotiated by some and be a source of authoritative and allocative resources for others.

Crowded Selves: The Blended Nature of Individual Identities

Approaches to participatory natural resource management tend to classify people into taxonomic groups (farmers, women, pastoralists, irrigators) and to overlook their rich social identities. Individual identities and associated motivations are multi-faceted, as are the channels through which resources are accessed. Plurality manifests in agents themselves and shapes people's behaviour in both public and private domains.

For example, evidence from a number of countries (Odgaard, 2002; Rao, 2003; Arora-Jonsson, 2005; Cleaver and Nyatsambo, 2011) suggests the complexity of identities and relationships through which women's land rights are exercised. Women may claim rights to natural resources as legal and equal citizens but also through their positions as daughters, wives, mothers, as members of a particular caste, religious or ethnic group. To these women, living their lives within marriages and kin groups, exercising their agency through public institutions may not always be the preferred option. Arora-Johnson (2005) found that women in communities in both India and Sweden saw forest issues as *inseparable* from social relationships and wider village issues; change required the exercise of agency in both domestic and public spheres. Understanding agency in collective action then requires focusing on social forms of organizing around everyday work and livelihood interests rather than solely on emphasizing agency exercised through public acts of participation or resistance.

The multiple elements of identity pose both challenges and opportunities to the exercise of agency. For example, in a study of the 'crowded selves' of women in squatter settlement in Istanbul, Turkey, women *primarily* identified themselves and conceptualized wellbeing in terms of their social relationships: 'they articulated their selfhood as their *fathers'* daughters, *brothers'* sisters, *husband's* wives, *families'* brides and mothers of *children*' (Uyan-Semerci, 2007, p209). The ways they exercised voice, fetched water, prepared food and expressed emotion were strongly influenced by patriarchal family norms and family and Muslim religious codes. For these women, parenthood gave them relative freedom and empowerment *and* increased their constraints and obligations. They were able to participate in public spaces as 'mothers' but continued to identify their needs and desires as inseparable from those of their families.

The recognition of such gendered opportunities and constraints in exercising agency poses a challenge to designed interventions supporting natural resource management. In a study of institutions for forest management in Ghana, Elizabeth Watson (2003) found that, due to the project's attempt to recognize gendered interests, income-generating activities were targeted at women. This resulted in men retaining prominence on formalized natural resource management committees (shaping resource-use rules and distribution), while women were limited to loosely associated self-help groups, addressing their practical and social needs but dislocated from formal decision-making processes.

Mainstream Institutionalist understandings of collective action are rule oriented – they see the creation of collective rules and the sanctions applied to rule breaking as essential to effective action. But how much capacity do people with different social identities have to exercise agency in respect of these rules – what shapes their room for manoeuvre? The agency of individuals is clearly exercised in relation to the perception by others of them. Dikito-Wachtmeister (2000) notes the tendency in the villages she studies for more powerful women to be excused from rule following. Her examples include someone associated with the ruling party – a woman who employed such 'vile language' that people were afraid to confront her – and a well-off woman who administered the church fund for people in misfortune. Social placement of an individual critically affects their ability to 'bend' collective rules.

Unequal Interdependence

Participatory approaches to resource management tend to assume that those sharing livelihood interests are more likely to craft effective collective action. Indeed, inter-relatedness is seen as fundamental to the building of social capital, the moulding of social norms, the generation of collective action and hence the further building of relations of trust and cooperation (Pretty, 2003). This assumption of equality of interest is underpinned by the myth that people following similar livelihood practices will be equally able to shape them. This clearly is not the case, as relations of unequal dependence distort the exercise of agency and its outcomes. For example, studies analyzing gender relations show us that the ability of men and women in a household or community to mobilize authoritative and allocative resources may be skewed in favour of men even where they perform similar tasks, have similar interests in the resource and are similarly recognized in formal decision-making arrangements.

Discussing indigenous forest management in Uganda, Nabanoga (2005) notes very similar knowledge about trees and practices of tree management between men and women. However, she suggests that prevailing cosmologies, myths that women are not significantly involved in tree protection and use, and land tenure arrangements which favour men mean that men dominate in decisions about tree planting (even of women's tree planting). Similarly, participation in tree-related activities often depends on social status, and the outcomes confer status: men's ownership of fig trees was historically an important status symbol and the ability to produce bark cloth in quantity conferred social status. By contrast, the production of handicrafts from palm trees and the collection of particular wild vegetables conferred social status on women, but were considered only the last resort of the poorest and unmarried men (Nabanoga, 2005).

Rao (2003) usefully points out, however, that the exercise of agency involves mutuality and interdependence as well as relations of domination and subordination. Indeed, the two are mutually implicated. Common interests are embedded in relations of unequal interdependence, often involving arrangements of patronage. For many poorer and subordinate individuals and groups, access to resources is *primarily* exercised through inequitable social arrangements. Thus, Joshi heard a dalit woman from India, excluded by higher-caste neighbours from equitable access to water, explaining why she would not object, even in the context of a gender-focused participatory development intervention: 'My neighbours are important to me, *no matter what they do*. I need their support for my family's daily existence' (Joshi *et al.*, 2003: 2, italics added).

Positions of relative power do not imply unfettered ability to exercise agency, as illustrated by research exploring the interaction between individuals, community-based workers and local institutions in participatory development initiatives in Tanzania and South Africa. Although the community-based workers were structurally relatively privileged, they frequently expressed frustration that community members did not 'play their part' properly. By absenting themselves, declining to cooperate or give full information, the community members constrained the effective exercise of agency by the workers (Understanding Community Action, 2006).

Another interesting exploration of skewed interdependence is offered by Masaki (2004) in his study of caste-based management of irrigation infrastructure in Nepal. The paper chronicles attempts by members of the labouring caste to exercise both individual and collective agency in reshaping 'customary' labour obligations to be less onerous to them. The landowning elite relied on the dissatisfied lower-caste villagers as labourers on their irrigated land and had certain ideas about their obligations as patrons, but the relationship was one of unequal interdependence, as the labourers were unlikely to survive at all without the patronage of the landowners. This then restricted the extent to which with labourers were willing or able to enter into confrontation with their patrons. Relations of interdependence may offer the possibility of negotiation of rights, but this is constrained by structural inequality. Immediate livelihood imperatives combined with unequal authoritative and allocative resources may shape the exercise of agency in directions productive of social harmony and conflict avoidance, rather than effective resistance or explicit negotiation of rights.

Relations of mutuality are plural in their manifestations, sites of decision-making and the generation of norms are dispersed. The intra-household dynamics shaping agency are often overlooked in institutional analyses. Bolt and Bird (2003) schematize the layers of overlapping factors (gender, age, birth order, physical ability and relationship to head of household) which may disadvantage individuals within households and render them less likely to shape decisions and to access resources. Livelihoods research in Tanzania showed how entrepreneurial women were restricted in their business activities by the location of their marital home and expectations of wifeliness (SMUWC, 2001) whilst young women declined to volunteer for training as Village Activators, citing the influence of elders as key restrictions on their choice of social and economic roles (Cleaver and Kaare, 1998).

Structure and Voice

The literature on participatory natural resource management is often optimistic about the possibilities of exercising voice in public fora; it is assumed that when given the chance people will use this opportunity to shape individually and collectively beneficial rules. As a result, dominant thinking in the field tends to underplay the ways in which social norms shape articulation, how participation is mediated through representatives and the ways in which less-powerful people are often muted in situations marked by significant power differentials (Jaworski, 2005). Post-tyranny literature on participation and gendered empowerment recognizes that the power relations imbue participatory spaces but is generally also optimistic that participatory methodologies can be used to disrupt 'business as usual' and facilitate the articulation of alternative views (Cornwall, 2004; Kesby, 2005).

How far is the exercise of voice in public institutions empowering? In the case of the Amei village in Tanzania, attempts to empower women in a pastoralist community through an NGO-funded participatory water project had mixed results. The aim of promoting women's role as active citizens was partially achieved – women increased their representation on the village council and on the water committee, and claimed greater confidence in discussions with men at village and household level. However, within the timescale of the project, their increased capacity to exercise agency and voice could not counter the wider relations of patriarchy in which they were embedded. Despite their gains in citizenship, they could not secure rights to water on equal terms with men, partly because men retained the ability to pay cash for preferential water access (House, 2003; Tukai, 2005).

Hierarchies amongst women, concepts of proper behaviour and virilocal marriage arrangements constrain the exercise of voice by some. In Zimbabwe, one young woman explained constraints on her participation in water management to a researcher thus:

> I cannot be seen to be taking a lead role at meetings attended by older women as this could be perceived as being disrespectful. I am a young woman who has just been married here for a few years, so I cannot be speaking often and taking a lead in these things. If you are still young and have young children like me, nobody takes you seriously, nobody respects you. (Dikito–Wachtmeister, 2000: 221)

However, we have already seen how ideas about the right way of doing things may unwittingly shape people's agency, but may also be consciously deployed and negotiated. Dikito-Wachtmeister (2000) postulates the transfer of household bargaining models, based on negotiations of proper gender roles, to the more public domain. The women she studied used the strategy of 'buttering' (or flattering) men both in the household and in public and invoked gendered norms of desirable behaviour to avoid water management work. In particular, Dikito-Wachtmeister documents a meeting in which women consciously and deliberately 'buttered' men through praise and positive reinforcement of their manliness in order to persuade one particular man to take on a water management leadership role. They adopted a humble demeanour in keeping with tradition and respect when doing this. The man then asserted his intention to be strong and strict in the role. Dikito-Wachtmeister also noted the strategic use on other occasions of gendered norms of mutedness; by deliberate and collective non-contributions to a meeting, women were able to gain the concerned attention of the chairman and an invitation to elucidate their views.

A concern with gendered participation and voice is often translated into the counting of numbers of women participating, but this throws little light on the gendered dynamics of articulation and representation at meetings. Research in Tanzania showed women participating in village meetings by nominating representatives (on the basis of their eloquence or social position) to speak for them whilst men participated and spoke for themselves as individuals. In one case a community meeting had decided to invest surplus village funds in a new water supply (the women's priority) rather than in the feast and beer drink favoured by many of the men who spoke (Cleaver and Kaare, 1998). However, in a study of village-level water committees in India, Ahmed (2008) tracked the formation of 'in-groups' amongst those men and women who could speak out. Women who found it difficult to be heard gradually dropped out of meetings, so increasing the influence of those comfortable with such public articulation.

The focus on negotiations in public institutional settings overlooks other ways in which voice is exercised, for example through gossip, everyday conversation and songs. In tracking the changing nature of women's walking songs in a border community in South Africa, Angela Impey (2009) found the expression of everyday experiences of life, love and livelihoods, environmental shocks, politics and poverty. These songs were performed whilst traversing long distances for trade, work and family networking and through them were expressed feelings towards nature and the landscape and changing spatial land use practices (for example, relating to the restriction on their livelihoods imposed by the extension of a national park area). Impey frames this socio-spatial exercise of voice in terms of the concept of 'ecological habitus', noting that the affective aspects of landscapes, belonging and practices are often overlooked in instrumental approaches to natural resource management. The case of walking songs well illustrates one way in which agency is embodied, a subject to which we now turn.

Embodiment

Accessing and using natural resources is often a very physical activity – distances must be travelled; water, firewood and thatching grass collected and carried. Participation in decision-making involves physical presence at particular times and in specific places. And yet the enacting of participatory natural resource management through corporeal human conduct is often neglected in analyses; little attention is given to how embodiment enables and constrains active participation (Jackson, 1998). Here I consider three aspects of embodiment which shape the exercise of agency: the physiological, social and political.

Natural resources are accessed and managed by sexed human beings who age, physically reproduce, and are of different sizes and strengths. This physiological embodiment shapes resource-related needs and access. The nature of the resource shapes the type of labour that must be performed, whilst technology may ameliorate or add to this burden (Wong, 2009). Where demands for labour increase, households may meet these requirements by increasing the *intensity* of their labour, possibly at the expense of the health and wellbeing (Jackson and Palmer-Jones, 1997).

It could be argued that, for many, able-bodiedness is key to the exercise of agency in participatory natural resource management. Public participation, using resources and interacting with others is shaped by physical capabilities; healthy and able-bodied individuals are most likely to be able to exercise effective agency in these respects. We have seen in Chapter 4 how poor families in Tanzania suffered multiple constraints on their physical ability to produce livelihoods, to travel and to engage socially. They gradually dropped out of associational life and became progressively more circumscribed in their natural resource use. Constraints on able-bodiedness and mobility ranged from diseases and disablement to the limitations imposed by caring for sick relatives, large numbers of very small children or carrying a difficult pregnancy. People suffering such problems were unable to contribute to collective action, attend meetings or social events or pay fees to clubs and associations. They were also unable to access distant resources, relied on very local supplies of grass, wood and water, or had to pay to buy these in small quantities (Cleaver, 2005). In other words, they were unable to fully exercise their agency in the maintenance of their livelihoods. Embodiment and agency are recursively linked. Campbell and Jovchelovitch (2000) also note the fact that people who lack the power to shape their lifecourses in strategic ways are significantly less likely to be healthy, a factor which can create a vicious cycle of disempowerment and poor health.

Even for healthy, mobile, able-bodied people, embodiment creates some challenges to the exercise of agency. In a project researching community-driven development in Tanzania and South Africa, community-based workers were asked to keep reflective diaries chronicling their work. The diaries detailing home visits, community mobilization and training activities are characterized by daily references to the workers' own physical states (being hungry, tired, hot, cold or wet) and the detrimental effects of this on their activities. The diaries well illustrate the ways in which both strategic action and everyday practice is shaped by embodied experiences as well as by personal interests and motivations (Boesten *et al.*, 2011).

Social positions are partly bodily defined and expressed through demeanour, voice or clothing. Such social markers are related to gendered divisions of labour and resource access, taboos and, as we have seen above, the ways in which people speak in public.

Bourdieu emphasizes the body in his discussion of habitus – for him the habitus moulds the human physique and the human body is an important signifier in social interaction, expressing social status and power as much as communicative intent. Deportment, ways of dressing and speaking are produced by and reproduce social structure (King, 2005: 223). This is well illustrated by the previous example of Zimbabwean women displaying physical expressions of humility, respectful forms of speech and silence in order to influence decision-making. Dikito-Wachtmeister further speculates about the impact of body size on the effective exercise of agency in participatory decision-making. Noting how the concept of a 'big man' or 'big woman' was used locally to denote wealth and prestige as well as physiology, she speculates that large body size often bestows authority in public decision-making contexts.

Access to natural resources is also enacted through *gendered* bodies. Taboos around menstruation, pregnancy and childbirth may restrict access to natural resources (particularly to water points), collective ceremonies and public appearances (Upperman, 2000). Additionally, gendered ideas about strength and physical ability, linked to divisions of labour and livelihood priorities, shape access and participation (Jackson, 1998, 2000). For example, in Zimbabwe, men rarely headload water, but generally deploy some means of transport (a wheelbarrow, cart, donkey or bicycle), whilst women and girl children carry heavy loads in buckets on their heads. Different physical norms of water carrying combined with gendered livelihood priorities shape preferences for using particular waterpoints. Men may be more willing to travel further to waterpoints with plentiful supply for livestock whereas women might weigh up the benefits of closeness with the constraints of queuing and the quality of water – definitions often also related to the amount of work implied in collection, queuing and use.

Not all agents have equal command over their physical selves. In India, higher-caste women may not collect water from public sources themselves, whilst scheduled caste and scheduled tribe women are socially constrained from accessing water in higher-caste public spaces and so incur additional work travelling further to other sources (Singh, 2008). Natural resources are often accessed through deploying the labour of others: children and junior wives sent to fetch water, herdsmen employed to take cattle to grazing lands, youth required to collect and carry firewood for their families. Such people are often the ones who shape, abide by or break the 'rules-in-use' relating to the natural resource, and yet may not be involved in participatory decision-making. How far the effective exercise of agency implies command over one's own labour and how far it can be exercised by commanding the labour of others is a moot point.

Within cosmologies which emphasize the connection between the living and the dead, between the world of natural resources, human beings and spirits, gods and ancestors the boundaries between the physical and spiritual become blurred. Supernatural forces may manifest through living people's physical bodies (most obviously when human mediums are possessed by spirits), through animals and things, and offer directions for the physical/social practices of those people. In the case of water, flow may be seen as positively or adversely affected by human/supernatural agency, and water can socially purify as well as be contaminated by witchcraft or socially polluting acts. Many people perceive connections between physical resource use, social behaviour and consequences in the natural world (for example on rainfall or water flows). Gendered meaning is encoded in cosmologies (Strang, 2005) and helps shape the parameters of individual behaviour.

The physiological and social aspects of resource access clearly have *political* ramifications, a point well illustrated by Ben Page in his account of the history of contested control over water in the Cameroonian town of Tombel. He documents a case of women taking to the streets in 1994 to protest against the government's attempts to close down public taps and charge users for water. At the front of this protest a few old women marched naked, urinated on the steps of the parastatal responsible for water supplies and threw down herbs with magical properties capable of transforming into poisonous snakes if anyone crossed the threshold. Men hid for fear of seeing the women naked and the parastatal staff fled, refusing to return to the office in fear of the wrath of the crowd and the old women's magic. The next day the government's engineers fled town. Page's analysis of this case includes the ways in which women used their naked bodies as the language of insult, reworking historic forms of protest in the modern era to speak to powerful actors (the government, politicians) by invoking worldviews emphasizing respect for elders and tradition (Page, 2005).

The social and territorial location of resource management has implications for power relations and political identities ranging from the everyday politics through which queues, rotations and collective labour are organized to the oppressive or empowering politics of the state (Mollinga, 2008, 2011). We have seen in Chapter 3 an example of the historical– political dimensions of embodiment in the ways in which the colonial experience of forced 'community' labour on water infrastructure shaped subsequent attitudes towards collective water labour and ideas about 'ownership' of that same infrastructure. Control over the labour of others and labour-saving, resource-shaping technology is also implicated in social and political influence. So in the Tanzanian irrigation schemes studies in Chapter 4, the wealthier farmers who owned power tillers were able to bring more land under cultivation, no longer relying simply of their own labour, and to rent out their power tillers to others. This command of technology and irrigated land, greater

productivity and resilience in markets was mirrored by their dispropor-
tionate influence in the management structures (a finding echoed by
Pant, 2005, for irrigation farmers in India).

Emotions and Reflexive Agency

We have already seen that social theorists conceptualize agency as more
complex than simply the exercise of 'rational choice' or even deliberate
reflection. They also recognize the importance of practical knowledge,
of unconscious motivations, the self-disciplining of agents and their
internalization of hegemonic norms (Giddens, 1984; Bourdieu 1977).
However, within such social theory approaches some argue that there
is a tendency to over-emphasize the discursive elements of agency and
to separate these out from other elements such as emotions (Holmes,
2010; Burkitt, forthcoming). Key to this debate is the nature of 'reflexivity'. For Margaret Archer (2003), reflexivity is synonymous with
self-reflection – it is the mental capacity of people, exercised through
an 'internal conversation', to consider themselves and their actions
in relation to their social context. For Anthony Giddens, reflexivity
is about how people, in circumstances where tradition has declined,
constantly adjust their lives in response to *knowledge* about changing
social circumstances. Such approaches, whilst richer than 'bounded
rationality' models of agency, still underplay the part emotions play in
people's social relationships and their responses to life's circumstances.
Holmes suggests that the exercise of agency is not simply about forming
and maintaining commitments to projects, but that reflexivity is 'an
emotional, embodied and cognitive process in which social actors have
feelings about and try to understand and alter their lives in relation to
their social and natural environment and to others' (Holmes, 2011:
140–42). Similarly, Burkitt argues against a model of agency that seems
to imply that knowledgeable agents are able to separate themselves from
the social world in order to monitor and reflect upon their choices
and actions. He suggests instead that feelings towards others, and our
perception of their judgements of us, centrally shape ourselves and our
own actions in social contexts (Burkitt, forthcoming).

How does this relate to the exercise of agency in natural resource
management and collective action? Both consciously and unconsciously
emotions are critical in shaping people's sense of self-efficacy, their social
relationships and therefore the extent to which they publicly engage
and assert their rights (Myers, 1996). Kabeer (2000) emphasizes that for
potential courses of action to become real, for example, for a woman
to claim her land rights, they must be both materially possible *and* be

conceived by the agent to be within the bounds of possibility. 'Imagined autonomy', also shaped by understanding of the perceptions of others, is therefore an important factor in people's idea of their own agency. Campbell and Jovchelovitch (2000), writing of the social psychology of health, link individuals' perception of self-efficacy to their placement in wider networks of social support and macro-social factors such as ethnicity, class and gender, which shape perceived self-efficacy. This layered analysis of the psychology of individuals in communities is a useful antidote to the methodological individualism of bounded rationality assumptions.

In this book we are interested in the ways that people's agency shapes and is shaped by institutions. Some insights can be gleaned from Mumby and Putnam's (1992) critique of understanding of behaviour in organizations. Questioning dominant bounded rationality assumptions about individual motivations, they bring these into dialogue with a concept of 'bounded emotionality' (although they reject a dichotomization of 'rationality' and 'emotionality'). They characterize bounded rationality as informed by intentional, reasoned and goal-directed models of human action, 'bounded' by the limitations of context and the ability to attain and process information. Institutionally, this model translates into the need for role-based hierarchies and rules, boundaries, the divorcing of physical labour and emotions from decision-making. By contrast (although carefully not counter-posed as an alternative), they suggest a model of bounded emotionality based on the recognition of inter-relatedness, tolerance of ambiguity, community and relational feelings and embodied self-identities. I suggest that several of these factors are evident in the ways that institutions formed through bricolage operate, as illustrated in Chapters 3 and 4. For example, they are prominent in people's general preference for bending the rules in the interests of conflict avoidance and reconciliation rather than 'impartially' upholding them through the rigorous exercise of monitoring and sanctions.

Some of the desire for relatedness, the importance of the judgement of others and the physicality of agency is this account given by a community grazing policeman from Zimbabwe. The role of this voluntary policeman in the village was to roam around the area seasonally prohibited to grazing, 'arresting' cattle encroaching on it and taking them to the headman's compound. He also acted as a community messenger. This young man did not directly benefit from the rotational grazing of cattle, did not own or control land and was not old enough or wealthy enough to ordinarily command respect. Nonetheless, he had volunteered for this role, about which he said:

To be a successful policeman you must catch offenders because then people will say 'that is a good policeman' and then they will confide in you and bring problems to you. I am very strict about devoting time to policing, even in the rainy season when there is plenty to do in the fields, because that is the only way to be a good policeman. (Cleaver, 1996: 212)

Holmes sees emotions as sensations that we manage according to socially shaped rules about emotional expression. 'Feeling rules' set out the norms of emotional behaviour in various situations. Examples might include the Turkish women in Uyan-Semerci's (2007) study who were socially 'prohibited' from laughing or talking loudly in public and expressed pleasure only through smiling; the feeling of humility expected of Zimbabwean women when dealing with elder men (Dikito-Wachtmeister, 2000); the self-disciplining of a Ghanaian woman who fears that if she is seen to inappropriately criticize authority she will be laughed at or become a target for witchcraft (Osei-Kufuor, 2010). The channelling of emotions through rituals and ceremonies can be construed a form of emotional labour by which people's behaviour is managed (and self-managed) in public contexts and aligned with 'rational' or instrumental approaches. For example, the common opening or handover ceremonies for new water infrastructure are often accompanied by pre-organized celebratory singing, expressions of praise for the implementing or funding agency, and statements of community worthiness, solidarity and responsibility. In these ways emotions are managed and govern public expression in a way which helps to secure public commitment to ongoing tasks of financing, maintenance and sustainability. Emotions can therefore be deployed as a form of power to bring about or to impede change. The invoking of feelings of caste-related shame and obligation in the village Joshi and Fawcett (2001) studied in India, or the invocation of feelings of humiliation and fear by the Tombel women in Page's study, seem to illustrate the ways in which both the powerful and the subaltern draw on emotions in their exercise of agency. 'Doing emotions well' is therefore a matter of work in public spaces and public decision-making, not just a privately exercised social skill, reproduced unconsciously.

Conclusion

This paper has raised and inevitably left unanswered a number of questions about agency. Conceptually, it leaves unresolved the question of where the boundaries of agency lie: are all actions constitutive of agency, whether conscious or unconscious, strategic or habitual? In thinking about the implications for the collective management of natural resources and the prospects for participatory governance, further questions and dilemmas arise. We need to think further about how far participatory development initiatives require people to exercise agency *within* the existing rules of the game, within the parameters of the programme or project on offer, the designed institutional arrangements. If we are interested in how institutions which shape access to rights and resources work, and how effective and equitable their outcomes are, we need better understandings of *why* and *how* individuals act and the balance between empowerment and constraint in such actions. Critically, we need to expand our gaze beyond visible public forums of decision-making to the places where agency is exercised through everyday practice. In particular, we need analyses which illuminate various aspects of agency in decision-making with a rigorous and differentiated scrutiny of the *effects* of such decision-making on different actors.

References

Adams, W., Watson, E. and Mutiso, S. (1997) 'Water, Rules and Gender: Water Rights in an Indigenous Irrigation System, Marakwet, Kenya', *Development and Change* 28, 4, pp. 707–30.

Agrawal, A. (2005) *Environmentality: Technologies of Government and the Making of Subjects.*

Ahlers, R. and Zwarteveen, M. (2009) 'The Water Question in Feminism: Water Control and Gender Inequities in a Neo-Liberal Era', *Gender, Place and Culture* 16, 4, pp. 409–26.

Ahmed, S. (2008) 'Challenging the Flow: Gendered Participation, Equity and Sustainability in Decentralised Water Governance in Gujarat', paper presented at SaciWATERs International Conference on Water Resources Policy in South Asia, Colombo, Sri Lanka, 17–20 December.

Arce, A. and Long, N. (2000) 'Reconfiguring Modernity and Development from an Anthropological Perspective', in A. Arce and N. Long (eds) *Anthropology, Development and Modernities: Exploring Discourses, Counter-Tendencies and Violence*, London, Routledge, pp. 1–30.

Archer, M. (2000) *Being Human: The Problem of Agency*, Cambridge, Cambridge University Press.

—(2003) *Structure, Agency and the Internal Conversation*, Cambridge, Cambridge University Press.

Arora-Jonsson, S. (2005) 'Unsettling the Order: Gendered Subjects and Grassroots Activism in Two Forest Communities', PhD thesis No. 2005: 70, Swedish University of Agricultural Sciences.

Ballet, J., Dubois, J.-L. and Mahieu, F.-R. (2007) 'Responsibility for Each Other's

Freedom: Agency as the Source of Collective Capability', *Journal of Human Development* 8, 2, pp. 185–201.

Bardhan, P. and Ray, I. (2006) 'Symposium on Anthropologists' Views on Common Resources: Methodological Approaches to the Question of the Commons', *Economic Development and Cultural Change* 54, 3, pp. 655–76.

Boelens, R. (2008) *The Rules of the Game and the Game of the Rules: Normalization and Resistance in Andean Water Control*, Wageningen, Wageningen University,

Boesten, J., Mdee, A., Cleaver, F. (2011) 'Service Delivery on the Cheap? Community-Based Workers in Development Interventions', *Development in Practice* 21, 1, pp. 41–58.

Bolt, V. and Bird, K. (2003) 'The Intra-Household Disadvantages Framework: A Framework for the Analysis of Intra-Household Difference and Inequality', *IDPM/Chronic Poverty Research Centre Working Paper Series* 32.

Bourdieu, P. (1977) *Outline of a Theory of Practice*, Cambridge, Cambridge University Press.

Burkitt, I. (2012) 'Emotional Reflexivity: Feeling, Emotion and Imagination in Reflexive Dialogues', *Sociology*, published online March 15, 2012. http://soc.sagepub.com/content/early/2012/03/14/0038038511422587.abstract.

Campbell, C. and Jovchelovitch, S. (2000) 'Health, Community and Development: Towards a Social Psychology of Participation', *Journal of Community and Applied Social Psychology* 10, pp. 255–70.

Cleaver, F. (2005) 'The Inequality of Social Capital and the Reproduction of Chronic Poverty', *World Development* 33, 6, pp. 893–906.

Cleaver, F. and Elson, D. (1995) 'Women and Water Resources: Continued Marginalisation and New Policies', IIED, Gatekeeper Series 49.

Cleaver, F. and Nyatsambo, R. (2011) 'Gender and Integrated Water Resource Management', in R. Grafton and K. Hussey (eds) *Water Resources Planning and Management*, Cambridge, Cambridge University Press, pp. 311–30.

Cornwall, A. (2004) 'Spaces for Transformation? Reflections in Issues of Power and Difference in Participation in Development', in S. Hickey and G. Mohan (eds) *Participation: From Tyranny to Transformation*, London, Zed Books.

De Herdt, T. and Abega, S. (2007) 'The Political Complexity of Pro-Poor Policy Processes in the Mandara Mountains, Cameroon', *Journal of Human Development* 8, 2, pp. 303–23.

Delgado, J. V. and Zwarteveen, M. (2007) 'The Public and Private Domain of the Everyday Politics of Water', *International Feminist Journal of Politics* 9, 4, pp. 503–11.

Deneulin, S. and De Herdt, T. (2007) 'Individual Freedoms as Relational Experiences: Guest Editors' Introduction', *Journal of Human Development and Capabilities* 8, 2, pp. 179–84.

Dikito-Wachtmeister, M. (2000) 'Women's Participation in Decision-Making Processes in Rural Water Projects, Makoni District, Zimbabwe', unpublished PhD thesis, University of Bradford.

Douglas, M. (1987) *How Institutions Think*, London, Routledge and Kegan Paul.

Giddens, A. (1984) *The Constitution of Society: Outline of the Theory of Structuration*, Cambridge, Polity Press.

—(1996) 'Affluence, Poverty and the Idea of a Post-Scarcity Society', *Development and Change* 27, 2, pp. 365–77.

Granovetter, M. (1985) 'Economic Action and Social Structure: The Problem of Embeddedness', *American Journal of Sociology* 91, pp. 481–93.

Greener, I. (2002) 'Agency, Social Theory and Social Policy', *Critical Social Policy* 22, 4, pp. 688–705.

Gross, N. (2005) 'The Detraditionalization of Intimacy Reconsidered', *Sociological Theory* 23, 3, pp. 286–311.

Henriques, J., Hollway, W., Urwin, C., Venn, C. and Walkerdine, V. (1984) *Changing the Subject: Psychology, Social Regulation and Subjectivity*, London. Methuen.

Hickey, S. and Mohan, G. (2004) 'Relocating Participation Within a Radical Politics of Development: Critical Modernism and Citizenship', in S. Hickey and G. Mohan (eds) *Participation: From Tyranny to Transformation? Exploring New Approaches to Participation in Development*, London, Zed Books.

Hoggett, P. (2001) 'Agency, Rationality and Social Policy', *Journal of Social Policy* 30, 1, pp. 37–56.

Holmes, M. (2010) 'The Emotionalization of Reflexivity', *Sociology* 44, 1, pp. 139–54.

House, S. (2003) 'Easier to Say, Harder to Do: Gender, Equity and Water', paper presented at the Alternative Water Forum, University of Bradford, 1–2 May.

Ibrahim, S. S. (2006) 'From Individual to Collective Capabilities: The Capability Approach as a Conceptual Framework for Self-Help', *Journal of Human Development* 7, 3, pp. 397–416.

Impey, A. (2009) 'Songs of Mobility and Belonging: Gender, Spatiality and the Local in Southern Africa's Transfrontier Conservation Development', paper presented at 54th Society for Ethnomusicology Conference, November 19–22, Mexico City.

Jackson, C. (1998) 'Gender, Irrigation and Environment: Arguing for Agency', *Agriculture and Human Values* 15, 4, pp. 313–24.

Jackson, C. and Palmer-Jones, R. (1997) 'Work Intensity, Poverty and Gender in Sustainable Development', *Food Policy* 22, 1, pp. 39–62.

Jaworski, A. (2005) 'Introduction: Silence in Institutional and Intercultural Contexts', *Multilingua* 24, pp. 1–6.

Johnson, C. (2004) 'Uncommon Ground: The "Poverty of History" in Common Property Discourse', *Development and Change* 35, 3, pp. 407–33.

Joshi, D. and Fawcett, B. (2001) 'Water, Hindu Mythology and an Unequal Social Order in India', paper presented at the Second Conference of the International Water History Association, Bergen, August.

—(2005) 'The Role of Water in an Unequal Social Order in India', in A. Coles and T. Wallace (eds) *Gender, Water and Development*, Oxford, Berg, pp. 39–56.

Joshi, D., Lloyd, M. and Fawcett, B. (2003) 'Voices from the Village: An Alternative Paper for the Alternative Water Forum', paper presented at the Alternative Water Forum, Bradford Centre for International Development, University of Bradford, 1–2 May.

Kabeer, N. (2000) 'Resources, Agency, Achievements: Reflections on the

Measurement of Women's Empowerment', in R. Shahra (ed.) *Gendered Poverty and Well-Being*, Oxford, Blackwell.

Kesby, M. (2005) 'Retheorising Empowerment-Through – Participation as a Performance in Space: Beyond Tyranny to Transformation', *Signs: Journal of Women in Culture and Society* 30, 4, pp. 2037–65.

King, A. (2005) 'Structure and Agency', in A. Harrington (ed.) *Modern Social Theory: An Introduction*, Oxford, OUP, pp. 215–32.

Levi, M. (1996) 'Social and Unsocial Capital: A Review Essay of Robert Putnam's Making Democracy Work', *Politics and Society* 24, 1, pp. 45–55.

Long, A. (1992) 'From Paradigm Lost to Paradigm Regained? The Case for an Actor-Oriented Sociology of Development', in N. Long and A. Long (eds) *Battlefields of Knowledge: The Interlocking of Theory and Practice in Social Research and Development*, London, Routledge, pp. 16–43.

Long, N. (2001) *Development Sociology: Actor Perspectives*, London, Routledge.

Lukes, S. (2005) *Power: A Radical View*, Basingstoke, Palgrave Macmillan, 2nd edition.

Maganga, F. (2003) 'Customary Systems and Water Governance: Insights from Southern Africa', Seminar 5 on Splash water governance website, University of Bradford, http://www.splash.bradford.ac.uk/project-four/.

Masaki, K. (2004) 'The Transformative Unfolding of Tyrannical Participation: The Corvée Tradition and Ongoing Local Politics in Western Nepal', in S. Hickey and G. Mohan (eds) *Participation: From Tyranny to Transformation? Exploring New Approaches to Participation*, London, Zed Books, pp. 125–39.

McNay, L. (2000) *Gender and Agency: Reconfiguring the Subject in Feminist and Social Theory*, Cambridge, Polity Press.

Merrey, D. J., Meinzen-Dick, R., Mollinga, P. and Karar, E. (2007) 'Policy and Institutional Reform: The Art of the Possible', in D. Molden (ed.) *Water for Food, Water for Life: A Comprehensive Assessment of Water Management in Agriculture*, London, Earthscan, pp. 193–231.

Mollinga, P. (2008) 'Water, Politics and Development: Framing a Political Sociology of Water Resources Management', *Water Alternatives* 1, 1, pp. 7–23.

Mollinga, P. (2011) 'The Material Conditions of a Polarized Discourse: Clamours and Silences in Critical Analysis of Agricultural Water Use in India', *Journal of Agrarian Change* 10, 3, pp. 414–36.

Mosse, D. (1997) 'The Symbolic Making of a Common Property Resource: History, Ecology and Locality in a Tank-Irrigated Landscape in South India', *Development and Change* 28, 3, pp. 467–504.

Mumby, D. K. and Putnam, L. (1992) 'The Politics of Emotion: A Feminist Reading of "Bounded Rationality"', *Academy of Management Review* 17, pp. 465–86.

Myers, D. (1996) *Social Psychology*, New York, McGraw-Hill.

Nabanoga, G. N. (2005) 'Transgressing Boundaries: Gendered Spaces, Species, and Indigenous Forest management in Uganda', PhD thesis, Wageningen University.

Odgaard, R. (2002) 'Scrambling for Land in Tanzania: Processes of Formalisation and Legitimisation of Land Rights', *The European Journal of Development Research* 14, 2, pp. 71–88.

Osei-Kufuor, P. (2010) 'Does Institutionalising Decentralisation Work? Rethinking Agency, Institutions and Authority in Local Governance: A Case Study Ntonaboma in Kwahu-North District, Ghana', unpublished PhD thesis, University of Bradford.

Ostrom, E. (2005) *Understanding Institutional Diversity*, Princeton, Princeton University Press.

Page, B. (2005) 'Naked Power: Women and the Social Production of Water in Anglophone Cameroon', in A. Coles and T. Wallace (eds) *Gender, Water and Development*, Oxford, Berg, pp. 57–76.

Pant, N. (2005) 'Control of an Access to Groundwater in UP', *Economic and Political Weekly*, pp. 30–36.

Pretty, J. (2003) 'Social Capital and the Collective Management of Resources', *Science* 302, pp. 1912–14.

Rao, N. (2003) 'Only Women Can and Will Represent Women's Interests: The Case of Land Rights', paper presented at the Workshop on Gender Myths and Feminist Fables: Repositioning Gender in Development Policy and Practice, Institute of Development Studies, University of Sussex, 2–4 July.

Rapport, N. and Overing, J. (2000) *Social and Cultural Anthropology: The Key Concepts*, London, Routledge.

Sen, A. (1999) *Development as Freedom*, Oxford, Oxford University Press.

Singh, N. (2008) 'Equitable Gender Participation in Local Water Governance: An Insight into Institutional Paradoxes', *Water Resources Management* 22, 7, pp. 925–42.

SMUWC (2001) 'SMUWC Final Report: Rural Livelihoods', http://www.usangu.org/reports/rural.pdf.

Strang, V. (2004) *The Meaning of Water*, Oxford, Berg.

—(2005) 'Taking the Waters: Cosmology, Gender and Material Culture in the Appropriation of Water Resources', in A. Coles and T. Wallace (eds) *Gender, Water and Development*, Oxford, Berg, Oxford, pp. 21–38.

Tukai, R. (2005) 'Gender and Access in Pastoral Communities: Re-evaluating Community Participation and Gender Empowerment', paper presented at the ESRC seminar Access, Poverty and Social Exclusion, ODI, London, 1 March.

Upperman, E. (2000) 'Gender Relations in a Traditional Irrigation Scheme in Northern Tanzania', in C. Creighton and C. Omari (eds) *Gender, Family and Work in Tanzania*, Aldershot, Ashgate, pp. 357–79.

Uyan-Semerci, P. (2007) 'A Relational Account of Nussbaum's List of Capabilities', *Journal of Human Development* 8, 2, pp. 203–22.

Van Hecken, G. and Bastiaensen, J. (2010) 'Payments for Ecosystem Services in Nicaragua: Do Market-based Approaches Work?' *Development and Change* 41, 3, pp. 421–44.

Vatn, A. (2009) 'Cooperative Behavior and Institutions', *Journal of Socio-Economics* 38, 1, pp. 188–96.

Von Benda-Beckman, F. and Von Benda-Beckman, K. (2006) 'The Dynamics of Change and Continuity in Plural Legal Orders', *Journal of Legal Pluralism* 53–4, pp. 1–44.

Watson, E. (2003) 'Examining the Potential of Indigenous Institutions for Development: The Case from Borana, Ethiopia', *Development and Change* 34, 2, pp. 287–309.

Wong, S. (2009) 'Climate Change and Sustainable Technology: Re-linking Nature, Governance and Gender', *Gender and Development* 17, 1, pp. 95–108.

6 Piecing Together Policy Knowledge: Promises and Pitfalls

Introduction

This chapter considers how policy is formed through processes of bricolage. By tracking policy formation over time, the chapter explores the role of policy-makers as bricoleurs and considers both the authoritative and negotiated nature of the process. The creation of epistemic communities around accepted knowledge is shown to be of relevance to the ways in which particular ideas about resource governance become accepted and legitimized. Tensions between the received need for continuity and innovation in policy are considered. The chapter illustrates these points with examples drawn from the author's experience of attempting to shape water governance policy as formed and implemented by the British Department for International Development.[1]

Is Policy Pieced Together or Designed?

So far, we have considered how people in local communities operate as bricoleurs, patching together joint arrangements for natural resource management, within patterns of structural constraint. Now, let us shift our focus to the domain of development planning and explore the ways in which knowledge is pieced together to form policy.

How far can the formation of policy be characterized as a process of rational and deliberate 'design' or one of 'bricolage'? The chapter draws on my own experience of generating knowledge about water governance and of trying to feed this into policy-making. It considers how ideas about resource governance and equity were understood in the policy-making process and examines the different perspectives of some of the actors involved.

Here I suggest that policy-making is only partly a matter of rational or evidence-based design. It is also pieced together in a more improvised way through bricolage (Freeman, 2007). Processes of path dependence ensure that some elements of policy remain largely unchanged over time. The shared meanings embedded in policy are shaped by assumptions about the nature of the world and by the powerful ways in which authoritative knowledge communities frame understandings. However, bricolage does not merely reproduce past policy or dominant models. The need to respond to topical political priorities, the influence of particular actors, time and resource availability can also prompt innovations and novel reconfigurations of policy. New or reinvented elements of policy are assembled and legitimized by reference to selected 'evidence' of what has worked in the past or to what is considered 'best practice'. Such processes can result in dominant policy models which are also littered with discontinuities and dissenting voices, as in the case of the global consensus on water policy.

Let us begin this exploration of policy-making as bricolage with a thumbnail sketch of elements of a water policy developed by the British Department for International Development (2008a). In the autumn of 2008 the department held a stakeholder meeting at which it launched its new water policy. The policy was the culmination of a process prompted by a number of factors, which included:

- The need to deliver on pledges set out in the 2006 White Paper and on international commitments; in particular the need to speed up progress towards meeting the Millennium Development Goals.
- Pressure to respond to a partly critical report from the Parliamentary Inquiry into Water and Sanitation (House of Commons, 2007).
- The need to relate water policy to DFID's new priority areas of economic growth, fragile states, climate change and international aid architecture. Also, the need to relate water to DFID's strong interest in 'good governance' (Department for International Development, 2006).
- Lobbying, particularly from NGOs, for a greater emphasis on sanitation.
- The actions of a Minister for International Development with a lively interest in water, endeavouring to increase its political and organizational prominence.

The publicly observable formulation of the policy had included the commissioning of thematic background papers from consultants and academics, the holding of stakeholder consultation meetings and e-mail discussions. There was much to admire in this policy, including the commitment to targeting funds to poor communities. The policy claimed to identify three new priority areas, these being sanitation, water resources management and governance. The latter covered areas of concern such as a perceived lack of political will and capability in recipient governments, and a lack of financing. However, overall, the new policy offered shifts in emphases rather than radical departures from previous policies; the impact of the commissioned background papers appeared minimal. At the official launch many of the stakeholders who had contributed during the consultation process reiterated points which they felt had been overlooked.

Previous policies, in line with an international consensus on water resource management, had emphasized community management, cost recovery, increased commercialization and private sector participation as essential to achieving the goals of water for all (Department for International Development, 2008b). The 2008 policy recognized the some of the shortcomings of these approaches but struggled to reconcile these with continued commitments to particular policies. So, for example, the policy document states on the one hand that:

> Donors, partner governments and NGOs have overestimated the capacity of communities to manage and maintain their own systems and recovering user fees from consumers to cover operation and maintenance has continued to prove difficult ... the private sector has not invested anywhere near as much in water as was anticipated ... something unlikely to change in the short term given global credit conditions. (DFID, 2008a: 7)

However, it goes on to reiterate the value of community contributions of cash and labour (for sustainable management) and the need for significant private sector involvement (for increased coverage). Tensions appear, particularly where the policy document struggles to reconcile the conventional wisdom of the international water consensus with a concern with the poorest. For example, it states that: 'evidence suggests that some contributions from communities, whether in the form of cash or labour, helps to provide a sense of ownership that ensure water supplies are maintained' (35). But, elaborating on approaches to ensure 'flexible payment arrangements for the poor', the document continues, 'We also recognise that at least in the short term, food shortages and price increases may limit the use of this approach because households simply do not have any money to spend on non-food items' (35). The document further acknowledging problems that the poorest people are unlikely to gain access to water and sanitation through contemporary policy approaches: 'those left unserved after the MDG target deadline of 2015 will include the poorest and most vulnerable and marginalised, often in the most remote or water-scarce areas, or in areas of conflict or fragility' (36).

So, the policy contains inconsistencies and uses 'evidence' to apparently make contradictory points. An emphasis on increased involvement of communities and the private sector sits uneasily beside the acknowledgement of the limitations of either approach in delivering water access for poor people. The co-existence in one document of apparently incompatible concerns and approaches is partly because policy is intended to speak in different ways to a number of audiences. In this case we could identify the targets as the UK government (the minister, the Parliamentary Committee for International Development, the Treasury), the domestic water stakeholder community (NGOs, academics, consultants), the British public (as taxpayers, voters), multi-lateral aid agencies (the EU, African Development Bank and World Bank, through which DFID channels half of its funds for water and sanitation), the bilaterals (such as the Dutch and Swedish development agencies amongst whom DFID see themselves as leaders) and recipient country governments (for example, those receiving direct budget support, such as Tanzania and Uganda).

The 'evidence' cited in this document, though, suggests that knowledge generation is an authoritative process with some stakeholders holding far more power to define the agenda than others. Evidence is cited in the form of illustrative text boxes of examples of success/best practice and in statistics mostly derived from the publications of international development agencies. About 50 per cent of the references cited (21 of 43) are to the publications and policy documents of multilateral development agencies (WHO, UNDP, World Bank, UNICEF etc.); another 25 per cent refer to DFID's own policy documents, UK policy documents or reports commissioned by DFID; and the final 25 per cent are publications produced by NGOs and a smattering of journal articles, mostly written by professionals with strong connections to DFID or to the multilaterals.

It is, then, clear that the policy was created through a process of consultation and negotiation between different stakeholders and in response to a variety of influences. This is reflected in shifts in emphasis in presentation of the problems and their solution, compared to previous policy statements. However, it is also very clear that the policy is formulated within an authoritative community of knowledge, which values and validates certain explanations of cause and effect above others. To reflect on policy-making as an authoritative process, let us now consider the nature of knowledge and the actors who generate it.

Knowledge Production and Epistemic Communities

In the piecing together of policy, not all knowledge is equally influential or valued. Burawoy's (2005) classification of types of knowledge produced in sociology provides a useful frame for reflecting on the dynamics of producing 'public' knowledge, including policy. Burawoy classifies knowledge production as dividing into four approaches arranged along two axes. One axis refers to whether the aim is to produce instrumental or reflexive knowledge and the other to whether the audience is academic or extra-academic. Burawoy (2006) characterizes policy knowledge as largely instrumental, characterized by its concrete, problem-solving and pragmatic nature. By contrast, 'critical knowledge' is produced for and by academics and involves examining the value assumptions underlying the identification of problems and their solutions. 'Critical knowledge' may therefore raise questions rather than simply offer solutions. Burawoy argues for a kind of synthesis of types of knowledge into a reflexive public knowledge which is communicative and concerned with understanding and addressing societal problems through dialogue. However, he notes that power relations mean that instrumental knowledge is often more valued and prevails over reflexive knowledge.

The generation of water knowledge often falls into the professional and policy categories of Burawoy's matrix, being concerned with resolving water related problems through development interventions. The dominance of instrumental knowledge (reinforced by the cultures of development agencies, regimes of funding, professional

Figure 6.1 Elaborating the types of sociological knowledge

	Academic audience	*Extra-academic audience*
Instrumental knowledge	*Professional sociology*	*Policy sociology*
Knowledge	Theoretical/empirical	Concrete
Truth	Correspondence	Pragmatic
Legitimacy	Scientific norms	Effectiveness
Accountability	Peers	Clients/Patrons
Pathology	Self-referentiality	Servility
Politics	Professional self-interest	Policy intervention
Reflexive knowledge	*Critical Sociology*	*Public Sociology*
Knowledge	Foundational	Communicative
Truth	Normative	Consensus
Legitimacy	Moral vision	Relevance
Accountability	Critical intellectuals	Designated publics
Pathology	Dogmatism	Faddishness
Politics	Internal debate	Public dialogue

Reproduced from Burawoy (2005) with permission from John Wiley & Sons Ltd.

career trajectories) results in the valorization of certain types of water knowledge above others. Critical knowledge, in the form of examining the worldviews and assumptions which underpin knowledge, is rather scarce in the field of water policy.

To understand how this categorization applies to water policy, consider the roles and perspectives of some of the different actors in the policy-making process. I categories these broadly as 'uncertainty reducers' and 'uncertainty creators', as illustrated by the following contrasting statements on water governance. In evidence to the parliamentary inquiry in 2006, my academic colleagues and I stressed the *complexity* of issues involved:

> Water governance works out at through dynamic political processes of power and negotiations, particularly at the interface between service providers and users. General principles must be balanced with context-specific initiatives and there is a need to work at the messy middle between policy-making and local level practices. (Cleaver *et al.*, 2005)

In contrast, at a consultation on DFID's new water policy (24 May 2007), one senior international policymaker emphasized the need, when formulating water governance policy, to 'debunk the language, simplify the ideas. No nuances, no problems, just solutions.'

In writing of epistemic communities (Haas, 1992) characterizes policy-makers as 'uncertainty reducers' who, in conditions of uncertainty, draw on networks of knowledge professionals to articulate cause–effect relationships, frame issues and propose policies. Such interlocking networks often become self-referential and self-reinforcing, creating mainstream 'consensus' views on the right direction for policy, as we shall see later. Civil servants tend to see themselves as 'uncertainty reducers'. In a study of civil servants in industrialized countries (Aberbach *et al.*, 1981, cited by Haas, 1992) showed that the majority of them considered themselves technicians, implementing practical solutions to problems, rather than brokers between competing ideas/solutions. In contrast, many researchers (particularly in social sciences) consider their role to be 'uncertainty creators' unsettling established categories, questioning assumptions of cause and effect, and problematizing and scrutinizing implied principles (Corbridge, 2005). Commenting on these different perceptions of what constitutes good evidence, one senior British civil servant observed that the qualifications and caveats surrounding academic work are of little interest to politicians and bureaucrats: 'Policy-makers will use any evidence that can help them make a decision that seems reasonable, has a clear message and is available at the right time' (Davis, 2005, quoted in Young and Mendizabal, 2009).

Some commentators perceive a fundamental mismatch between the needs of policy and the requirements of good quality research. For Collingridge and Reeve (1986), the dysfunctionality of the research/policy relationship derives from adherence to two unsustainable myths. Firstly, the *rationality myth* supposes that policy decisions must be informed by significant data collection (treated as evidence), which reduces uncertainty. Secondly, the *power of science* myth holds that the research community has the ability to provide data at such times and in forms useful to policy-makers. Collingridge and Reeve propose instead that policy decisions, being political, can readily be made with scanty initial information; mistakes are unavoidable (even with vast quantities of information); and therefore it makes sense to favour choices which are flexible and to implement decision-making systems which allow for the early detection of errors and modification of policy.

The model of policy decision-making as a rational bureaucratic exercise that shapes development interventions has also been challenged, for example by David Mosse (2004). He sees policy as primarily used as a legitimizing and authoritative tool for development practices which are more directly shaped by personal relationships and organizational cultures in different contexts. Policy-making as rational design is situated in the 'perpetual present' rather than the longer historical perspective, so overlooking or under-emphasizing key elements of societal experience which may shape its efficacy (Lewis, 2009).

Further, all types of knowledge generation, collection and translation are shaped by the organizational context and by the ways in which brico-leurs learn. Discussing human decision-making in a business context, David Snowden (2003) suggests that people in organizations do not make logical decisions based on information input. Rather, they pattern match with their own experience and with collective or institutional experience expressed as stories (often 'best practice' stories). Shared context is vital to knowledge exchange and this usually involves some kind of authoritative validation of information from a trusted human contact. People fail to perceive or significantly acknowledge relation-ships, phenomena and outcomes which do not match their expectations.

For example, at the time the water policy was produced, the internal procedures of DFID required policy to be supported by 'evidence' for it to pass through various stages of approval. In a model borrowed from medical knowledge, there have been various attempts made to undertake 'systematic reviews' of evidence of the efficacy of particular development interventions. Such approaches involve addressing very narrowly defined cause-and-effect questions and assessing the 'robustness' of sources and data which apparently address them. However, studies of the way knowledge is used in DFID (Mendizabal and Jones, 2010) shows a rather unreflexive preference for certain types of 'evidence' above others. In this study the informants, all DFID staff employed across a range of level of seniority and functions, strongly preferred to draw evidence from:

- Studies they already know.
- Studies that validate existing knowledge, especially 'mainstream' approaches within the organization.
- Their own experience.
- Information from trusted personal contacts.

In addition the types of data preferred were:

- Quantitative.
- Concerned with value for money.
- Expressed in short form.
- Illustrations of best practice.

Types of knowledge which were less valued, and were not sought were:

- Studies searched for from the organizational database.
- Studies tangential to their direct focus/problem.
- Qualitative evidence.
- Examples of 'bad practice' or failure.
- Alternative or contesting voices/evidence.

Whilst this highly instrumental approach to knowledge is understandable within the expectations and constraints of a particular organizational culture, and in a specific political climate, it has certain potentially detrimental outcomes. As Mendizabal and Jones (2010) point out, there is a strong tendency to 'reinvent the wheel': certain types of knowledge and evidence are recycled and reinvested with authority, dissenting voices (including innovatory insights from tangential areas) blocked out. Moreover, 'evidence' which suggests a broader political economy approach to addressing water problems is often sidelined in favour of much narrower technical or managerial fixes.

Negotiating instrumental and reflexive knowledge

Generating the evidence to press into the service of knowledge is not a neutral exercise but reflects the patternings of social structure. Piecing together policy through 'bricolage' means there is potential to include new insights and innovations, but the ways that understandings of the world are cognitively institutionalized often means that policy reproduces dominant views and power relations.

To explore how knowledge is generated by various actors, pieced together through bricolage and amplified or muted through relations of power, let us consider the case of knowledge production about the Usangu plains in Tanzania. The example is drawn from the DFID-funded project, the Sustainable Management of the Usangu Wetland and its Catchment (SMUWC), introduced in Chapter 4.

The project explicitly attempted to generate knowledge to address development problems. It aimed to diagnose the causes of the shrinking of the Usangu wetlands and reduced flows downstream in the Ruaha River. At the start of the project the dominant views amongst policy-makers were that the depletion and degradation of the resources was caused by the irresponsible livelihood practices of pastoralists allowing their large herds of cattle to overgraze the wetland. The project was designed to produce instrumental knowledge to guide local policy-makers in the sustainable management of the wetland and to feed this into training and capacity building for local government.

The project produced a substantial body of data, generating greater knowledge and understanding of the multiple causes of changes in the wetlands (Lankford *et al.*, 2004). However, the project had very limited success in influencing policy because it was unable to formulate knowledge consistent with the worldviews of policy-makers. The research team struggled to communicate findings to the policy-makers for a number of reasons.

Firstly, there was a perception that the research had little relationship to action as represented by the views of one District Commissioner on project start up, who said 'No more studies. We want action.'

Secondly, the study team were unable to shift the policy bias against pastoralists. The project discovered that cattle numbers had been grossly overestimated by the authorities and that water resource depletion was largely the result of dry season irrigated agriculture. However, this finding challenged locally held prejudices as well as institutionalized ideas about the need for modernization and development (epitomized by irrigated agriculture) and the backwardness of pastoralist values and practices. Dominant views proved difficult to shift, even in the face of such 'evidence', because they were embedded in institutionalized power relations permeating the state from national to local levels (Walsh, 2007, 2008, 2012). These dominant views leaked into other areas of social categorization; for example, the presumed pastoralism/agriculture divide was also expressed in ethnic categorizations even where the evidence was these identities were blurred and fluctuating.

Thirdly, the study team, having spent the duration of the project generating in-depth knowledge of people–environment interlinkages, were uncomfortable about engaging in the gross abstractions and generalizations required to translate the local-level findings into lessons for national-level policy. Such simplifications are a necessary part of policy formulation, but inevitably involve the authoritative selection and amplification of some knowledge and the sidelining of other evidence. The case also illustrates the different perceptions, motivations and practices even of categorically similar actors in 'knowledge bricolage'. For example, at the end of the project, there were varied views from the different academics involved about the amounts of data produced. Lankford (a specialist in irrigation water management) and his colleagues argued for the need for *more* data generation from large-scale, long-term interdisciplinary research, centred on hydrological studies and irrigation, linked to action–research initiatives to increase the likely uptake of results (Lankford *et al.*, 2004). By contrast, Walsh, an anthropologist, confessed how he struggled to disentangle his role as academic and development practitioner in Usangu. He gives an account of how the politics of knowledge production (and insufficient reflexivity) about Usangu results in the reproduction, over time, of ignorance about the major fault lines of social inequality (Walsh, 2006).

It is simplistic to suggest clearly demarcated perspectives between different actors and discrete reservoirs of knowledge which only need to be commensurated to produce rational and integrated policy. Rather, the plural nature of water governance arrangements, stakeholders and practices suggest more polycentric processes of knowledge production. Policy is shaped by diverse and unequal stakeholders, pieced together from various arrangements and sources of knowledge (Court and Young, 2004; Merrey *et al.*, 2007).

In water management literature significant attention *is* paid to how different groups of actors conceptualize problems and negotiate agreements about how to deal with them (Wegerich and Warner, 2010). Such processes do not necessarily result in more 'democratic' knowledge or in policy approaches which ensure fairness of resource distribution. Public spaces intended for the negotiation of different interests (often called multi-stakeholder platforms) are imbued with power relations (Warner, 2007). In the interests of avoiding conflicts and securing agreements, different groups of actors may 'foreground' issues on which they can agree and avoid or 'background' more contentious issues or the deeper fault-lines which divide them. Lukes (2005) cogently defines power as partly consisting of the ability to define the agenda, to shape what is publicly addressed, *and* what goes unsaid and unexamined. It is to the relationship between 'evidence' and 'power' in knowledge production and the challenges of maintaining reflexivity in processes of bricolage that we now turn.

From Social Ontologies to Success Stories

Here I draw on social theory and examples to illustrate how instrumental knowledge is always underpinned by particular assumptions about the nature of the world and cause–effect relationships. These unspoken assumptions and models, and the relationships of power through which they are perpetuated, shape policy knowledge in particular ways. Assumptions about the nature of the world are institutionalized in organizations and communities of knowledge so that it becomes very difficult to approach policy with a clean slate. In this way policy is not simply a process of deliberate rational design but contains many shadowy places in which are hidden the assumptions and worldviews which also shape knowledge production.

In attempting to understand how policy is made, it is easy to concentrate entirely on the sort of instrumental knowledge that is articulated in policy documents. Margaret Archer's (1998) analysis of social theory provides some useful critical pointers here. Writing of social policy, she suggests that instrumental approaches detach practical explanations of events and outcomes from wider understandings of cause effect relationships and the nature of the world. Rather she suggests that three elements of the construction of social theory and policy are necessarily interlinked. These are shown in in Figure 6.2.

For Archer, each element is indispensible to generating understandings of the social world and each shapes the others. However, she suggests that instrumentalism (a common approach in policy-making and policy-related research) uncouples the last element (the category

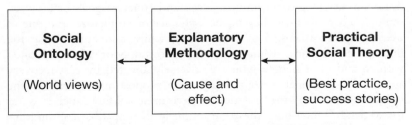

Figure 6.2 Linking social theory and social policy (Adapted from Archer, 1998)

of 'practical social theory' or best practices) from the first two. Policy approaches to knowledge in the project of 'development' are largely instrumentalist: worldviews are unacknowledged or taken for granted; explanatory methodologies become a collection of indices with demonstrable workability through their an apparent capacity to attribute effects to causes; and practical social theory becomes an amalgamation of assorted and often contradictory 'best practices' or 'success stories'. For Archer, this approach of practical utility generates theoretical inconsistency, as there is nothing to guarantee mutual coherence of the multiple examples of best practice. This results in the policy being an amalgamation of incompatible concepts retained because of their apparent workability (Archer, 1998).

Let us consider some of these points with reference to water policy. Policies often are often a collection of mutually incompatible concepts, as we have seen for example in the case of water policy where a concern for ensuring the poorest gain access to water is contradicted by an emphasis on payments for water services. Incompatible elements of policy may be retained for various reasons: because of their individual utility (some evidence of success exists); because of path dependence (the authority of what has gone before); or because of the hegemony of dominant ideas within epistemic communities. The inherent contradictions in policy are then glossed over in public presentation in order to legitimise and gain support for policy-making processes.

Whilst policy-makers may be rightly interested in 'what works' and see theory as irrelevant, underlying concepts *are* central to shaping understandings of how and why certain outcomes are obtained. Approaches which 'decouple' success stories from worldviews and cause–effect explanations detach discrete contextualized experiences from any means of understanding their broader relevance.

Reflecting on the shortcomings of understandings of environmental governance Fischer *et al.*, (2007) highlight the normative assumptions which shape interventions but also point out that these assumptions are often unspoken in policy statements. They show how contradictions can occur between implicit ideals and concrete goals or between multiple goals. Thus, policy in the water sector emphasizes the role of user payments in ensuring sustainability, whilst also highlighting the importance of gender, equity and support for the poor, when it is often women and poor people who are adversely affected by cost-recovery approaches. National water policies often propose investments in the irrigation sector and the retention of environmental flows such as water for wetlands, when both these are mutually incompatible consumptive uses. In the SMUWC example, the Tanzanian government proposed to restore year-round flows in the river Ruaha, whilst simultaneously advocating increased use of dry-season flows for irrigation. It was dry-season diversion of river water that diminished overall flows in the river. Within the irrigation sector itself, there are continuing inherent tensions between concepts of efficiency and equity. In theory water flows may be effectively controlled and monitored (using canal gates) by those farmers who cultivate at the head-end of the irrigation scheme, who are in a good position to easily monitor the opening and closing of the gates. However, downstream farmers may receive fairer allocations of water if head-end irrigators have less control of the gates and water flows.

The importance of ontologies or worldviews in shaping policy models of governance and associated actions is illustrated in Moretto's (2007) article on urban water governance. This argues that differing underlying views of society shape the different models of urban water governance promoted by the World Bank and UN-Habitat. Whilst both avowedly aim to facilitate equitable and efficient access to urban water services through support to small- scale providers, their diverging ontological assumptions about the desirability of market choices or community ownership, competition and cooperation, economic and social performance shape the forms of their interventions. For example, the World Bank policy emphasizes the importance of supporting private, independent providers whilst UN-Habitat's approach rather emphasizes support to communities in managing and regulating water supply arrangements.

Policy, then, is not just rationally crafted, guided by evidence, but also is shaped by underlying worldviews which often reflect structural allocations of power and resources in society.

Are best practices a useful guide for policy-making?

A rational approach to 'crafting' policy suggests drawing on evidence of best practice and success stories as advocated by many policy-makers. In a consultation meeting on water resource management, aimed at informing DFID's new water policy, a senior water advisor suggested that policy would be pragmatically shaped by experience of what has worked in the past. He called for those present to share their experience of 'success stories' in water resource management, to identify 'points of illumination' to elucidate policy direction.

There are, however, a number of problems with assuming that policy can be shaped through assorted collections of best practice. David Snowden argues that 'best practice' is often simply institutionally entrained past practice and that 'worst practice' evidence may provide more resilient lessons to guide future practice. One difficulty is that 'success' is difficult to identify and define. As Moser and Sollis (1991) demonstrated, for a slum upgrading and environmental health project in Ecuador, the notion that planned interventions succeed or fail or that such outcomes are the intentional results of intervention is questionable. In their case, whilst the success of the project in securing community-based environmental health management was limited (a 'failure' to the donor agency), local leaders perceived it to be a success as it had increased their visibility, advocacy and leadership capacities.

Another example of a 'success story' also containing elements of failure is documented by (Tukai, 2005). She details a community-based water project in Tanzania, which through the intense application of resources achieved apparent success in facilitating community management of the supply and in increasing women's participation in water management and village affairs. However, these successes did not equate to greater equity of access to water for women, nor did they substantially change women's disadvantage in decision-making and livelihood generation. Whether or not this example could be cited as a 'success story' for replication elsewhere depends on how widely or narrowly the outcomes of the project are defined.

Piecing together policy from different sources often overlooks the deep patterning of unequal social conditions which shape outcomes. Let us consider in some more detail the case of designing policy and interventions to ensure that poor people get access to water. Mainstream water policy, avowedly pro-poor, advocates a focus on various practices and interventions for increasing access to water for the poor and their increased representation in decision-making. However, these approaches can be criticized for their focus on limited mechanisms for inclusion of poor people (assuming a direct relationship between participation and beneficial outcomes) rather than for addressing interrelated patterns of constraint (Cleaver *et al.*, 2005).

This emphasis on best practices is associated with the idea that these can be replicated across contexts and 'scaled up' to different levels of operation. This is very evident in the prevalence of 'best practice' cases in water governance 'toolkits' or 'toolboxes', often a practical manifestation of design principles. These resources, often internet-based and intended as a guide to policy and practice, generally include best-practice cases, reference materials and links to relevant organizations and websites (GWP, 2008). Such toolboxes are generally so heavily focused on providing guidance for national-level or senior policy-makers that they tend to be formulated in terms of water subsectors (irrigation, sanitation, river basin management) and mostly fail to address water–poverty interlinkages. For example, the Global Water Partnerships toolbox is shaped around three themes providing guidance on water policy and the enabling environment, institutional roles and management instruments. The toolboxes perpetuate a managerial/technical approach to water governance policy and practice in which 'models' and 'best practices' provide the primary guide for action. Nyatsambo suggests a disconnection between such prescriptive approaches and the need for flexible strategies for working with plurality at the local level (Meinzen-Dick, 2007; Ostrom, 2007; Nyatsambo, 2009).

Research suggests that chronic poverty is characterized both by depth and duration; that poor people are systematically disadvantaged in interlinked ways over long periods of time (generations) and in particular locations. Increasingly, critics argue that 'pro-poor' interventions are particularly hard to achieve within taken-for-granted assumptions of market-based economic growth. A focus on mechanisms for increased participation and representation, without interrogating the conditions (resources/structures) which shape them, might well further marginalize rather than empower the poor (Green, 2006; Harris, 2006; Harriss-White, 2006). Practitioners' accounts of attempts to secure pro-poor water governance emphasize the need to look beyond simple measures or 'best practices' to improve water access. Rather, they suggested that a constant reiteration of an equity focus was required, combined with ongoing adjustments of approach in order to improve access for poor people (Cleaver *et al.*, 2005). Successes were only ever patchy and incremental over fairly long timescales; the processes of achieving them a combination of design, adaptation and improvisation. For example, in their accounts of establishing water-user schools in Nepal, Simon Howarth and Gladys Nott (2005) emphasize the constant review and readjustment of interventions needed to support the involvement of poor people in local decision-making. They detail their experience of trying to ensure that an irrigation management scheme in Nepal included poor people. Measures included broadening farmer groups to include landless labourers who worked on the fields of irrigation farmers and training people in how to participate and exercise voice, adapting the name, timing and curriculum of such training, repeatedly targeting particular poor households and women within these households. This example highlights the persistence required in such readjustment – the need for pragmatic adaptation and creative improvisation goes on and on (Howarth *et al.*, 2004; Howarth and Nott, 2005). Compared to this dynamic process approach, 'best practice' models represent rather static snapshots of configurations of practices in a particular place and time. A focus on success stories is in danger of leading us to believe that we can reproduce certain beneficial outcomes by selective reiteration of certain practices without addressing the wider societal factors and multiple relationships which shape the cause–effect relationship.

Nott and Howarth also emphasize the different supporting actions and processes across a range of scales if local processes promoting inclusion are to be sustained, including, for example, the role of champions of change at local national and international levels, multidisciplinary studies to understand the place of water in people's livelihoods, the decentralizing and strengthening of financial management, reform of irrigation agencies and strong political support. Emerging insights into the nature of poverty and disadvantage suggest that addressing the complexity of water and social relations requires both strategic direction and incremental reflexive practice. Policy-making tends towards incrementalism; 'doing more and doing it better' is favoured over 'doing it differently'. But neither a focus on increased supply and access nor more participation of the marginalized alone is likely to transform the situation of the chronically poor. Rather, there are arguments for linking these processes to redistributive policies, livelihood security, and basic service and social welfare provision. Such redistributive and welfare policies can provide the platform from which political voice and empowerment and demands for socially inclusive measures can be built (Hickey and Mohan, 2004; Cleaver, 2005; Wateraid, 2007).

A bricolage approach suggests that policy-making is both rational design *and* a less-conscious piecing together of approaches that 'fit' in a particular time and place, strongly influenced by authoritative actors. If this is so, how can we assess the extent to which processes of policy bricolage are actively managed and the degree to which they are shaped by factors beyond the control of individual actors?

Knowledge and Power

In this chapter so far I have referred in passing to the authoritative nature of epistemic communities and the versions of knowledge they produce. In this section I consider how such processes work to shape a dominant consensus on water governance, and I also raise the question about how much room for manoeuvre there is within dominant policy models. To introduce this, let us briefly return to the making of the 2008 DFID water policy, introduced at the beginning of the chapter.

At a consultation meeting that discussed the theme of governance in DFID's new water policy, contributions from participants were required to fit into DFID's general framework for understanding governance (comprising a set of normative principles: capability, accountability and responsiveness) published in the 2006 White Paper. The nature of the framework (known as the CAR framework) and its relevance to water governance were not for discussion, as this was the accepted way of conceptualizing governance within the DFID. This approach was partially justified by water advisors as increasing the chances of other more powerful departments within the DFID taking water seriously. However, it posed a challenge to external participants trying to contribute insights from perspectives (human rights, poverty, conflict) which were not framed in the language of the CAR framework.

It is clear that the power dimensions of who defines the subject matter of governance and who sets the parameters of the subjects to be included are critical. Haas (1992) considers the role of epistemic communities in shaping policy decisions. He defines an epistemic community as a network of professionals with a shared set of causal and principled (analytical and normative) beliefs, a consensual knowledge base and a common policy enterprise (common interests). The role of such networks is critical when policy-makers face conditions of uncertainty. Policy-makers as 'uncertainty reducers' may call on networks of knowledge-based experts to articulate the cause-and-effect relationships of complex problems, frame the issues for collective debate, and propose specific policies and salient points for negotiation. Such a framing of the terms of collective debate may be self-reinforcing, in the sense that the boundaries (assumed or defined) shape subsequent negotiations, thereby bringing about preferred outcomes to the exclusion of all others. As Haas points out, the drawing of 'science' into policy-making does not reduce the political nature of policy choices, which, being concerned with who gets what in society and at what cost, are highly political in their allocative consequences.

How do certain policy models and particular narratives of cause and effect become dominant? Francois Molle (2008) examines why the 'vision' of Integrated Water Resources Management (IWRM) has become so ubiquitously adopted in policy and looks at some of the problems of this dominant model. He suggests that it is an attractive and woolly consensual concept that obscures the political nature of natural resource management in favour of technical/managerial fixes and is easily hijacked by powerful groups for their own agendas. Narratives and storylines, like policies, are self-validating, as they tend to produce evidence. The snowballing effect, the embedding of particular models in interlinked epistemic communities, the resources attached to dominant concepts/policies and the organizational (self-)disciplining of professionals all contribute to the evolution of hegemonic policy models.

The impetus to retain dominant concepts in policy and not to subject them to too much critical scrutiny was well illustrated in discussions on reformulating DFID's water policy. Some debate was expended on the desirability of retaining 'woolly consensual' terms like 'Integrated Water Resources Management' (IWRM). For senior managers, such concepts, despite or maybe because of their ambiguity, have significant authoritative weight. Thus a senior official of the Global Water Partnership (GWP) commented:

> In GWP we recognize the term has been overused, however it would be foolish to ignore something agreed at so many high level summits, where there is a very strong momentum in many countries with support from many donors ... The support provided by donors on IWRM has had a major impact on refocusing thinking on the non-structural aspects of IWRM and also to help cohesion across sectors and policies as well as bringing in the voice of stakeholders. (Cleaver and Franks, 2008: 169)

In a similar way, the concept of water governance emerged from ideas of IWRM, 'managing water wisely' and the World Water Vision of the second World Water Forum to become accepted currency amongst water professionals. In the early stages little effort was made to define what 'water governance' meant. It sounded like a good idea, and nobody would argue against it, so it was rapidly taken up by different groups to represent their particular interest. For example, the first World Water Development Report (2003) included public–private partnerships in the chapter on good governance, whilst for others water governance became a synonym for water management. When, my colleague Tom Franks and I organized a seminar series 'Water Governance: Challenging the Consensus' we found that within the watery epistemic community there were commonalities in the much-promulgated international policy statements on water governance. These included the understanding of governance primarily as a managerial solution to water problems (rather than one which involved addressing the allocation of resources in society). Characterized by one participant as a 'waterish Washington consensus', the policy statements seemingly combined neo-liberal perspectives (viewing water as an economic good) with an emphasis on neo-populism and representative democracy (water users are expected to directly participate and to be represented in water governance).[2]

Throughout the course of the seminar series on water governance, which was set up in order to unpick the concept and test some of these ideas, we found that the epistemic community around water governance was not so consensual, dominant discourses were strongly challenged by commentators from different disciplines and even the existence of an international consensus of water governance was disputed. Differences between the academic discourse and the focus of policy emerged. For example, a dominant element of policy on water governance (based on unspoken neo-liberal assumptions) is on overcoming state corruption, whereas this was not a major concern of most of the seminar papers. In first drafts of DFID's new water policy, anti-corruption measures and strengthening the role of private providers were strongly emphasized, whereas several academics and practitioner (NGO) commentators felt that this underemphasized the necessary regulatory role of the state and need for strengthening public sector provision.

So the dominance of particular models and approaches over others is a reflection of power relations within processes of bricolage – certain bricoleurs and their worldviews exercise considerably more authoritative weight than others. Other understandings exist, and may sometimes provide the material for innovation or shifts in dominant policies, but rarely transform them. An example of knowledge shaping policy in unanticipated ways is provided by the example of one of the background papers prepared to inform the 2008 water policy. This paper, 'Rethinking Governance in Water Services' (Plummer and Slaymaker, 2007), took existing DFID frameworks for under-standing governance (CAR and the Drivers of Change framework) and considered how these applied to water services. However, little of the lengthy report was reflected in the policy, which made only very brief reference to governance. However, the background paper did enable the water section to speak the authoritative language of governance to more influential departments in DFID. Additionally, country studies (in Ethiopia and Bangladesh) were commissioned in an attempt to apply such grand and abstracted frameworks and NGOs such as Wateraid and Tearfund used some ideas/frameworks from the background paper to guide their analysis of country programmes. This spreading of unantici-pated/unintended outcomes and the leakage of meaning from one arena to others is a key feature of processes of bricolage.

'Locking Down' Complex Problems

At a meeting with DFID advisors in London I was asked to report on emerging findings from a study 'Water Governance and Poverty: What Works for the Poor?' Halfway through a brief outline of six key thematic points, the presentation was halted by the Chief Scientific Officer. He claimed that six points were too many and too complex – that it was the excessive complexity of issues that had hitherto prevented prioritization of water in DFID policy, and approaches based on complexity that had failed to produce results.

In a paper addressing development professionalism, thinking and practice, Robert Chambers (2010) elaborates two paradigms. A dominant paradigm he classifies as neo-Newtonian and is concerned with the relationships between things. This approach is equated with the powerful 'normal professionalism' of development practice. Premised on assumptions of universality and linear predictability, this paradigm values clarity and measurement, best practices and codifications. By contrast, a paradigm of adaptive pluralism, primarily focused on under-standing relationships between people, assumes diversity, dynamism and complexity. In this paradigm, measurement is less important, but creative improvisation and adaptation is emphasized along with partici-patory methods and democratic relationships.

Chambers favours the second paradigm as an approach to devel-opment thinking, claiming that it more closely reflects the dynamic complexities of people's lives. However, dominant policy models require significant abstraction, simplification and generalization of knowledge. Such processes are particularly important for policy-makers, in order to render the complexities of the social relations around water legible, to make it possible to formulate generic rather than site-specific policy. The lens through which state actors view water governance tends towards prescriptions for codification, formalization and clarification of complex webs of relationships, in accordance with Scott's analysis of state perspectives on complexity (Scott, 1998).

Necessary simplification of policy direction can give rise to tension at the interface with research and with practice. As we have seen when discussing ontologies, policy models are often informed by an implicit normative vision – a hypothetical presumption about an idealized state of affairs, often the photo-negative of existing inadequacies. Thus the vision of 'integrated water resource management' is assumed to replace fragmented and unsustainable existing forms of water management (Molle, 2007). In critiquing such 'visioning' for formulating policy, Mowles (2007, 2008) suggests that these processes create idealized models of the future, the realization of which would require radical and qualitative discontinuities with the past. He argues that such visioning processes are based on naive and unrealistic views of how change comes about and increasingly informed by systems theory. Mowles charac-terizes systems theories as ideas that organizations or societies are wholes with boundaries, and that wholesale change is possible by making changes to the way the parts interact with the whole, based on assumptions of predictability and control. Though useful in spheres where they assist in the modelling of known cause and effect (such as engineering), he argues that they are less useful in accounting for change, complexity and the unpredictability of human interactions. Contributing to the growing literature critical of the dominant discourse of managerialism in development, he suggests instead an approach based on the recognition of complexity and the need for reflexivity, for seeing strategy-making as the continuous and skilful improvisation with others and the repeated re-exploration of the consequences of that improvisation (a kind of reflexive bricolage!). Such an approach would, of course, have implications for the ways in which organizations operate, requiring a flexible learning approach to policy formulation and the successes and failures of practice (Bainbridge *et al.*, 2002). The challenges of managing such learning ecologies are great, but for some hold out the promise of the active management of creative connections and innovation (Snowden, 2003).

Let us consider the case of water governance as a complex or wicked problem and so briefly examine 'neo-Newtonian' and 'adaptive pluralist' approaches to it. The latter more clearly recognizes the need to see policy-making as bricolage rather than design, but the imperatives of development intervention mean that the two actually overlap. Some element of purposive design is crucial if the inequalities reproduced through processes of bricolage are to be addressed.

Addressing water governance as a 'wicked' problem

Reducing policy or interventions to over-simplified abstractions (free of context) and replicating disparate best practice is unlikely to generate good results. Water governance can justifiably be seen as a 'wicked problem' (Franks and Cleaver, 2009), so posing considerable challenges for designed interventions.

The concept of 'wicked problems' coined by Rittel and Webber (1973) has come to prominence in analysis of complex environmental problems. These are problems which partially defy definition, where potential analyses and solutions differ, where there is unlikely to be an agreed end point. They are unlikely to be resolved by science or technology alone as they cannot be separated from issues of values, equity and social justice. Water governance fits this definition as it is characterized by a plurality of perspectives, social complexity and a lack of one clear outcome when the problem can be said to be 'solved'.

Wicked problems are characterized by a number of stakeholder perspectives and competing values. For example, is the priority outcome of governance arrangements to secure water for domestic or productive uses, or to preserve ecosystems? Is the goal of sustainability financial (to ensure the efficiency of water services) or social (the effectiveness of those services in securing positive health, livelihood and wellbeing outcomes)? The differing values of stakeholders are well reflected in the debate about private sector participation in water management in which advocates may claim increased efficiency and coverage whilst critics see detrimental effects on the water poor, and on the environment.

The socially complex nature of the water sustainability challenge is partly a consequence of such multiple viewpoints. People and water relationships are defined by unequal inter-dependencies; between different groups of people and between people, technology, natural resources and society. Relationships around water are thus socially entwined and multi-scalar. Merrey and colleagues (2007) identify three dimensions of plurality, encompassing multiple stakeholders, a variety of uses of water and plural institutional arrangements to regulate them. Multi-dimensional complexity means that arrangements for managing water are likely to be variable, dynamic and critically related to other issues like access to land and the exercise of political power.

There is therefore unlikely to be a single or final 'solution' to water sustainability. Ensuring adequately functioning and affordable water supplies and balancing the needs of people with the environment is likely to involve continuous and variable effort over indefinite time periods. Variability (performance of technology, of rainfall, of demand) and unpredictability (environmental and economic shocks) may increase the pressure on arrangements for water governance and require the constant exercise of flexible and adaptive approaches to problem solving. Such approaches may in themselves generate unanticipated and undesirable consequences.

The complexity or 'wicked' nature of the problem of water governance seems obvious. But the nature of policymaking and the exigencies of practice (the need for action and clarity of direction, within short timescales and with limited resources) often mean that complex problems are 'locked down' or 'tamed'. Problems are narrowly defined, with uni-dimensional solutions suggested as once-and-for-all answers. For water governance, 'locking down' tends to result in a focus on effective management or on responsive government whilst at the more local level particular mechanisms, such as tariffs, or constitutions or committees, may be seen as the 'answer'.

The common elision of the concepts of government and governance in policy (Batterbury and Fernando, 2006) is no accident. Governments see themselves as prime facilitators; the main actors in securing 'good' governance and development agencies such as DFID are statist organizations. To a large degree, policy-making is an activity carried out by governments. As we have seen in a previous section, 'seeing like a state' involves a certain tunnel vision when it comes to the complexity of social relationships. This is no surprise when we examine the mechanisms at the disposal of governments in devising and implementing policy; mainly, this includes dialogue with national governments and through established organizational structures.

So typical of a mainstream approach to formulating water governance policy is a focus on reshaping institutions in relation to the state. For example, the Global Water Partnership's toolbox has a section on 'reforming institutions for better governance', with a strong emphasis on the institutional basis of water governance, and closely linked to integrated water resources management. Similarly UNESCO's 2006 World Water Assessment Report focuses on ways of shaping governance arrangements through national water policies, water rights, privatization, tackling corruption and decentralization of decision-making.

The level at which policy-making happens is significant. This can be illustrated by returning to my experiences at the consultation meetings for DFID's 2008 water policy. At one of these a civil servant suggested the need for 'local policy committees' to critically examine the proposed water policy and translate it into contextualized plans for local action. After some discussion it gradually emerged that for the civil servant 'local' did not mean village, district or even regional level, but committees operating at recipient country level. 'Local policy committee' therefore was conceived as a forum for translating London-generated policy into a nationally acceptable shape in the country receiving development aid. By contrast, many of the water professionals in the room were concerned with water governance processes at sub-national levels, where they interacted more directly with people's livelihoods.

Such formally structured and hierarchical approaches to forming policy ill reflect both the distributed nature of water governance and the overlapping of scales and boundaries of social and political action (Mollinga, 2008). Policy may indeed influence action in different domains. For example, when people in a Zimbabwean village contest the levying of user fees for water by claiming access to water as a human right, they are drawing on debates from the domain of international policy (Chapter 7). Conversely, when the Swedish Ministry of

Environment uses the example of the collective action in a number of Swedish villages to promote their environmental approaches (Chapter 8), national policy is being shaped by the politics of everyday lives in the villages.

Conclusion

So it seems that policy is made through a combination of design and bricolage. The promise of such hybrid processes of policy-making is that of 'managed serendipity' (Snowden, 2003) – the deliberate facilitation of multiple and creative encounters between different types of knowledge and the flexibility that goes with this. The pitfalls, however, are that processes of design and bricolage, being inextricably tied into historical, social, economic and political power relations, all too often reproduce inequalities, filter out dissenting voices and institutionalize dominant ideas.

References

Archer, M. (1998) 'Social Theory and the Analysis of Society', in T. May and M. Williams (eds) *Knowing the Social World*, Buckingham, Open University Press, pp. 69–85.

Bainbridge, V., Foerster, S., Pasteur, K., Pimbert, M., Pratt, G. and Arroyo, I. Y. (2002) 'Transforming Bureaucracies: Institutionalising Participation and People-Centred Processes in Natural Resource Management – an Annotated Bibliography', IDS and IIED, http://pubs.iied.org/pdfs/6342IIED.pdf.

Batterbury, S. and Fernando, J. (2006) 'Rescaling Governance and the Impacts of Political and Environmental Decentralisation: An Introduction', *World Development* 34, 11, pp. 1851–63.

Burawoy, M. (2005) 2004 American Sociological Association Presidential Address: For Public Sociology. The British Journal of Sociology, 56: 259–94 (June).

—(2005) 'For Public Sociology', *American Sociological Review* 70, pp. 4–28.

—(2006) 'Open the Social Sciences: To Whom and for What?' Address to the Portuguese Sociological Association, 30 March, http://sociology.berkeley.edu/faculty/burawoy/burawoy_pdfburawoy-open_thesocialsciences.pdf.

Chambers, R. (2010) 'Paradigms, Poverty and Adaptive Pluralism', *IDS Working Papers* vol. 344, pp. 1–57.

Cleaver, F. (2005) 'The Inequality of Social Capital and the Reproduction of Chronic Poverty', *World Development* 33, 6, pp. 893–906.

Cleaver, F., Franks, T., Boesten, J. and Kiire, A. (2005) 'Water Governance and Poverty: What Works for the Poor?' A Report to DFID, University of Bradford, http://www.splash.bradford.ac.uk/files/PDF%20Water%20Governance%20and%20Poverty%20Final%20Report%2006.05.pdf.

Collingridge, D. and Reeve, C. (1986) *Science Speaks to Power: The Role of Experts in Policy Making*, New York. St Martin's Press, New York.

Corbridge, S. (2005) *Seeing the State: Governance and Governmentality in India*, Cambridge, Cambridge University Press.

Court, J. and Young, J. (2004) 'Bridging Research and Policy in International Development: Context, Evidence and Links', in D. Stone and S. Maxwell (eds) *Global Knowledge Networks and International Development: Bridges Across Boundaries*, London, Routledge.

Department for International Development (2006) *White Paper: Making Governance Work for the Poor*, London, Department for International Development.

—(2008a) *Water: An Increasingly Precious Resource. Sanitation: A Matter of Dignity*, London, Department for International Development.

—(2008b) *Meeting our Promises: A Fourth Update on DFID's Work in Water and Sanitation Since the 2004 Water Action Plan*, London, Department for International Development.

Fischer, A., Petersen, L., Feldkotter, C. and Huppert, W. (2007) 'Sustainable Governance of Natural Resources and Institutional Change: An Analytical Framework', *Public Administration and Development* 27, pp. 123–37.

Franks, T. and Cleaver, F. (2009) 'Analysing Water Governance: A Tool for Sustainability', *Engineering Sustainability* 162, 4, pp. 207–14.

Freeman, R. (2007) 'Epistemological Bricolage: How Practitioners Make Sense of Learning', *Administration and Society* 39, 4, pp. 476–96.

Green, M. (2006) 'Thinking Through Chronic Poverty and Destitution: Theorizing Social Relations and Social Ordering', paper presented at the Workshop on Concepts and Methods for Analysing Poverty Dynamics and Chronic Poverty, University of Manchester, 23–25 October.

GWP (2008) 'IWRM Toolbox, version 2', Global Water Partnership, http://www.gwptoolbox.org/images/stories/Docs/toolboxeng.pdf.

Haas, P. M. (1992) 'Introduction: Epistemic Communities and International Policy Coordination', *International Organisation* 46, 1, pp. 1–35.

Harris, J. (2006) 'Why Understanding of Social Relations Matters More for Policy on Chronic Poverty than Measurement', paper presented at the Workshop on Concepts and Methods for Analysing Poverty Dynamics and Chronic Poverty, University of Manchester, 23–25 October.

Harriss-White, B. (2006) 'Poverty and Capitalism', *Economic and Political Weekly*, pp. 1241–6.

Hickey, S. and Mohan, G. (2004) 'Relocating Participation within a Radical Politics of Development: Critical Modernism and Citizenship', in S. Hickey and G. Mohan (eds) *Participation: From Tyranny to Transformation? Exploring New Approaches to Participation in Development*, London, Zed Books.

House of Commons (2007) *Sanitation and Water: Sixth Report of the Session 2006–2007, Volume 1*, London, The Stationery Office Limited.

Howarth, S. and Nott, G. (2005) 'Practitioner Input Form 6', in F. Cleaver, T. Franks, J. Boesten and A. Kiire, 'Water Governance and Poverty: What Works for the Poor?' Report to the Department for International Development, http://

www.splash.bradford.ac.uk/files/PDF%20Water%20Governance%20and%20 Poverty%20Final%20Report%2006.05.pdf.

Howarth, S., Parajuli, U. N., Baral, J. R., Nott, G. A., Adhikari, B. R., Gautam, D. R. and Menuka, K. C. (2004) 'Promoting Good Governance of Water Users' Associations in Nepal', www.research4development.info/pdf/outputs/k80233. pdf.

Lankford, B., Van Koppen, B., Franks, T. and Mahoo, H. (2004) 'Entrenched Views or Insufficient Science? Contested Causes and Solutions of Water Allocation: Insights from the Great Ruaha River Basin, Tanzania', *Agricultural Water Management* 69, 2, pp. 135–53.

Lewis, D. (2009) 'International Development and the "Perpetual Present": Anthropological Approaches to the Re-Historicization of Policy', *European Journal of Development Research*, 21, 1, pp. 32–46.

Lukes, S. (2005) *Power: A Radical View*, Basingstoke, Palgrave Macmillan, 2nd edition.

Meinzen-Dick, Ruth (2007) 'Beyond Panaceas in Water Institutions', *Proceedings of the National Academy of Sciences of the United States of America* 104, 39, pp. 15200–5.

Mendizabal, E. and Jones, H. (2010) 'Strengthening Learning from Research and Evaluation: Going with the Grain', ODI Report, http://www.odi.org.uk/ resources/feedback.asp?id=5154&title=learning;-research;-evaluation;-dfid.

Merrey, D. J., Meinzen-Dick, R., Mollinga, P. and Karar, E. (2007) 'Policy and Institutional Reform: The Art of the Possible', in D. Molden (ed.) *Water for Food, Water for Life: A Comprehensive Assessment of Water Management in Agriculture*, London, Earthscan, pp. 193–231.

Molle, F. (2007) 'Sacred Cows, Storylines and Nirvana Concepts: Insights from the Water Sector (Draft Paper)', paper presented at the Workshop on Water, Politics and Development, ZEF, University of Bonn, Germany, March.

—(2008) 'Nirvana Concepts, Storylines and Policy Models: Insights from the Water Sector', *Water Alternatives* 1, 1, pp. 131–56.

Mollinga, P. (2008) 'Water, Politics and Development: Framing a Political Sociology of Water Resources Management', *Water Alternatives* 1, 1, pp. 7–23.

Moretto, L. (2007) 'Urban Governance and Multilateral Aid Organisations: The Case of Informal Water Supply Systems', *The Review of International Organisations* 2, 4, pp. 345–70.

Moser, C. and Sollis, P. (1991) 'Did the Project Fail? A Community Perspective on a Participatory Primary Health Care Project in Ecuador', *Development in Practice* 1, 1, pp. 19–33.

Mosse, D. (2004) 'Is Good Policy Unimplementable? Reflections on the Ethnography of Aid Policy and Practice', *Development and Change* 35, 4, pp. 639–71.

Mowles, C. (2007) 'Promises of Transformation: Just How Different are Development INGOs?' *Journal of International Development* 19, 3, pp. 383–8.

—(2008) 'Values in International Development Organisations: Negotiating Non-Negotiables', *Development in Practice* 18, 1, pp. 5–16.

Nyatsambo, R. (2009) 'Making "Targeting the Poor" Effective: A Review of Water and Poverty Toolboxes', unpublished working paper, SOAS.

Ostrom, Elinor (2007) 'A Diagnostic Approach for Going Beyond Panaceas', *Proceedings of the National Academy of Sciences of the United States of America* 104, 39, pp. 15181–7.

Plummer, J. and Slaymaker, T. (2007) 'Rethinking Governance in Water Services', ODI Working Paper 284.

Rittel, H. and Webber, M. (1973) 'Dilemmas in a General Theory of Planning', *Policy Sciences* 4, 2, pp. 155–69.

Scott, J. (1998) *Seeing Like a State: How Certain Schemes to Improve the Human Condition Have Failed*, New Haven, CT, Yale University Press.

Snowden, D. (2003) 'Managing for Serendipity: Why We Should Lay Off "Best Practice" in K.M.' Cynefin Centre, http://www.cognitive-edge.com/articledetails.php?articleid=39.

Tukai, R. (2005) 'Gender and Access in Pastoral Communities: Re-evaluating Community Participation and Gender Empowerment', paper presented at the ESRC seminar 'Access, Poverty and Social Exclusion', ODI, London, 1 March.

Walsh, M. (2006) 'The Production of Knowledge and Reproduction of Ignorance about Usangu, Mbarali District, Tanzania', paper presented at the Workshop on Equalities and Inequalities in Tanzania: Past and Present, Darwin College, University of Cambridge, 9 June.

—(2007) 'Pangolins and Politics in the Great Ruaha Valley, Tanzania: Symbol, Ritual and Difference', in E. Dounias, E. Motte-Florac and M. Dunham (eds) *Animal Symbolism: Animals, Keystone of the Relationship between Man and Nature?*, Paris, IRD, pp. 1003–44.

—(2008) 'Study on the Options for Pastoralists to Secure their Livelihoods: Pastoralism and Policy Process in Tanzania – Mbarali Case Study', Report Submitted to TNRF.

—(2012) 'The Not-so-Great Ruaha and hidden histories of an environmental panic in Tanzania, Journal of East African Studies, forthcoming.

Wateraid (2007) 'End Water Poverty: Sanitation and Water for All', WaterAid, www.endwaterpoverty.org.

Wegerich, K. and Warner, J. (eds) (2010) *The Politics of Water: A Survey*, London, Routledge.

World Water Assessment Programme (2003) *Water for People, Water for Life*, Oxford, UNESCO and Berghahn Books.

Young, J. and Mendizabal, E. (2009) 'Helping Researchers become Policy Entrepreneurs', ODI Briefing Papers 53, http://www.odi.org.uk/resources/details.asp?id=1127&title=become-policy-entrepreneur-roma.

Notes

1 This chapter builds on previously published papers, most notably Cleaver and Franks 2008. I gratefully acknowledge the contributions of colleagues at Bradford (Tom Franks) and SOAS (Rose Nyatsambo, Kate Bayliss and Kristin Hamada) to the analysis presented here. I also benefitted from conversations with Tom Slaymaker and various DFID staff about policy-making processes for water.

2 See the University of Bradford's Water Governance Research Group website at http//www.splash.bradford.ac.uk. The term 'Waterish Washington Consensus' was coined by Dr Stephen Merrett.

7 Remapping the Institutional Landscape

Introduction: Examining Development at the State–Community Interface

In the last chapter we explored policy-making at the national level as shaped by processes of bricolage. In this chapter I re-focus on community-level life and collective action to examine the evolution of local institutions and their effects over time. Re-examining the institutional landscape of Eguqeni village in Nkayi district nearly two decades after the scenarios presented in Chapter 3 allows me to situate local processes of bricolage in the context of wider societal trends. Using this material, I review some of the key themes of institutional bricolage set out in previous chapters, and in so doing touch on ideas about the nature and role of the state in development.

Authoritative accounts of the development of Nkayi district, collected in 2010,[1] eerily resonate with reports from previous eras. For example, in an interview in February 2010 the Chief Nkalakatha observed that Nkayi district was 'under-developed, under-skilled and under-financed'. Very similar sentiments were expressed by a series of Native Commissioners in the first half of the twentieth century, reporting on the 'uphill struggle to develop a backward district', the lack of infrastructure and the reluctance of residents to provide labour for development works. The five-year strategic plan for Nkayi (under revision by the Rural District Council in 2010) bemoaned the unwillingness of residents to pay rates: 'There is a lack of equipment for maintenance of public goods/ service delivery ... a dangerous dependency syndrome ... has encroached into people's culture ... Free food handouts and Food for Work programmes have also added to this dependency dilemma.'

The repeated assertion that lack of development in the district is caused by patterns of under-resourcing and non-participation over many decades paints a dismal picture but raises numerous questions.

If the district is so beset by state incapacity and community inactivity (persisting over decades), how then are livelihoods secured, resources managed, the social order maintained; through what institutions are such arrangements mediated? I have argued in this book that to understand institutional dynamics we need to expand our focus away from narrowly functional designed arrangements to explore the wider landscape in which they are situated. From a bricolage perspective, institutional formation is socially located, shaped in the interplay between deliberate design, everyday practices and relationships and societal processes. The boundaries of institutions are porous and arrangements made defy simple categorization as modern/traditional, formal/informal, community/state. Decisions about natural resource management are made consciously and non-consciously and the legitimacy of innovations are established through reference to authoritative discourses, often drawing on the past, the natural order and the 'right way of doing things'. Institutions are also shaped by the ways in which wider societal resource allocations and trends inscribe on to local life and public spaces. Before exploring how these themes work out in Eguqeni, let us briefly consider the influence of the state and development initiatives on local level arrangements.

Between High Modernism and Romanticism

The possibilities of designing or engineering schemes to improve the human condition are well reflected in 'high modern' ideas about the developmental state. 'Seeing like a state' suggests that valued goals can be achieved through the planned and logical organization of people and resources. For Scott, writing of grand state directed programmes, such as *ujaama* in Tanzania, such schemes are doomed to fail as they ignore the informal or social knowledge and informal networks that would be crucial to their success (Scott, 1998).

Mainstream Institutional thinking applied to natural resource management focuses on the state primarily as ineffective, often because of its centralizing tendencies, and is more concerned with understanding and supporting community-level action, which can make up for such deficiencies. However, Mainstream Institutionalism does incorporate features of such 'high modern' perspectives through its focus on planning and design, on ensuring the legibility and codification of institutional arrangements and its concern with nested layers of public authority and collective action. Such optimism about the designability of institutions fits well with contemporary policy emphases that stress the possibility of engineering 'good' governance arrangements.

Evidence presented in this book suggests that the rational, modernist project of designing institutions (and systems) for natural resource management is partially doomed to failure. Designed institutions often sit lightly superimposed on the institutional landscape with little purchase on the way decisions are actually made. Or they are colonized and cannibalized for their resources of authority and symbols of legitimacy; resources pressed into service in the do-it-yourself assembly of institutions through bricolage. We cannot guarantee that the designed institutions of development interventions produce the results intended.

Moral economy perspectives usefully offer a balance to state-centric analyses pointing to the importance and robustness of social relationships and tradition (Hyden, 2006). However, I have also argued that questioning the claims made for institutional design do not necessarily mean uncritically embracing over-romantic myths of communities and their potential for self-development. In addition to admiring the richness and creativity of local collective action, we have seen its limits: the constraints of resources and effectiveness, the reproduction of inequality. Such insights inform contemporary political and institutional analyses, which endeavour to understand how public authority and citizenship is enacted through relationships of belonging and believing. Hagmann and Péclard (2010) suggest that such relationships are shaped by history, the embeddedness of bureaucratic institutions in society, symbolic and material factors and claims to legitimacy. For them, statehood is practically negotiated between a multitude of social actors competing over resources and claims to legitimacy.

In his study of social institutions in rural Uganda, Jones (2009) highlights the enduring importance of social institutions (burial societies, clan and lineage organizations, churches) as the sites through which everyday livelihood strategies, the allocation of resources and struggles over power are enacted (Berry, 2005). Even when the state is unable to function in terms of basic service delivery, or is outwardly focused (towards donor agencies, other states), it is still an important factor in shaping the authoritative configuration of institutions at local level. Taking a broader brush comparative approach, Chabal (2009) understands wider political institutions and processes of state formation as moulded by local people's struggle to secure livelihoods within frameworks of 'belonging' (social identities, obligations and networks) and believing (cosmologies). So, in keeping with ideas about the 'everyday state' (Fuller and Benei, 2001), I suggest that institutions, the ideology and disciplinary practices of the state are interwoven into everyday relations. The question then arises: to what extent can such negotiations and the exercise of agency by citizens, reconfigure the workings of the state?

From a Critical Institutionalist perspective, institutions are the arenas where the state comes into engagement with locally generated meanings and configurations of authority through the actions and practices of bricoleurs. The boundaries between different institutional arrangements and domains of governance overlap – meaning and authority leaks in and out of institutions and across scales. So to understand the ways that institutions work we have to understand the weft and warp of local social and political life, and the way these become woven into the broadcloth of societal patterns of allocation and authority. We also need to examine the wider resources of governance (configured at national and international levels) available for the assembly of institutions through bricolage and how they are deployed to legitimize old and new arrangements.

Critical Institutionalist thinking is in danger of falling into an impasse in which facilitating positive social change through institutions seems impossible because of the infinitely complex and negotiated ways in which human relations are conducted. Avoiding this impasse requires a tricky balancing act. This involves steering a path between over-simplified 'rational design' perspectives, over-romantic ideas about community resourcefulness, and post-structural emphases on diversity and negotiability. Such a position would enable us to identify opportunities for shaping governance arrangements in emancipatory directions, while simultaneously maintaining an awareness that such arrangements are likely to evolve in unintended ways.

Remapping the Institutional Landscape in a Zimbabwean Village

Let us return to Eguqeni village in Zimbabwe, the location of my analysis in Chapter 3, to consider some of these issues and challenges. Returning to Eguqeni in 2010 after a gap of almost sixteen years, I had the chance to review the institutional landscape, to piece together how arrangements for communal management of water and grazing had evolved in the intervening years. This offered a golden opportunity for tracking institutional continuity and change at the local level, in the context of some very dramatic changes to Zimbabwean society and to the broader governance context.

This longer view of institutional arrangements in one village offers us the chance to review the ways in which institutions evolve through bricolage, the creativity and the limits of community-level action and the ways these link positively and negatively to societal governance arrangements and directed development efforts.

In this chapter I consider the formation of local-level institutions in the context of a government unable to perform its practical functions, but nonetheless concerned with maintaining its authoritative reach. In this area of Zimbabwe the 'development machine' (Ferguson, 1990) was also largely absent, though still influential as an idea or future possibility. These absences help to bring into focus more clearly the local social institutions which shape governance arrangements. In scrutinizing these institutions a number of questions are pertinent. How are authoritative and material resources configured in the evolution of institutional arrangements over time? How are interpretations of the past and present used to invest institutions with pedigree of the 'right way of doing things'? And does a crisis in national governance trigger similar crises in local governance?

In Chapter 3 I tracked the features of water management focusing on villages in Nkayi district using data collected between 1992 and 1994. At that time, a decade or so after independence, the institutional landscape was characterized by a dual system of modern and traditional authority with an explicit division of responsibility between them. Formal public decision-making was embedded in social institutions which prioritized consensus decision-making, conflict avoidance and universal partici-pation in collective cultural ceremonies like rain-making. 'Traditional' principles of access to all were approximately upheld with a certain tolerance of free riding (depending on social identity). The limited reach of community initiatives was extended by vertical links to service delivery branches of the state, as for example in the three-tier system for handpump maintenance. The influence of national and international development discourses was strong in shaping discussions about rights and participation and in the requirement for formal committees, trans-parently operated, as a pre-condition of receiving aid. Let us consider how far this profile of local governance arrangements changed over subsequent years.

The national governance context – years of crisis and change

The national framework of governance in Zimbabwe since the 1990s had been a troubled one. Between the end of the 1990s and 2010 Zimbabwe suffered a precipitate decline in reputation from being a leading post-independence state to one epitomizing the worst of African malfeasance. Despite increasing evidence of violent repression and authoritarianism, in the early 1990s Zimbabwe could feasibly still be characterized as a modernizing developmental state. Great progress had been made post-independence with managing the infrastructure and economy, improving indicators of education and child mortality. Within a decade development had ground to a halt.

From the late 1990s the cracks in the post-independence developmental state began to widen into gaping chasms. The government bankrupted itself making payments to war veterans and through structural adjustment policies divested itself of many of its functions, and introduced user fees for health and education. The dire effects on poor people were compounded by the devastating impact of the HIV/ Aids epidemic and increased economic stresses on livelihoods and family structures. The crisis deepened with political conflict over the emergence of an opposition movement in the 1990s and the takeover of commercial farms in the early 2000s, accompanied by the increasing use of violence by the ruling party. By 2000/2001 (following disputed elections) international sanctions were imposed on the regime and donor agencies provided only very limited humanitarian relief through non-governmental organizations. The country entered a downward spiral of crisis characterized by economic collapse, hyper-inflation, political oppression and out-migration of skilled people. The crisis apparently peaked in the election year of 2008, which was characterized by widespread violence, shortages of food and basic commodities, the breakdown of infrastructure and outbreaks of cholera (Potts, 2010).

From the vantage point of 2010, the previous year seemed to represent a turning point. With mediation, a government of national unity (of sorts) was established, and the Zimbabwe dollar was abandoned for hard foreign currencies, resulting in improved availability of goods and services. However, rehabilitation of the infrastructure, economy and political system was clearly going to be a massive and long-term challenge. Slow progress on political governance issues meant that external donor support was still limited; development had not yet restarted.

During the late 1990s the Zimbabwean government, in accordance with the international water consensus, had adopted a national policy of integrated water resources management. Water sector reforms were underpinned by ideas about the management of water on the basis of hydrological boundaries (catchments), decentralization, stakeholder participation and the treatment of water as an economic good. However, in the Zimbabwean context these policy principles interacted with ideas about the need to redress colonial injustices in access to water and to promote the needs of previously disadvantaged users, particularly communal, resettlement and small-scale farmers (Bolding *et al.*, 1998). The water reforms built around neo-liberal principles, the concept of integrated water resource management and decentralization were implemented from the end of the 1990s, coinciding with a radical trans-formation of state governance as outlined above (Mtisi, 2011; Mapedza and Geheb, 2010). In this chapter I track water management from the perspective of one village and reflect on the extent to which local-level processes are influenced by such national policies and trends.

The post-independence experience of much of Matabeleland (the regional location of Nkayi district) never fully reflected the national trajectory. Inadequate infrastructure, more marginal land and a history of political and ethnic difference from the ruling Zanu-PF counted against Matabeleland. 'Development' was only experienced briefly after independence; from 1983 until 1987 the government deployed its notorious Fifth Brigade (Gukhurahundi) in Matabeleland ostensibly to crush 'dissidents' claiming loyalty to ZAPU (Zimbabwe African People's Union), in so doing killing and terrorizing thousands of people (Catholic Commission for Justice and Peace, 1999). Following an amnesty in 1988, the revival of development was tentative, and set back in 1992 when the severest drought of the century hit Matabeleland particularly badly. The withdrawal of donor-funded development aid and the emergence of a national political opposition resulted in the further marginalization of Matabeleland over the subsequent years. This situation clearly shaped the ways in which local institutions functioned. The need for self-reliant creativity was imperative, but so was the necessity to demonstrate the legitimacy of their improvised arrange-ments, as we shall see in the following sections.

Development in Nkayi: the uphill struggle continues ...

Picture Eguqeni village in Nkayi district as it appeared to me in February of 2010. The road bisecting the village was almost empty, save for a few donkey carts and pedestrians. Most of the water sources were broken, or only partially functioning. In many houses thatch had not been renewed, nor mud walls re-plastered, and chicken hutches were derelict, all the chickens having been bartered in place of money. The manufactured items of everyday life – shoes and clothes, buckets, bowls, cup and plates – were scarce and often in poor condition. Many graves had appeared around the village since my last visit.

There was a positive sense that people were just beginning to emerge from years of deep crisis, but this tentative hope was balanced by anxiety about the patchy rains and the fate of growing crops. The district, though largely supporting the opposition, was mostly spared the national political violence of the last decade. It suffered severely though from economic crisis compounded by years of low crop production, outmigration and the collapse of government. By early 2010 some optimism sprang from the ability to buy some goods and the expectation of a resumption of 'development'. However, signs of re-emergence of the state were barely visible. The district administration was minimally functional, with empty offices and absent staff. The Nkayi Rural District Council had just begun to revive after some years of total paralysis due to lack of funds, political tensions and demoralization. Neither operated beyond the district centre. The lowest tier of government, village development committees, had collapsed during the height of national political strife. Communications and infrastructure were minimal, the telephone system had collapsed due to lack of maintenance, and the cellular network from Bulawayo only intermittently covered Nkayi. Of the eighty-one dams in the district eighty were silted up (and only two held water throughout the year). An estimated eighty per cent of the boreholes were dysfunctional, the reticulated water supply to Nkayi growth point operated intermittently and sanitation coverage was estimated by the council (optimistically) at thirteen per cent. Transport within the district and connecting it to Kwekwe and Bulawayo towns was limited.

In terms of the governance of water, the water supply and sanitation sub-committee of the district council was non-functional, and the district development fund (DDF), responsible for maintaining rural infrastructure, had no vehicles and no budget for rehabilitation of boreholes. The pump minders, technicians previously employed to support community maintenance of water supplies, had been retrenched; many had out-migrated, leaving a skills shortage in pump maintenance.

What did all this mean for the livelihoods of ordinary poor people in Nkayi? Households had relied on remittances from relatives in South Africa or Botswana but also had endeavoured to keep household members in Zimbabwe's urban areas supplied with food. The preponderance of women over men in the population of the district, high dependency ratios and Aids-related morbidity and mortality severely restricted availability of labour for agricultural work. In 2010 there were no large-scale development projects in the district, though some small-scale NGO activity (supporting people with HIV/Aids and promoting sustainable agriculture) was just beginning. Food relief was provided through the World Food Programme to orphans and vulnerable households, but this ceased mid-2010 following a controversial report by a national agency judging that Nkayi was not food insecure.

Despite variable rainfall conditions, people still relied on rain-fed maize as their main crop, but had survived years of crisis partly through the barter economy. In 2010 both money and goods were being used in transactions;

US dollars were used for large transactions, South African rand, Botswana pula or desirable goods for small change. The price my local research assistants paid for two chickens in February 2010 was US $5, half a loaf of bread and two sheets of paracetamol tablets!

Water management: a serious business

So, in this context of precipitate national decline and crisis, how had the social institutions of resource management fared at village level? Did the changes at national level reconfigure the 'stock repertoire' of institutional furniture available for bricolage? Let us begin, as we did in Chapter 3, with considering the interplay between design and improvisation in water management.

In Eguqeni village in 2010 only two boreholes of the nine waterpoints were functioning properly. Two more wells produced minimal amounts of water, the rest were in need of total rehabilitation. Mtswirini Well, the site of much community effort in the 1990s, was derelict, but just a few metres away a new borehole known as 'Creche' was in good condition and had recently been fenced by the community. In February I observed a notice pinned to the borehole which, when translated, read:

Box 7.1 Borehole Notice

To Parents we are asking for borehole money.
I no longer go around people's homes. Each person should bring theirs.
I am serious. I am serious.

It's me Mother of Sikhululekile.

The notice piqued my interest, as it suggested that the community was regularly collecting funds for borehole maintenance but that people needed to be prompted to pay up. In contrast to this seriousness, the message was couched in social terms of address, and the writer signed herself as 'Mother of Sikhululekile' rather than as 'Treasurer of the Waterpoint Committee' or by her formal name.

The following day the treasurer and secretary of the waterpoint committee (both women) took turns to stand at the borehole from 6am to 7pm to collect the monthly borehole maintenance fees from people as they fetched water. Dues were collected (in dollars, rand or maize) from about a quarter of the registered eighty-six user households, with others promising to pay up soon. Two days later, some of this money was used to contract the local freelance pump minder to service the pump.

The collection of water fees marked a departure from the situation in the early 1990s. Then, under the leadership of the village development committee (VIDCO) chairman, the community considered establishing a multi-purpose 'village purse'. Universal free access to water was generally considered the right way of doing things, though in practice gradations in access rights existed. The drought and development policy messages advocating 'community ownership' had caused some communities to introduce restrictions contrary to these principles. These were, however, resisted by people calling on tradition and on messages of equal citizenship promoted through development initiatives. The more formalized ways in which water maintenance fees were levied in 2010 illustrates the continued re-negotiation of norms towards more exclusivity, but this was still hotly disputed, as we shall see below.

Two trends were apparent in the evolution of arrangements over time. The first was a certain amount of innovation, negotiation of rules and norms and flexibility in application. The second was a growing concern, in the face of wider governance crisis, for public accounting and the demonstration of legitimacy, as the examples below suggest.

Shifting norms: fees, negotiating access and exemptions

In 2009 the local Red Cross had rehabilitated the Crèche borehole to facilitate their home-based care for people living with HIV/Aids. They had also trained the community in how to organize maintenance. The community had quickly established a waterpoint committee, constitution and tariff in response to the Red Cross initiative, as they were eager to be seen to be enthusiastic about development opportunities.

In setting the tariff (which included a one-off household registration fee and a monthly maintenance fee), the committee introduced graded payments. They set themselves an exemplary higher rate of registration fee (US $1 as compared to South African R5 for other villagers). The highest rate (US $5) was reserved for those intermittently coming to the village by car from the district centre to collect water. Villagers could negotiate to pay their monthly fee of R5 in kind (2kg of maize or equivalent in chicks) if they did not have the cash. Compliance with fee payment was patchy – in February 2010 a quarter of villagers paid up on the day and some were observed to be paying three-months-back subscriptions.

The validity of the new arrangements, which had been agreed at a public meeting, was subject to some debate. Our enquiries about fee exemptions for the poorest households sparked a heated discussion amongst a group of people gathered in one part of the village. An older woman objected to the 'no exemptions' policy as inhumane. One senior man objected vigorously, on the basis that fees had been agreed at a community meeting, when anyone who objected could have spoken out. He also doubted that any villagers would be willing to pay to cover the shortfall caused by exemptions, given ongoing economic crisis. During the course of debate the women present gradually started voicing disagreement with the 'no exemptions' policy. The case was cited of a poor neighbour, caring for her orphaned grandchildren, who had allegedly been scolded at the Creche pump the day before for not paying her fees. Desperate to maintain good reputation with neighbours and avoid being excluded from collecting water, she had rushed home to fetch her last kilos of food relief maize as payment-in-kind. This left her household with no staple food until the next food relief distribution the following week.

In this example we see the two opposing views in this debate drawing of different legitimizing discourses – on the one hand 'traditional' ideas of access for all supplemented by notions of human rights, and on the other the assertion of the over-riding jurisdictional reach of a community meeting, and a claiming that rules should be equally and impersonally applied. We can also glean some interesting insights into community dynamics here. Why had women's reservations about the effect of the rules not been more strongly expressed at the whole community meeting? And how had the poor grandmother assessed the relative costs and benefits of paying with scarce food, or facing community sanctions?

In fact, throughout 2010 the community avoided imposing strict sanctions for non-payment. In the opinion of the treasurer, this was partly because villagers needed to get used to the system, and partly because they considered it 'ethically and constitutionally wrong to exclude people from public communal facilities'. Compliance was therefore sought by lengthy processes of persuasion; minutes of the waterpoint committee meetings record that on more than one occasion it referred the matter to the (traditional) headman and elders, requesting them to hold a meeting to persuade people to pay up. By October of 2010 the dry season had depleted water supplies, and food aid had been withdrawn from the district, reducing people's capacity to pay in kind. The committee had suspended the collection of funds (recording a healthy balance of cash, chickens and maize) and turned its attention to issues of rationing instead.

Within these evolving arrangements there was a deep concern with public accountability. This was undoubtedly heightened by the recent experience of economic chaos and political contestation. Money collected from registered households was noted in an exercise book kept by the secretary. Following hyper-inflation and conversion to foreign currency (when all savings were 'frozen'), people had lost faith in the banking system. Rather, the treasurer kept the funds in a plastic bag, with the sum written on a piece of paper. Some of the money collected in February was used very quickly to commission maintenance from a freelance pump minder, at a cost of US $40. The community gathered to assist with the repair, and once completed the treasurer counted out the money in front of other committee members, it was handed it over to the caretaker (the senior man on the committee), who in turn ceremoniously paid it to the pump minder. The caretaker then announced to the public that in two days' time there would be a community meeting at which the funds collected and spent would be accounted for.

This waterpoint committee regarded communal rules as flexible tools, their application to be varied according to circumstances rather than upheld impersonally and swiftly. Flexibility in interpreting the rules is a key feature of institutions formed through bricolage – a certain amount of socially sanctioned free riding avoids unpleasant confrontation with neighbours and facilitates peaceful living together. Conflicting evidence as to whether such flexibility was threatened or reinforced by the experience of economic crisis is illustrated by the debate over 'no exemptions'. The concern for public accountability and legitimacy was undoubtedly a response to political crisis, but it is clear that this resulted in an assertion of 'traditional' and patriarchal relations of authority.

Community decision-making and jurisdiction

A concern with public accountability was mirrored by a concern for demonstrating that institutional arrangements were transparent and legitimate. Shifting norms were also apparent here, with a modification of the model of consensus as the sole way of making decisions in the village. However, such changes to the right way of doing things had to be specifically justified and legitimized, as the following example shows.

Old arrangements (whole community meetings) still retained their significance even as variations were introduced. The committee had proposed a constitution, subsequently approved by a community meeting and written up in an exercise book, as shown below.

Box 7.2 Constitution of village water committee (translated)

Constitution 11/12/2009

1. Water time: Opens 6am. Closes 7pm.
2. We agreed to make a roster to clean the water point.
3. Children below 10 years should not come to the borehole.
4. Persons who never came on workday to borehole $5 *(fine)*.
5. Those moulding bricks for sale not allowed.
6. Fund raising: (i) Committee $1
                 (ii) People R5
                 (iii) Those with cars $5
                 (iv) Monthly subscription R5
7. Rule breakers who defy the committee will be taken to the headman.

In the minutes of the meeting of the waterpoint committee when this constitution was mooted it says: 'We agreed that the constitution should be made *even if all household representatives are not present*' (my emphasis added).

During the 1990s great effort was put into ensuring incorporative decision-making; meetings were organized on days when everyone could attend, consensus was considered important to ensure compliance, and decision-making often took place over a considerable timescale to accommodate this. A number of changes may have contributed to shifting this norm including significant out-migration and adult morbidity, the stresses of securing livelihoods during the economic crisis and the need for the community to position itself quickly in response to any NGO initiatives.

The 2009 constitution, written by hand on paper torn from an exercise book, bore two very official-looking stamps, one from the ('modern') elected ward councillor and one from the ('traditional') Chief Nkalakatha. At another nearby borehole the constitution had these two stamps *and* that of the Zimbabwe Republic Police. A concern with collecting various stamps of authority may reflect anxiety about shifting balances of power in a politically unstable context and the need to demonstrate legitimacy for public meetings which otherwise may be regarded suspiciously. Where the community was changing the norms of decision-making and forming new rules, the emphasis on support from authorities was even more important.

Throughout this book we have seen how processes of bricolage make new arrangements seem natural, a continuation of right ways of doing things. Old arrangements have a remarkable tenacity, informing

and shaping apparent innovations. In Eguqeni, despite the newly introduced levying of fees and listing of sanctions, underlying principles
shaping collective action persisted. The deeply held principle of conflict
avoidance (prominent in the material presented in Chapter 3) was made
explicit in the 2010 arrangements. Kept in the same file as the constitution was a list of roles of the water committee and prominent amongst
them was 'ensuring peaceful relations between people'. A review
of waterpoint committee minutes throughout 2009/2010 reveals a
constant concern for 'respect', a dislike of publicly expressed opposition
or non-cooperation, and requests for the headman and elders to hold
meetings of the people to explain matters to them.

So, alongside the conscious redesign of collective action rules around
water, the 'right way of doing things' was reiterated. Offenders against
the rules were to be referred to the village headman, who would hear
their case at a whole community meeting. The six-person waterpoint
committee, set up at the instigation of the Red Cross, also represented
continuity of authority in social relationships. The chair of the committee
and the caretaker were daughter and son of the previous chairman (now
deceased), one of the dominant triumvirate of patriarchs of the village in
the 1990s. Although the chair was a woman, the caretaker, as senior man of
that part of the village, actually was the leading authority figure. He played
a prominent role in public management, supervising collective maintenance work and paying the pump minder. Notably, the local Red Cross
was also strongly linked to the ruling party through its patrons and funding
and its operations in the district were rather contentious. This example
leads us neatly to the issue of authority in the evolution of institutions.

Authority and Agency

Earlier in this book we saw how institutions formed by bricolage draw
on authoritative resources – relationships of power which bolster and
legitimize rules, norms and practices. Such authority may reside in
humans with the power to command people and resources, in symbolic
references, for example, to past behaviour, or to 'tradition' and in supernatural agents such as the spirits of ancestors essential to the proper
functioning of the wider cosmological order. Here the role of authority
is to link individual human and domestic actions to the collective good.
The leakage of meaning helps to ensure that authority in institutions,
even where invented, must be naturalized so it becomes embedded in
everyday norms and practices. Drawing (consciously and unconsciously)
on general social organizing principles of lineage, seniority, respect, and
on the resources of the state, helps to ensure the legitimacy of those in

authority. However, such borrowing and naturalization, though tending to reproduce the social order, also allows scope for re-negotiation and room for manoeuvre. There is rarely only one channel of authority or source of legitimization – for example, at local level people may turn variously to 'traditional' figures (elders and leaders, spirit mediums and witch doctors) or 'modern' figures (councillors, MPs, development workers, school teachers), or to religious authorities. The ebb and flow of power between different stakeholders over time and the ways in which particular authoritative individuals exercise agency over changing lifecourses is also significant.

Here I draw on some notable authority figures in Eguqeni's institutional landscape to explore these points further. Investigating authoritative relations requires us to recognize that domains of jurisdiction over social life, collective action and natural resources can rarely be neatly confined to definable entities such as the village. Rather, they incorporate overlapping domains (here resource boundaries, social networks, the chiefly area, ward, district and region as well as religious congregations and social networks). Configurations of power are not static but may shift over time, and the longer-term tracking of processes of bricolage allow us to understand both continuity and change in authoritative relations.

Continuity in lineage

I have already suggested how, in the 1990s, a variety of people holding offices related to the state were publicly prominent in authoritative decision-making but that by 2010 traditional authority figures dominated at local level. However, the extent of ebb and flow of authority is difficult to pin down, as office holding does not necessarily convey power, and tradition and modernity are inaccurate terms covering a range of positions that have been invented or reinvented. So chiefs and headmen exist partly as colonial and post-independence reinterpretations of 'traditional' authority – attempts by the state to rule through legible 'native' structures. In Nkayi, due to the troubled local experiences of the liberation war and the post-independence period of political dissent and oppression by the Fifth Brigade of the Zimbabwean army, the workings of authority were also hampered by a reluctance to nominate the real holders of power to prominent posts.

The intermeshing of the old and the new and the waxing and waning of particular positions of authority can be well illustrated through the fate of the modern village development committees (VIDCOs) and the changing role of the village headmen. For many years, until the end of the 1990s, authority in Eguqeni had been embodied in three brothers of the dominant family in the village, the sons of different mothers. In their late seventies and eighties, they dominated the village by holding the posts of headman, chairman of the village development committee (VIDCO) and chairman of the waterpoint committee. By 2010 they were all deceased, but lineage still mattered. The sons of these three retained prominent positions in the community as headman, caretaker of the waterpoint committee and respected elder. With the passing away of the VIDCOs the authority of the headman extended to all village activities. It could be argued that VIDCOs were only ever an externally imposed arrangement, a design folly of the 1980s developmental state, never fully embedded in village life. Thus even in the 1990s the VIDCO did not meet separately as a committee but was convened as incorporative 'meetings of the people', an arrangement claiming pedigree from the nineteenth-century Ndebele state. Retrospectively, it is easy to see how the dominant patriarchal authority figures in the village extended their reach over the modern imported institutions. In this sense, the decentralized village development committee, introduced as the lowest tier of government, became another source of authority that could be deployed in the organization of village life and blended with the existing resources of authority derived from lineage and from 'traditional' status.

The intermeshing of modern and traditional and the blurring of the boundaries between state and society is well illustrated by the case of the local chief. His role and reputation had changed through government action and as a result of his own lifecourse and actions. In the 1990s the chief had been a young man who had inherited the chieftainship from his older brother. People regarded him as a youth, not a full adult, and he was often to be found drinking beer at Nkayi centre. The system of administration introduced by the developmental state in the post-independence 1980s more or less bypassed the chiefs. Instead, the district council, ward councillors and village development committees led in local development, and traditional authorities were seen as less important but having a role in community mobilization and social control.

In the succeeding decades the chief had grown up and Mugabe's government, attempting to extend its support in the rural areas, had enhanced the authority of all chiefs, who were given tractors and four-wheel-drive vehicles. Chief Nkalakatha, living in the regional town but returning to Nkayi every Tuesday and Wednesday to deal with chiefly matters, was now a far more prominent figure than he had been in the 1990s. As commissioner of oaths, he had his own stamp of authority, and the six headmen of his area reported to him through his assistant, the Mlisa. Reports and files of the village hearings of the headmen were passed to the chief. From his point of view the village development committees had been 'scrapped off' and now the proper lines of authority ran through the headmen to himself. The chief executive officer of the Nkayi Rural District Council confirmed the contemporary importance of the chiefs – in attempting to revive the activities of the council he saw the need to bring chiefs and councillors 'to sit together to get development working again'.

Community police

A profile of one of the community policemen in the village nicely illustrates the some of the themes of this chapter; the intertwined strands of authority over collective action, natural resource regulation and the social order, the leakage of authoritative meaning from one domain to another and the variation arising from the exercise of individual agency.

In the 1990s half a dozen young men roamed around the village, exercising their duties as grazing policemen – ensuring that the village rules designating areas seasonally closed to livestock were not breached and 'arresting' offending cattle. They also, in the course of these duties, acted as messengers, giving people notice of village meetings. By 2010 the number of community police had expanded considerably to nine men and eleven women, one of them being Sophie Nyoni. She had become a policewoman five years earlier when the headman proposed her for the position at a meeting of the people. She was given original training by the Zimbabwe Republic Police at Nkayi growth point, and was also initially promised payment for her duties by the community. She described her duties as:

- Fetching people to hearings at the headman's place and assisting there.
- Maintaining order at public gatherings such as for food distribution and borehole maintenance.
- Monitoring the grazing rules.
- Catching criminals.
- Maintaining social order.

The action she took depended on the nature of the offence. If she found someone smoking marijuana she would just warn him or her; if people were fighting she would report to the headman. For cattle grazing offenses she would write down the name and give it to the headman – a fine of $2 would be levied, of which she received half. In the past the grazing fines were used for upkeep of the Headman's compound, where community hearings are held, but now they go into the community purse. Fines for other offences are sent to the chief. Although a key role of the policemen was to monitor natural resource use, Sophie particularly relished her part in mediating domestic disputes. She felt that that was where she could really make a difference and 'get things straight', either by giving advice to the warring parties or by calling them to the community gathering place under the mopane tree to receive advice from the headman and elders. In performing her duties, Sophie was sure that her large body size, reputation for strength and loud voice were an asset – she noted how in meetings, when she spoke, people fell silent and really listened.

According to Sophie, the tariff for any fine is 'given' by the chief, but the headmen make adjustments for the nature of the crime and for the social status of the offender. Sanctions, when imposed, tended to combine punishment with reconciliation. When a man was caught grazing his cattle on post-harvest stover, before that area was open for grazing, the elders fined him four chickens, which were cooked and eaten by all the *men* at the headman's place!

Sophie told us a story of a criminal she had apprehended, illustrating the overlapping nature of authority in the village. The story began when a homestead was burnt down and all its contents lost. The woman of the house suspected her brother-in-law, so she consulted the prophets of her Pentecostal church on the other side of the Shangani River. As it happened, the arsonist had also been to the prophets to ask for cleansing of his crime through prayer, so they were able to confirm that the arsonist was indeed the brother-in-law. When the woman reported this to the headman and elders they disbelieved her, as they could not comprehend how a man could burn his own brother's house. So the woman gave them a few dollars to consult the *inyanga* (the traditional 'witch doctor'). He threw bones and divined that the brother-in-law was indeed the culprit. With the weight of authoritative opinion from 'traditional' healer and church prophets against him, the man was arrested on the orders of the village elders and handed over to the Zimbabwe Republic Police, eventually being tried and imprisoned in Nkayi. He served a short sentence after repaying some of the cost of the burnt goods.

Shifting but enduring moral rationalities

The example of community justice above should not be used to imply that because there are multiple sources of authority then any source is legitimate. Authoritative relations are embedded in wider systems of meaning, which both legitimize and naturalize them. In Chapter 3 we saw the central role of moral–ecological explanations in conveying continuity in a shifting social order; we also saw how such under-standings were interwoven with discourses of 'development'. By 2010, the grip of traditional practice on collective life seemed to have ebbed, though as we shall see the underlying principles and legitimacy of this way of doing things were tenacious.

In early 2010 Eguqeni village had not recently held a major rain-making ceremony, despite the combination of natural and manmade drought. This may have partly been to do with the nature of the preceding political and economic crisis, the government ban on meeting together, and the expense of providing hospitality to the mediums, offerings to the spirits, and beer to the people. The spirit medium who had conducted the major ceremony I attended in 1992 was afterwards deemed a cheat and the local medium had moved away to be married, so connections with the Njelele rain shrine had been lost.

In various discussions in the village, people attributed the decline of such ceremonies, and the lack of rains to the rise of new (Pentecostal) churches. The explanation commonly went that people were no longer respecting the old traditions because whereas the 'old churches (Catholic, Lutherans, 'London'[2]) were tolerant of traditional beliefs and let people practice them alongside Christianity, the new ones were not. New churches often banned people from participating in traditional ceremonies; rest days in honour of the spirits were no longer universally respected, and some people avoided collective labour obligations.

However, this shift was perhaps not as radical as it first seemed. In discussions people still emphasized the importance of belief, of living together and the continuity of tradition. As one man said, 'But really, you can't get away from culture – it's like your surname, it never leaves you.' There was a common feeling that as the rains appeared to be failing, people would see it as a warning and start returning to traditional collective ceremonies. Many villagers were relaxed with holding both sets of beliefs. In another village in the district, a woman holding the post of 'headman regent' on behalf of her nephew (who was working in South Africa) was also an elder of an apostolic church. She claimed that there was an easy co-existence between her Christian and tradi-tional beliefs – for example, in both, rain-making ceremonies were held involving offerings of maize, cloth and chickens. For a Christian ceremony the people bring the offerings to church and pray; for the traditional ceremony they take them to the Mtolo tree site and sing and dance. As she said, 'For us, the really important thing whether it is in church or at a traditional ceremony is the offering and asking for blessings and togetherness. They are the same wherever you do them.' An important element of this women's dual role as traditional and Christian elder was ensuring the proper behaviour of children and youth, through moral guidance.

Such overlaps in cosmological beliefs were also noted by a group of women singing traditional songs indoors in Eguqeni one rainy afternoon. They pointed out that Selitshe, the special place in the Shangani River reserved for traditional rain making ceremonies, was also used by churches new and old for meetings and fasts for rain. The women said, though, that increasingly they believe that it is God, rather than the spirits of ancestors, who will punish them with drought if they fail to respect each other and cause conflicts.

So it seems that certain principles of living together carry authoritative weight as the right way of doing things – authority is not simply vested in powerful individuals but in claims to particular symbols, practices and relationships. Authority and meaning leaks across institutional arrangements and contexts, so that it becomes difficult to see what is old and what is new.

Collective work, community management and its limits

It is easy to become immersed in the rich details of local institutional life and the continuity of arrangements and to be distracted from addressing questions of the effectiveness of local organization. Many social institutions in Nkayi were able to survive and adapt in years of crisis (even if contracting in scope), and collective action maintained the semblance of sameness. However, the ongoing the crisis of government and the curtailment of development activities severely impacted on the outcomes of institutional arrangements. This is unsurprising. If we refer back to the framework for analyzing water governance set out in Chapter 2, we see institutional arrangements shaped by the configuration of authoritative and allocative resources in society. Where these become weak or distorted the variety of institutional channels also becomes restricted, so in turn limiting outcomes. People's scope for initiating actions that will be transformatory become seriously reduced. In Nkayi the lack of support of state institutions, or other development agencies such as non-governmental organizations, meant that local effort and the resilient local forms of collective action were stuck in a dead-end. A plurality of overlapping arrangements does not necessarily compensate for linkages to significant enabling institutions and resources.

In Jingeni, the village neighbouring Eguqeni, a women's burial society was actively functioning in early 2010. The members met regularly, dressed in their blue and white uniforms, to discuss society business and to socialize. Before the economic crisis the burial society had plans to generate cash through sewing uniforms, but now they could not afford a sewing machine or materials. Where possible, they were practising hand sewing their own clothes in anticipation of an improvement in fortunes.

Several of the ladies of the burial society in Jingeni were also members of the dam committee. This represented a wider community effort to locate and prepare a site for a small dam, to be used primarily for livestock watering. The community (in this case comprising seventy listed households spread across the villages in the area) had initiated the plan by making a request through an inter-denominational church body and a Catholic non-governmental organisation had agreed to provide support. Over a period of two years the community cleared site of trees, dug a lot of gravel and moved it to the site. Contributions of labour by each of the seventy households were recorded in the same book as the burial society records by the woman who acted as secretary to both sets of activities. However, at the time when the community could proceed no further without needed mechanical digging equipment, the NGO was suffering crippling resource constraints and withdrew support from the project. By early 2010 the site of the dam was overgrown with scrub, much of the community labour wasted. The lack of a dam in the area meant that the people of Jingeni village had to risk infringing the area grazing rules. The absence of other water sources within easy reach meant they had to drive their cattle through the 'closed' grazing areas to water them at the Shangani River. This they only did every other day so as not to be suspected of lingering in the area in contravention of the grazing rules.

So we can see how different institutional arrangements, the burial society, the dam committee and the grazing rules are interlinked in practice and through particular people and variously constrained by lack of resources. For poor communities there are crippling limits to what can be achieved through collective action, in the absence of productive connections to authoritative and resourceful agencies. This point becomes clearer when we return to consider the outcome of efforts to manage Creche borehole in Eguqeni village.

In addition to collecting fees, the community adopted a do-it-yourself approach to maintenance, replacing broken parts, mending fencing. We have also seen that they commissioned the local pump minder to perform maintenance, replacing the worn-out parts of the pump mechanism with the community's help. As there was only one pump minder in the area, now working as a private contractor, the community had little choice but to use him, although they believed that they were being over-charged. Two problems were apparent here. In the 1990s the pump minder had operated as part of a three-tier system, working with village waterpoint committees on preventative and minor corrective maintenance and calling in the skilled district maintenance team and its heavy equipment for major repairs. Now, the privatized pump minder had no interest in preventative maintenance and offered no guarantee for his repairs – each job was charged separately even if closely related to a previous one. So all the community efforts at organization, collection of maintenance fees and DIY maintenance only secured minor repairs at relatively high cost. At numerous other waterpoints in the district communities were similarly well organized but unable to rehabilitate their dysfunctional boreholes without specialist help and additional resources.

Conclusion: Institutions, Bricolage and Social Meaning

The example of the evolution of village-level institutions in Eguqeni village allows us to reflect on the nature of institutional evolution in the context of a state in crisis. The presence (or absence) of the state clearly matters, in terms of providing a discourse of development to draw on, authoritative resources to legitimize arrangements and allocative resources in the form of expertise, manpower, service delivery, linking local action to wider domains. In the context of a withdrawn or ineffective state we could suggest that the institutional stock is narrowed down – there is less furniture in the store for bricoleurs to rearrange into apparently fresh room layouts. However, the uncertainty about the authority of the state in Nkayi animated vigorous processes of legitimation of institutional arrangements at the local level. In 2010 it seemed even more important than in the early 1990s to formally demonstrate the authority upholding local institutions (as in the collecting of a variety of stamps on the constitution). New and shifting arrangements were also legitimized by reference to the proper practices of social life and tradition, even where these were evolving too. However, we should be cautious of attributing too much to such processes of legitimation as many of the parameters of governance are decided at non-local levels, and negotiations through local institutions often benefit those with the greatest power (Doornbos, 2010).

There is no easily determined link between macro-level 'good governance' and effective local action. Good or bad governance does not simply trickle down through intermediary layers to state and the people. Local-level arrangements do not simply mirror those at national level on a micro scale. Rather, macro-level governance arrangements shape local institutional life in less obvious ways, by reconfiguring the institutional stock from which local arrangements can be drawn. In Eguqeni 'bad' national-level governance created uncertainty and villagers responded by investing more time and effort in demonstrating the validity of their local arrangements, the legitimacy of authority, the enduring meaning attached to practices and the continuity of proper behaviour and roles. In other words, bad governance at the national level seems to have resulted here in a reassertion at local level of some of the core principles of local social organization. This seems to be a different sort of robustness than implied in institutional design models. Robustness manifests in enduring ideas about living together, which shape institutional arrangements and natural resource practices, respect for social position, neighbourliness, conditional tolerance of free riding and the placing of human action in broader frameworks of meaning involving the natural and supernatural worlds.

Can *designed* arrangements of rules, regulations and constitutions be robust in the same way? The answer is both no and yes, for even where the reach of the state is tenuous and intermittent it does shape the ways in which village-level institutions constitute authority, and position themselves in relation to those in power. Designed institutions may be imposed by the state or development agencies and are subject to dual processes. In addition to performing the tasks for which they were designed, they may become institutional resources which can be mined for authoritative symbols and discourses. Particular arrangements (roles, committees, contracts, tariffs, elections etc.) may be borrowed for other purposes or their meaning leak less consciously into other areas of collective life, just as accepted ways of doing things come to reshape the designed institution. As this happens, their content and processes become naturalized; they become woven into the fabric of institutional life so that the boundaries between old and new institutions, traditional and modern, formal and informal is always difficult to detect.

The diversity *and* the sameness of institutional life well illustrates the endless activity of bricoleurs in making sense of their world – in creatively generating livelihood arrangements that are deeply imbued with meaning. But when we look at the outcomes we see such community-level action as severely limited; without intervention and design, without measures to redistribute at scale, without specified measures of equality and without an investment of resources beyond the scope of the villagers, such action is likely to be limited in its impact both on environmental management and on equity of access and other socially desirable outcomes.

References

Berry, S. (2005) 'Poverty Counts: Living with Poverty and Poverty Measures', paper presented at the International Conference on the Many Dimensions of Poverty, Carlton Hotel, Brasilia, Brazil, 29–31 August.

Catholic Commission for Justice and Peace (1999) 'Breaking the Silence, Building True Peace: A Report on the Disturbances in Matabeleland and the Midlands 1980–1988', Harare, Zimbabwe, Catholic Commission for Justice and Peace/ Legal Resources Foundation.

Chabal, P. (2009) *Africa: The Politics of Suffering and Smiling*, London, Zed Books.

Doornbos, M. (2010) 'Researching African Statehood Dynamics: Negotiability and its Limits', *Development and Change* 41, 4, pp. 747–69.

Ferguson, J. (1990) *The Anti-Politics Machine: Development, Depoliticization and Bureaucratic Power in Lesotho*, Cambridge, Cambridge University Press.

Fuller, C. and Benei, V. (eds) (2001) *The Everyday State and Society in Modern India*, London, C. Hurst & Co.

Hagmann, T. and Péclard, D. (2010) 'Negotiating Statehood: Dynamics of Power and Domination in Africa', *Development and Change* 41, 4, pp. 539–62.

Hyden, G. (2006) 'Introduction and Overview to the Special Issue on Africa's Moral and Affective Economy', *African Studies Quarterly* 9, 1 & 2, pp. 1–8.

Jones, B. (2009) *Beyond the State in Rural Uganda: Development in Rural Uganda*, Edinburgh, Edinburgh University Press.

Mapedza, E. and Geheb, K. (2010) 'Power Dynamics and Water Reform in the Zimbabwean Context: Implications for the Poor', *Water Policy* 12, 4, pp. 517–27.

Mtsi, Sobona (2011) 'Water Reforms During the Crisis and Beyond: Understanding Policy and Political Challenges of Reforming the Water Sector in Zimbabwe', ODI Working Papers 333.

Potts, D. (2010) *Circular Migration in Zimbabwe and Contemporary Sub-Saharan Africa*, Oxford, James Currey.

Scott, J. (1998) *Seeing Like a State: How Certain Schemes to Improve the Human Condition Have Failed*, New Haven. CT, Yale University Press.

Notes

1 The research on which this is based was undertaken in three periods of fieldwork in February, June and October 2010. This was made possible by the support of Noma Neseni and the Institute of Water and Sanitation Development in Harare. I was ably assisted by Henry Nyoni, Tabholwethu Nyoni and Belladonah Musavazi and many long-standing friends and colleagues in Nkayi District. The research was supported by funds from the School of Oriental and African Studies London and the University of Bradford.

2 'London' is the name used in Nkayi for the United Congregational Church of Southern Africa, the successor to the London Missionary Society, which had operated in Matabeleland since the early nineteenth century.

8 Transforming Institutions?

Introduction: The Possibilities of Progressive Change

In this final chapter I reflect on whether adopting a bricolage analysis offers reasons for hope or for despair. Many of the examples considered in the previous chapters illustrate the ways in which invented institutions are shaped by past arrangements and relationships of authority. Such a perspective was captured in a well-known passage written by Marx (1934: 10):

> Men make their own history, but they do not make it as they please; they do not make it under self-selected circumstances, but under circumstances existing already, given and transmitted from the past. The tradition of all dead generations weighs like a nightmare on the brains of the living. And just as they seem to be occupied with revolutionizing themselves and things, creating something that did not exist before, precisely in such epochs of revolutionary crisis they anxiously conjure up the spirits of the past to their service, borrowing from them names, battle slogans, and costumes in order to present this new scene in world history in time-honored disguise and borrowed language.

In other chapters I have illustrated the ways in which people re-form institutions in response to changing circumstances. They do this exactly by conjuring up the spirits of the past to their service, asserting that adapted arrangements are in fact manifestations of the customary, legitimized by 'tradition'. I have deliberately concentrated on these aspects of bricolage for a number of reasons. Firstly, such a focus helps to counter models of institutional design that assume a 'blank slate' upon which new social arrangements can be designed for purpose with little regard for how the past shapes current relations. Secondly, an emphasis on reinvention and leakage of meaning helps to balance romantic ideas about individual and collective action that take little account of context and of the imperative of social fit. Thirdly, analyzing such processes has helped to highlight institutional formation as involving the exercise of power, the authoritative assertion of some particular claims to resources and versions of the social order over others. In short, a focus on reinvention demonstrates the workings of social structure and shows how processes of bricolage are disciplinary, shaping people's interactions in particular ways.

However, we have also seen that the essence of bricolage is that such processes often create something different, albeit that new arrangements are cloaked in 'time-honoured disguises'. How far then are they *also* transformatory, and how can we better understand the possibilities for effecting positive change through processes of bricolage? Indeed, to what extent can bricolage processes be deliberately managed to produce desirable outcomes? These are questions that, for the moment, remain unanswered.

In this book I have attempted to address a gap that exists in understanding community-based natural resource management as a wider governance process, through which relationships between society and individuals are mediated. Adopting a governance perspective to examine natural resource regimes helps to address the challenges of institutional analysis (outlined in Chapter 1) as it widens the gaze to incorporate plural, interlinked institutional arrangements and their outcomes. Additionally, the governance perspective situates these arrangements in a global–local nexus and significantly facilitates an analysis of power relations. To further consider these points I begin within a case drawn from Emil Sandström's research on community-based natural resource management in northern Sweden (Sandström, 2006, 2008). I choose this because he explicitly adopts a governance frame to understand local community action *and* is positive about the potentially transformatory effects of such processes. He specifically states: 'self organising community groups may set society in motion towards an institutional re-organisation' (Sandström, 2006: 232). In Sandström's analysis, institutions are formed in praxis, when globalization processes (environmental change, policy trends towards decentralization and democratization) tie into everyday life and require people to reflect and reshape their circumstances. However, he does not overemphasize the role of creative agency, but also considers the role of ideologies, particularly of 'place politics' as key shapers of such processes. According to Sandström, such self-organizing groups are also partly animated by 'outside' influences and actors.

Does the inevitability of adaptation through processes of bricolage, then, mean that formal institutional design has no meaningful role in shaping the allocation and distribution of resources? Alternatively, does the introduction of new institutions provide fresh resources, elements of which can be recombined and altered, so shifting old arrangements and producing something new and different? How can we reconceptualize the concept of institutional robustness so that it captures the endurance of particular elements or logics underlying social organization rather than just the persistence of particular institutional forms?

A promising case: the Coastal Ring organisation

Sandström's (2008) study of the Coastal Ring organisation is framed in the context of a long history of strong state intervention in property rights. The delimitation of Crown lands by the Swedish state in the nineteenth century was significant in setting out individual and collective property rights, though many informal rights of use continued following this. Despite such attempts at codification contemporary property and natural resource rights are overlapping and complex, informal and formal claims co-exist. The push to urbanize Sweden in the 1960s resulted in rural depopulation, but by the 1970s and 1980s ideas about the need to develop the rural areas were becoming more prominent. Policy envisaged natural resources (particularly forests) both as economic resources for rural development and as ecosystems in need of protection. A more recent shift away from state-centred control of conservation mirrors global policy discourses about the environment, sustainable development and the potential for the co-management of resources with communities. Alongside strong state intervention, a history of people's movements seeking protection for local concerns and for the environment shape the possibilities for local institutional emergence.

This case study is framed in the context of a shift from government control of natural resources towards de-centralization and co-management, in line with international policy discourses. Sandström characterizes the emergence of community-led institutions as a process of creating *shared* understandings and responsibilities.

Background to the Coastal Ring

The Coastal Ring is a three-village organization for co-management of natural resources in an area of northern Sweden, bordering the Gulf of Bothnia. At the time of Sandström's study, livelihoods related to seal hunting, fishing, agriculture and forestry had lost their economic significance, with many residents employed in nearby towns. Natural resources remained centrally important, though, to recreational and associational life. Various land redistributions in the three villages over centuries resulted in complex patterns of private land and village commons with associated rights, for example to fishing.

The Coastal Ring emerged through an affiliation of three villages in response to a 1998 proposal by the County Administrative Board (CAB) to protect the mouth of the Kalix River. This area was to be included in the European Commission's Natura 2000 Environmental Protection Network with the aim of preserving features of the natural environment and maintaining important bird habitats.

The emergence of local institutions began with village meetings mobilized in response to the Natura 2000 proposals and developed through study groups, networking, affiliation and negotiation with government authorities. By 2002 the Coastal Ring had a charter and a governing board of 5–7 members, with 20–25 people actively involved in its work and another 100–200 attending meetings.

In 2003 the Coastal Ring organisation had negotiated an informal mandate to manage the Liskär's island nature reserve, carrying out practical management activities as a subcontractor to the County Administrative Board (CAB). By 2004 a formal management agreement was reached under which the Coastal Ring received money from the CAB each year for day-to-day maintenance activities in the reserve.

Whilst formal co-management was being negotiated, the three constituent villages, through their 'traditional' institutions, became more dynamic in managing their land and water commons. They reinvented village byelaws, set aside fishing and wildlife conservation areas, developed public bathing areas, picnic sites and cabins, reconstructed paths and shelters and established a carbon sink project in the forest.

Response to a regulatory state: conflict and cooperation

The local–state relationships influence institutional emergence in complex ways. This case shows how people's suspicion of a 'distant' regulatory state prompted local action. But the authoritative and allocative resources of the state were also influential (and necessary) in shaping the institutions formed through bricolage.

The Coastal Ring organization developed local management partly as a way of safeguarding against state intervention, with national Swedish and European government seen as remote and threatening, lacking the appropriate sensibilities to manage local resources. Thus the response from one village chairman to the Natura 2000 proposals: 'We do not want the bigwigs in Brussels to write a framework of rules on how we should steward and care for nature' (Sandström, 2008: 86). The same person stated:

> the natural resources that surround our villages belong to us. They are ours irrespective of what the authorities say ... and you see ... we need to steward them because the authorities do not have the right kind of place connection. (Sandström, 2008: 118)

Although the idea of local stewardship was developed in *opposition* to distant state and European intervention, it was operationalized through varying degrees of *cooperation* with state structures. For example, initial mobilization included establishing study circles. These scrutinized Swedish policy and legal documents to find sanction for local management of natural resources, to identify precedents for pilot projects, and room for manoeuvre for co-management initiatives. They identified promising spaces for local management in fishing and marine policies, the Environment Act and the budget bill.

In relations between the state and community the configuration of authority was implicitly and explicitly being questioned – even possibly re-configured. Under the formalized co-management agreement the CAB undertook to pay the Coastal Ring organization for certain resource management activities. Whilst the CAB was reluctant to let go of its decision-making powers, the Coastal Ring wanted *more* power to manage local natural resources and saw this agreement as only the beginning of this process. Here it had to tread carefully not to alienate the CAB. The 'official' legitimacy bestowed through the agreement enabled the Coastal Ring to claim authority in dealing with other large land owners, like the forest companies and the church.

Issues of competence and legitimacy were prominent in the Coastal Ring's negotiations about co-management with the CAB. At one stage the CAB requested the curriculum vitae of Coastal Ring board members to establish their competence to manage natural resources. In response, the Coastal Ring board members stressed their legitimacy through knowledge, commitment and place connection. The chairperson of the Coastal Ring asked:

> What kind of competence do we lack? ... In our community we have all kinds of competence, practical and theoretical and we are even blessed with a person that has worked on these types of issues for the United Nations in India ... but this is not the most

important thing. It is rather about having good knowledge about the place and that we want to take responsibility (Sandström, 2008: 94)

It is notable that these relationships did not only involve the community struggling to wrest allocative and authoritative resources from the state. In developing local management arrangements and promoting innovative projects like the carbon sink in the forest, the Coastal Ring Organization also itself became a resource for the Ministry of the Environment in the promotion of their nature conservation policy. Representatives of the Coastal Ring were invited to national conferences and seminars and became involved in influencing government policy on local management, and in showcasing this to international audiences.

Intersecting networks and domains

Whilst the co-management agreement was an obvious attempt to engage with the state, the arrangements pieced together by Coastal Ring bricoleurs did not neatly fit into nested hierarchies of authoritative institutions. Rather, the arrangements drew on an uneven network of state and non-governmental institutions at different scales. For example, members of the Coastal Ring activated links with the Swedish University of Agricultural Sciences at Uppsala, the Kalix Agricultural College, Swedish Popular Movement Council for Rural Development, the Gaia Foundation, Swedish International Development Agency (SIDA) and the UN's Food and Agriculture Organisation. Such links were furthered by well-connected members who were also able to draw on national and international experience of community management as a resource for mobilization; these significant actors were institutional brokers of connections. The blurred boundaries, personal networks and overlapping domains of action here served to assist the communities by providing multiple channels, across which meaning leaked and through which they could access information and influence.

In addition to material assistance these links provided legitimizing discourses for community resource stewardship. The slogan 'Think global, act local' expanded the domain from which legitimacy was drawn, so framing Coastal Ring activities in terms of the global public good rather than insular localism.

The Coastal Ring's attempts to manage local fisheries illustrates the ways in which bricoleurs can consciously draw on certain authorities and bypass others in their attempts to find the room for manoeuvre for local management. In local fishery management there was history of conflict between the National Board of Fisheries, CAB and village landowners. This conflict had amplified differences between professional fishermen and local fishing rights holders on the village commons.

In 2004 the Coastal Ring started to look at the possibility of developing local management for fishing. They applied to the National Board of Fisheries to become a pilot project for the co-management of fisheries (a possibility they found out about through their study groups). However, the organization of professional fishermen refused to cooperate, seeing the Coastal Ring as environmental fundamentalists, and instead developed their own competing proposal. Both were turned down by the National Board of Fisheries. The Coastal Ring then changed strategy – instead of negotiating further with CAB and National Board of Fisheries, they contacted the National Property Board (the formal owner of the nature reserves and several other islands close to the villages). The outcome was a declaration of intent, where the Coastal Ring organization and the National Property Board agreed to investigate whether the Coastal Ring should manage some of the islands.

Parallel to this process the Coastal Ring was encouraging the reinvention of village bye-laws which also had the effect of regulating local fisheries by banning fishing in areas set aside areas for fish regeneration and fish passage. The case of fisheries well illustrates that processes of bricolage cross boundaries and may involve action and consequences in a number of inter-related domains.

Re-invention of tradition, creation of new shared meanings

Sandström defines institutionalization as 'a social process in which individuals come to accept a shared understanding of local reality'. Such understanding was partly invented by local stakeholders through reinterpretation of a shared but divergent past history, and legitimized through connection to wider cultural frames, norms and rules.

Whereas the official management plan for Liskär's nature reserve, drawn up in 1969, stressed biological values, the local management plan developed by the Coastal Ring underscored cultural and historical aspects of nature resource management. The shared understandings of the Coastal Ring members identified local management as inextricably linked to history, culture and place, and to sustainable living. Thus it stated:

> local management shall further strengthen the local and cultural identity ... Our villages are by tradition connected to the sea,

the archipelago and fishing and we believe we have the required knowledge to take care of and steward the culture or the archipelago that remains ... (Sandström, 2008: 114)

Sanction for these claims was sought from history and legitimacy claimed through the link to ancestors; the past was explicitly linked to a vision of sustainable management for the future:

> we have more and more come to realise that understanding our cultural heritage is the most important thing in order for us to develop our place ... understanding how ancestors utilised the natural resources provides us with useful tools on how we can plan for future local management in a responsible way. (Sandström, 2008: 115)

The mechanisms through which local management was formalized well illustrate the improvisation involved in bricolage and the ways in which the resources of tradition are drawn upon and reinvented.

The Coastal Ring organization was based on an adaptation of ancient village institution of the *byalag*,[1] historically comprising landowners entitled to a share in the village commons through possession of a farm unit. Such an arrangement may appear conservative, but the Coastal Ring reinvented the ancient *byalag* by *expanding* the property qualification to include anyone residing in the area, or with a local connection. Membership could be secured through voluntary work or paying small fee. The board members included one representative from each *byalag*, the remaining members being elected by annual assembly.

Bye-laws for village commons – drawn from an era when commons were an important source of income – were reinstated or reinvented, thus contemporary local management was legitimized by reference to historic continuity, even though economic and social conditions had changed significantly. But tradition is not the only legitimizing authority that is asserted – in this quote from a board member of the Coastal Ring, we see the authority of history being *combined* with that of state policies on environmental protection:

> We re-shape old village bye-laws. We work with our cultural history by investigating the framework of social rules that have existed earlier in the area ... And we reshape them and write them down ... and they are the foundations of the local management and for the biological values that the authorities want to protect. (Sandström, 2008: 109)

Processes of bricolage are not neatly bounded, and it seems that practices and actions (as well as meaning) leak across domains. So, in re-inventing ancient bye-laws and shared identities, the three villages of the Coastal Ring became more proactive in managing the village commons, effectively creating *new* rules for the fisheries, managing open-air bathing spaces and picnic areas, constructing log cabins, paths, wind and firewood shelters in the forest, and inventing the carbon sink project. The assertion of tradition was then instrumental to pursuing innovative arrangements and providing a fit with the directions of national and international natural resource management policies.

The example is more complex than that, though, as processes of reshaping and inventing involved constant negotiation and contestation between different authoritative actors and discourses. For example, the community's attempts to claim a natural legitimacy for institutions continuing a cultural tradition did not impress government authorities. The CAB was little interested in such arguments, more worried about the limits of delegated responsibility, the potential precedents set for the claims of other groups and the legal niceties of ownership of infra-structure being managed by the community. One official, talking of the ongoing negotiations with the Coastal Ring, said: 'It feels as if we can never be clear enough because we live in two different worlds.' Talking of the ambiguities inherent in legislation and policy, he stated:

> then we have the question concerning the right to make decisions and that is an important issue … and it is difficult to say how far you can go there … and that is an issue that you as a management authority cannot let go. (Sandström, 2008: 99)

This example highlights the contestations involved in legitimizing institutions and suggests some of the difficulties inherent to the 'nesting' or interaction of institutions with differing mandates and imbued with different world views. It suggests that we should be cautious of assuming that formalization equates with clarity. Boundaries and the categories of legitimate discourse are under constant re-negotiation; constant effort is required to invent shared meanings and common ground for formal agreements.

Comparative reflections

Sandström (2008) also studies in depth another Swedish community in which two Sami (reindeer herder) villages and two business associations joined together to form the Ammarnäs council in response to municipal plans to develop the Vindel Mountain Nature Reserve. Space prohibits an elaboration of this interesting, though less optimistic case. However, when read together with the Coastal Ring example outlined above and Arora-Johnson's study of the village association and women's forum in Drevdagen (Chapter 5), these cases support some general points about processes of bricolage.

Institutions emerge and evolve through both generic and context specific processes. Other examples discussed in this book suggest that local institutions are formed through bricolage when there is a governance vacuum, particularly when the state is weak or absent. From a 'democratic deficit' perspective, people 'make do' with improvised arrangements, which are inevitably a weak substitute for official and designed institutions. However, the Swedish examples offer alternative evidence of local institutions evolving in opposition to, but also drawing on, the resources of a strong state. Here the state supplies some of the institutional furniture (policy, legislated rights, co-management frameworks, technical knowledge) that are adapted in the piecing together of local arrangements.

New institutions are path dependent in that they are not inscribed on to a blank slate but rather are channelled into particular forms by the authoritative force of what has gone before. New institutions build on the past, even whilst resisting it.

The creation and legitimization of shared understandings and the re-making of norms are fundamental to the processes of institutional emergence explored in these cases. Both leakage of meaning and the reinvention of tradition allow for the creation of shared understandings between very different stakeholders. So, for example, actors from different backgrounds can invent or rediscover a *shared* heritage and articulate a collective claim to joint environmental stewardship. This is made possible by borrowing from each other's experiences and perspectives of resistance to the state, and by foregrounding past memories of past symbiosis, whilst backgrounding local histories of conflict. In this way, both consciously and unconsciously an authoritative discourse of responsible local stewardship rooted in the shared history of place is created. This provides the legitimizing frame for *new* institutional arrangements.

The Swedish studies illustrate that the emergence of local institutions are shaped not just by economic livelihood concerns. In the modern Swedish economy, contested ideas about resource management are not necessarily prompted by scarcity, or resource dependence for rural livelihoods. Rather, they are shaped by debates over what local management means, how it relates to preferred ways of life, wellbeing and attachment to place. The actions of institutional bricoleurs in Sweden are as much about 'being' and 'belonging' as they are in Zimbabwe or Tanzania;

their social identities are complex, tenacious but also amenable to change. Social identities and configurations of power matter in institutional formation – even where there is a strong societal presumption of equality. We saw in Chapter 5 how gendered priorities and norms shape engagement in public spaces and prompted the formation of alternative institutional forms.

Agency matters to the form institutions take. Individuals are resource appropriators but their actions are also shaped in relation to identity, attachments and the configuration of societal structures. Agency is operationalized in collective contexts; not just in public decision-making spaces, but through intersecting networks of social, political and professional relationships at a variety of scales. It is also strongly shaped by the ability of local actors to link their local initiatives to wider authoritative discourses – in these cases, international discourses about decentralization, democratization and globalised environmental management. The local arrangements that emerged in the Swedish cases became linked through overlapping domains of governance to national and global arenas for resource management.

Analogies to Aid Analysis of Bricolage

Viewing the preceding examples through a bricolage lens, we have seen how natural resource governance is enacted through a plurality of institutions and that the agency of bricoleurs is shaped by unequal relationships and structural constraints. This confirms the findings of previous chapters but still does not really help us to delineate the room for manoeuvre in forming institutions. Just how far are actors constrained or enabled by the wider governance framework in which they operate? How can we analyze this? Can the governance conditions be created which foster creative institutional bricolage?

The literature abounds with colourful analogies used to try to reflect the ways in which new arrangements are produced from a variety of parts. These include the concept of cultivation or gardening (Bastiaensen *et al.*, 2003), redecorating and DIY (Duncan, 2011), reconfiguring furniture to new layouts (Douglas, 1987), assembling junk items into new objects (Levi-Strauss, 2004), playing a game of football or stitching a patchwork (de Koning, 2011), even cooking a stew (Merrey and Cook, 2012)! Common to these analogies are ideas about a mix of intentional and improvised action, adaptation and making do, the dynamic nature of process and the variability of outcome. These analogies, while lively and engaging, go only so far in delineating the wider context which enables and constrains institutional formation and the constituent processes of bricolage which take place within such parameters. How broad is the frame within which bricolage takes place, and how far can it facilitate institutional transformation? Here I draw on two studies, both of which use analogies to good effect – one to map out the spaces available for bricolage, the other to track constituent processes of institutional formation.

Defining the institutional corridor

Firstly let us consider Jenniver Sehring's (2009) analysis of processes of bricolage in post-Soviet water governance over the period 1991–2005 in which she attempts to delineate the space within which arrangements are adapted and reformed.

Her comparative study of the Central Asian states of Kyrgyzstan and Tajikistan considers the factors shaping the effectiveness of post-Soviet water reforms. She considers two perspectives; firstly that path dependencies limit reform effectiveness as institutionalized Soviet and pre-Soviet patterns of behaviour continue to shape actors responses so undermining new rules and institutions. The second perspective suggests that the operation of such new institutions is partly facilitated by the adaptation of old institutional arrangements and logics. By recombining elements of different institutional logics, actors change both old and new institutional forms and alter their meanings.

Sehring usefully characterizes the way institutional arrangements are both constrained and dynamic by drawing on the analogy of the institutional corridor. The corridor is shaped by current governance relations – the degree to which a variety of actors are involved in decision-making, the configuration of laws, policies and administrative arrangements and the degree of plurality of these. The width of this corridor suggests the room for manoeuvre that different actors have for indentifying alternative paths and for reshaping institutions. Sehring's analysis suggests that the institutional corridor is broader in Kyrgyzstan than in Tajikistan, due to a greater degree of democratization of decision-making, privatization of agriculture, decentralization of local government and a greater variety of governance arrangements that broaden the options and strategies for different actors (Sehring, 2009).

Background to the cases

Let consider in a little more detail how Sehring delineates the institutional corridor and the processes which occur in it. The cases studies concern Kyrgyzstan and Tajikistan, both small, mountainous landlocked states heavily dependent on irrigated agriculture. Both countries share a similar legacy of water governance arrangements derived from past Russian and then Soviet rule. Following collapse of the Soviet Union and the unified Central Asian water-energy system, new national approaches to water governance were required. The formulation of new governance arrangements took place in the context of economic crisis, outmigration of professionals and infrastructure collapse.

In both Kyrgyzstan and Tajikistan the governments, highly influenced by international aid agencies, introduced reforms intended to establish good water governance by shifting away from a state-managed, sectoral and centralized system towards an integrated decentralized system with strong user participation. In accordance with the international consensus on good water governance an integral part of these reforms was the establishment of local water user associations and the levying of irrigation service fees.

Both countries developed new legal frameworks covering water rights, water user associations and contracts of water delivery with newly privatized farms. However, according to Sehring, these were not accompanied by sufficient implementation mechanisms (in the form of bye-laws and administrative arrangements) or knowledge dissemination to facilitate their adoption. Additionally, there was a lack of 'ownership', with a strong feeling amongst national experts and bureaucrats that international donors had written the law.

In both counties water user associations were established mainly in relation to donor-funded projects and could be seen as largely counterpart structures. In accordance with the normative objectives of the 'good governance' agenda, such associations were expected to be self-financing institutions responsible for operation and maintenance of infrastructure and for the fair distribution of water, accountable to their own members. Success in introducing water user associations was mixed – Sehring suggests that by 2004 59 per cent of irrigated land in Kyrgyzstan was managed by 353 water user associations whilst in Tajikistan an estimated 100 water user associations existed by 2005, managing less than 20 per cent of irrigated land.

The introduction of irrigation service fees had similarly only partial success: actual collection of fees was patchy and estimated at about 50 per cent. By 2005 only between 20 and 30 per cent of actual costs were covered by fees collected in both countries.

Mixed institutional logics

Sehring explains this patchy impact of new institutional arrangements by the coexistence of newly introduced pseudo-democratic mechanisms on the one hand and older authoritarian and patronage based arrangements on the other. In both states decision-making was strongly dominated by the President and his circle, by influential interest groups and by influential international donors. In Kyrgyzstan the institutional corridor was wider, as a variety of other actors were involved in policy formulation (though their role was largely limited to exercising veto).

In both countries attempts had been made at land reform with the breaking up of a large sate or collective farms. However, in Kyrgyzstan the privatized plots were too small for cash crops and were mainly used for subsistence, whereas in Tajikistan the quasi-privatized farms were often operated in the same ways as they had been in Soviet times. Economic crisis meant that many people relied primarily of subsistence agriculture and barter, and the breakdown of centralized systems also meant that agriculture became de-capitalized and infrastructure suffered. Many farmers were too poor to pay their irrigation fees, and officials, influenced by the Soviet-era norms of access to basic service for all, did not sanction non-payment. Unauthorized water withdrawal was therefore tolerated at the level that it became informally institutionalized in some places. The barter economy extended to water fees, which were often paid in kind, in the form of crops and other agricultural products and in labour (maintaining water canals). Such payments increased the transaction costs for local agencies.

A lack of knowledge of irrigation by the farmers (many of whom had previously been workers in state farms) led to inefficient water use and privatization was accompanied by injustices in land allocation. Influential and wealthy people could acquire better and larger land plots due to their networks and better knowledge of procedures and laws. Reforms addressing local governance dissolved the state and communal farms, which had been a principal unit of social organization in rural areas. In both countries formal local self-government was introduced with only limited budgets and competencies. Despite this potentially transformatory redesign of local governance, Sehring sees rather the continuation of organization through relations of authority and patronage from pre-Soviet and Soviet times. In other words, at the local level, the institutional corridor remained quite narrow.

New water user associations were unable to function as purely independent entities but drew on legacies of state/collective farm organization of the Soviet era and on the institutionalized authority of elders surviving from pre-Soviet times. Sehring suggests that local courts of elders, tolerated in the USSR, gained more importance in the post-Soviet transformation phase. In Kyrgyzstan the court of leaders was even formalized under the new governance regime. The authority of elders overlapped with the legacy of state farm organization through personalized leadership and patronage politics. The water user associations were seen by many as successors of collective farm organization, or as a part of local government, into which existing authority structures were interwoven. For example, the officials from local government or senior staff of the cooperative (successor of the collective farms) might take the position of chair of the water user association, with other key actors in the village filling other important positions. The key players in the water users association felt largely accountable to the donors and NGOs because of their financial support, and many ordinary farmers interviewed by Sehring were not even aware that they were members of a water user association.

Continuity and change within the institutional corridor

The case study and analysis offered by Sehring is complex in that it offers evidence of both opportunity and constraint. In interlinked processes the breadth of the institutional corridor was increased in the post-Soviet era, but at the same time old (Soviet and pre-Soviet) relations of authority and forms of organization channelled local people's engagement in governance along familiar lines. Sehring thus sees the introduction of new water user associations as enabling further power accumulation amongst already powerful actors at local level. However, she also highlights the flip side of this embedding of new institutions in pre-existing authoritative relationships. Acceptance of new arrangements and compliance with designed rules may be secured by drawing on old institutional authorities. So, when irrigation service fees were paid, it was not necessarily because of a market logic, but because the patron demanded such payment. In her research the most active water user associations were the ones where the leading local patrons were committed to their operation.

However, shifts in policy, legislation, administrative arrangements and the influence of new actors such as donor agencies and non-governmental organizations (the expansion of the institutional corridor) meant that old arrangements at local level were also changed and adapted. For example, the local patrons' role shifted to development brokerage, with a significant 'external' focus; traditional collective labour became a formalized participation mechanism in donor-funded projects. Sehring well illustrates how in processes of bricolage different logics and institutional legacies are mixed. Authoritative actors selectively adopted some new rules that seem appropriate or economically instrumental (such as water fees) but neglected others incompatible with existing logics (such as the democratic operation of water user associations). In this context, new and old arrangements interface – for example, a new water user association distributes water, but the way it does so is pre-figured by the way land has previously been allocated by longstanding village elites.

So, do the cases presented by Sehring suggest that the failure of water reform is due to path dependency (where the workings of old institutional arrangements dominate the new), or do they rather suggest that the introduction of new institutional arrangements and new actors provide additional resources for processes of bricolage in which both the old and new are reworked and combined in novel ways? The answer is both. For both Kyrgyzstan and Tajikistan, the outcome of policy reforms and the introduction of new institutional arrangements reflected the pre-Soviet legacy (resource distribution through clientilist patronage), Soviet-era arrangements (the centralized administrative culture, the key role of the collective farms, free access to basic services and resources) and post-Soviet initiatives (combining market mechanisms with participatory ones and strongly influenced by international donors). The institutional corridor was indeed widened through reform processes, through the introduction of more plural governance arrangements. However, in many cases it was people who had exercised authority in previous regimes who were able to utilize this greater room for manoeuvre, and so to ensure that local institutional arrangements retained their past character, particularly in the ways resources were accessed and distributed. Notably, the increased plurality of governance arrangements was not wholly beneficial. Due to the variety of actors involved, legislation policy and administrative reforms took a lot longer to formulate in Kyrgyzstan than in Tajikistan where there was less plurality, a narrower institutional corridor. This possibly increased the opportunities for the local elites to extend and consolidate their power.

The 'Rock-in-pond' analogy

In her work on bricolage processes in smallholder forestry in the Amazon, Jessica de Koning (2011) uses the analogy of a rock thrown into a pond to elaborate three constituent processes of bricolage. Drawing on studies from Bolivia and Ecuador, she considers the ways in which regulative frameworks for decentralized forest management, introduced by governments, have led to a multiplicity of institutions, rules and players (an expansion of the institutional corridor in Sehring's terms). New forest governance arrangements are characterized by bureaucratic decentralization (to local authorities) and by increased roles for markets, community groups and NGOs. However, the configuration of parts varies in different contexts. For example, in Bolivia, the resulting governance regimes feature community forest management strongly supported by NGOs as promoters, facilitators and brokers of forest law. By contrast, in Ecuador, reform processes result in an emphasis on individual forest management plans.

In her study de Koning tracks the processes which occur at local level when 'external' actors – the government, an NGO, a development agency – try to introduce new institutional arrangements, in this case for the management of forests and land. She uses the 'rock-in-pond' analogy to explore three key processes: aggregation, alteration and articulation.

Three scenarios: aggregation, alteration, articulation

In de Koning's analogy, the pond is the pre-existing setting comprising knowledge, technologies and conditions into which a new element of a designed institution (the rock) is thrown. The surface of the water represents the interface between the 'external' environment (the state, development initiatives and so on) and the community milieu. The nature of this surface or interface varies over time and with circumstance – it may be watery and porous, defined by a covering of soft or slushy ice, or bound by a layer of thick ice. de Koning suggests that there are three possible outcomes of attempting to introduce the rock (institution) into the water (the community). Firstly, the rock could enter the water, but then dissolve or disintegrate as the constituent parts are broken down and blended into the existing institutional milieu. This she calls a process of aggregation, and this happens when the logic and elements of an introduced arrangement such as a forest management

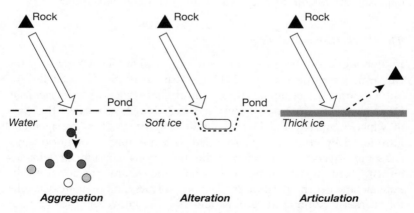

Figure 8.1 de Koning's rock-in-pond diagram (de Koning 2011: 215)

plan are disassembled, reshaped and blended with the local 'right way of doing things'.

So, aggregation consists of a process of combination where some of the external regulations and are adopted and combined with the rules, norms, and practices of local institutions. The hybrid institutions so formed may economize on transaction costs, particularly through the legitimacy derived from leakage of meaning, and combination or borrowing of authority. Here some elements of formal bureaucratic institutional principles become entwined with local, socially embedded arrangements.

A second possibility of throwing the rock in the pond is that the rock does not enter the water, but merely dents or marks the surface, as if it comes into contact with a layer of soft ice. In this case, the newly introduced institution is not fully blended into the social milieu; it mostly retains its newly designed shape, but is altered where it interfaces with existing arrangements (the surface of the pond). Alteration is where bricoleurs tweak or tinker with designed institutions, adjusting them slightly to better fit their livelihood practices. Such adaptation may include, for example, the bending of rules or partial engagement with them.

A third possibility, according to de Koning, is when the rock bounces off a layer of thick ice on the surface of the pond. This represents a process in which local people reject the introduction of the designed institution as unacceptable, irrelevant or socially inappropriate. de Koning links such rejection to processes of articulation, when bricoleurs emphasize local or traditional rules, norms and beliefs and identities as a form of resistance against institutional arrangements imposed by the authorities. Here 'tradition' or everyday practices may be asserted and invested with greater authority/legitimacy in opposition to the new imposed arrangements.

I find de Koning's delineation of overlapping processes of aggregation, alteration and articulation useful in helping us to think about the processes which might take place *within* institutional corridors. de Koning emphasizes that institutions partially elude design – there is no guarantee that designed arrangements will work out as intended. Institutions will be re-formed through various combinations of aggregation, alteration and articulation in different contexts resulting in a plurality of possible outcomes. In this sense, transformation and change is always possible through bricolage, but facilitating it through designed interventions requires a flexible and constantly adaptive approach that crosses scales and is able to address the exercise of both visible and invisible power.

Further Challenges of Institutional Analysis

In Chapter 1, I outlined a number of challenges to institutional analysis, and suggested that adopting the lens of institutional bricolage helps us to bring these into focus. In reviewing these challenges I argue that institutional bricolage cannot be understood as a purely micro-level process, comprised of local level practices. Rather, is an articulation of structure–agency relations, and can better be approached by analyzing institutional functioning within the frame of governance arrangements in society more generally. Adopting such a framework enables us to address challenges of complexity, scale and focus by analyzing the linkages and intersections (rather than the boundaries) between resources, networks of actors, institutions and domains of action. Tracking the leakage of power, knowledge and meaning between such arrangements, identifying the ways that mechanisms are borrowed and adapted, does not necessarily mean becoming mired in contextual complexity. Rather, it allows us to map *patterns* of adaptation and their outcomes for different people over time. I suggest clarity of analysis is achieved not by reducing institutional functioning to a few clear principles but rather by shining light into shadowy places to illuminate the processes through which institutional *outcomes* are formed.

Addressing the politics of agency-in-place enables us to link material and social dimensions of institutional functioning, to understand individual *and* collective action. We have seen from the previous examples how place politics and identities are highly significant in shaping people's engagement with resources and decision-making and in creating the links between individual and collective interests. Such identities and politics have the potential to be transformatory – for example, 'new' collective identities of environmental stewardship can be created from disparate interests. However, they are also likely to be disciplinary, shaping actions, claims to legitimacy and to resources along lines of social fit, of 'old' patterns in the allocation of resources. A key task for institutional analysis therefore is to try to assess the balance between constraint and opportunity in particular institutional configurations. How do disciplining processes and those generative of progressive social change interact to produce outcomes? Do shocks and pressures in the wider governance environment open up opportunities for positive change, or rather leave the field open for already powerful actors to extend their reach over allocative and authoritative resources?

It is clear, then, that in addressing the challenges to institutional analysis we need to place institutions in a wider governance framework that links scales and domains of action. Focusing on the constituent processes and practices of institutional bricolage helps us to understand the ways in which actors both reproduce and reconfigure such governance arrangements. Most critically, we need to link our analysis of governance context and institutional practices to outcomes in terms of ecosystem wellbeing and social justice. In the spirit of sustainable development, we should be as concerned with understanding outcomes for the wellbeing of people as well as for effective natural resource management.

To conclude, I argue that the concept of bricolage, underpinned by the idea that institutions are animated by socially situated people, offers a useful way to understand the interface between structure and agency in natural resource management. The concept of bricolage offers a number of insights for institutional analysis while simultaneously raising questions which point to areas for further research:

- The numerous dimensions of plurality in governance mean that institutional arrangements for natural resource management are multi-stranded, overlapping and imbued with a variety of meanings and interests. This plurality raises questions as to how far processes of bricolage can be managed, and to what extent institutions elude design.
- Recognizing the interplay between the creative exercise of agency, the constraining effects of social relationships and designed rules leaves us with the tricky task of tracking just how much room for manoeuvre specific institutions offer to different actors.
- Institutional analysis from a bricolage perspective is centrally concerned with tracking the effects of such arrangements on social justice as well as resource optimization. This usefully situates institutional analysis within broader processes of governance and raises questions about where the boundaries of analysis for natural resource management should be drawn.
- A bricolage perspective reveals the centrality of power relations to both the functioning and outcomes of institutional processes and so moves beyond over- instrumental 'technical' approaches to natural resource management, which are bound to fail. Illuminating the operation of power in everyday relationships, as well as through authority exercised by the state, poses further challenges to those concerned with better resource management. To what extent can this power be channelled to effect equitable and sustainable natural resource management without reproducing entrenched inequalities?

Bibliography

Bastiaensen, J., De Herdt, T. and D'Exelle, B. (2003) 'Poverty Reduction as Local Institutional Process', paper presented at Staying Poor: Chronic Poverty and Development Policy, Institute for Development and Policy Management, University of Manchester, 7–9 April.

de Koning, J. (2011) 'Reshaping Institutions: Bricolage Processes in Smallholder Forestry in the Amazon', Wageningen, Wageningen University.

Douglas, Mary (1987) *How Institutions Think*, London, Routledge & Kegan Paul.

Duncan, S. (2011) 'Personal Life, Pragmatism and Bricolage', *Sociological Review Online*. Vol 4, Issue 16.

Levi-Strauss, C. (2004) *The Savage Mind: Nature of Human Society*, Oxford, Oxford University Press.

Marx, K. (1934) *18th Brumaire of Louis Bonaparte*, Moscow, Progress Publishers.

Merrey, D. and Cook, S. (2012) 'Festering Institutional Creativity at Multiple Levels: Towards Facilitated Institutional Bricolage, Water Alternatives 5(1): pp. 1–19.

Sandström, E. (2006) 'Formation of Local Governance Arrangements for Natural Resources in the Age of Globalisation', in K. Havnevik, T. Negash and A. Beyene (eds) *Of Global Concern: Rural Livelihood Dynamics and Natural Resource Governance*, Stockholm, SIDA.

—(2008) 'Reinventing the Commons: Exploring the Emergence of the Local Natural Resource Management Arrangements', PhD Thesis, Swedish University of Agricultural Sciences.

Sehring, J. (2009) 'Path Dependencies and Institutional Bricolage in Post-Soviet Water Governance', *Water Alternatives* 2, 1, pp. 61–81.

Notes

1　The English word 'byelaw' is derived from the Swedish '*byalag*', probably via the Vikings (personal communication, Emil Sandström, 2011).

Index